Thom Braun is a marketing director for a large multi-national consumer goods business, and also a parish priest. His other books include *Holy Orders* (1995) and *Free Spirits* (1996).

# kingdom.com

## Thom Braun

CANTERBURY
PRESS

Norwich

© Thom Braun 2003

First published in 2003 by the
Canterbury Press Norwich
(a publishing imprint of
Hymns Ancient & Modern Limited,
a registered charity)
St Mary's Works, St Mary's Plain,
Norwich, Norfolk NR3 3BH

www.scm-canterburypress.co.uk

British Library Cataloguing in Publication data

A catalogue record for this book is available
from the British Library

ISBN 1-85311-554-1

Typeset by Regent Typesetting
Printed and bound by
Bookmarque, Croydon, Surrey

Jesus is Lord.

(I Corinthians 12.3)

The customer is king.

(John Wanamaker, a founder of the department store)

# I

April 1st. The newspaper story was headed 'Angel of Death'.

The day before. Early morning. The bright red sports car stopped outside the apartment building in Highgate. The large and burly driver, draped in a long, dark overcoat, climbed out. He started to walk, but stopped a few yards short of the gate. His arrival was expected. He had been observed from the first-floor flat. Almost at once the front door of the building closed behind a small, slim, dark figure in a trench coat. Within seconds the two men were travelling towards the city centre as fast as the traffic would allow.

'This is it,' said Noel Fear gruffly, gripping the steering wheel with fat white hands. 'The dawn of a new age.'

Robin Angel stared at his watch. Three minutes past seven. He would normally have been in bed. His routine was to rise at seven-thirty and catch the tube an hour later.

'How many should there be?' he said.

'One,' said Noel. Robin wasn't sure whether the word conveyed pleasure or disappointment. 'There should have been two, but one rang in last night with Delhi Belly.'

'Delhi?'

'Well, Crawley more like,' said Noel. 'But that doesn't rhyme with Belly.'

Robin nodded as if he understood what Noel was talking about. 'A man?' he asked. 'The one we're expecting. Man or woman?'

'A man,' said Noel. 'Blue overcoat. Respectable. He's been vetted.'

'Arriving?'

'Just before eight. We should be OK.'

Robin sat back in the moulded seat and watched the dimly pink sky turning to blue. Noel, he reflected, would normally have had a lot more to say. But then it *was* early.

Half an hour later, Noel backed the car into a meter bay close to Victoria Station. 'Got any money?' he said, plunging his hands into every deep and dark corner of his very large coat. 'For the meter.'

'Only notes,' said Robin apologetically.

Noel grimaced and started burrowing around under his seat. He emerged with a handful of cards which he pushed towards Robin.

'Here. Choose one of these.'

Robin looked at the collection of cards which were of different sizes and colours.

' "Disabled." "Doctor on Call." "Diplomatic Service." "Abandoned Vehicle: Police Aware." ' Robin muttered the words on the cards. 'Where did you get these?'

'Had the studio mock them up. Come on, let's go.'

Robin chose the 'Doctor on Call' card as the safest, and positioned it on the dashboard before stashing the other cards back below the seat.

'Have you ever seen a car with a sign on it saying "Abandoned Vehicle: Police Aware"?' continued Robin, as they hurried back in the direction of the train terminus.

'No,' said Noel, grimacing once more and showing off his large and uneven teeth. 'But someone in the studio claimed it was for real. Mind you, they also came up with "Priest on Compassionate Visit Caring for Elderly Woman". I thought that was a bit too wordy.'

'You could be right,' agreed Robin, before adding thoughtfully, 'and there probably aren't too many priests who drive red Porsches.'

'Too true. In fact, the whole scam's less than perfect,' said Noel. 'After all, that one about the police being aware ought to be on the outside of the windscreen, not the inside.

But what the hell. It's all a game. Life. Death. Where to park in between.'

They had reached the entrance to the station, and Noel's philosophical reflections were brought to a sudden halt.

'This way,' he said, weaving a path through the on-coming crowd of commuters. 'I know which platform. Just can't remember the number. Five minutes. We've got five minutes. Then it starts.'

Marianne Maddeley picked up the telephone, dialled Stuart's number and waited for the familiar deep voice. After the opening exchange of pleasantries, she got straight down to business.

'It's the thermometer, Stu. We've got to do something about the thermometer.'

'What's the matter with him then?' Stuart always called inanimate objects 'he' or 'him'.

'He's . . . I mean, it's fallen over.'

'Fallen over?'

'That's what I said, Stu.'

'What's caused that then?'

'Boredom, I should think.'

'Boredom?'

'Oh, for goodness' sake! I don't know, Stu. Woodworm. Subsidence. Deathwatch beetle. Metal fatigue. Vandalism. An act of God. I don't know. That's why I rang you.'

'If it's an act of God, the insurance won't pay for him,' commented Stuart flatly and with no hint of humour.

'God, Stu!' gasped Marianne in her best exasperated manner. 'He's not insured anyway.'

'Who? God?'

'What? No. *Him*. I mean "it". The thermometer. It's not insured.'

'It's not?'

'No, of course not. We're trying to save money, not spend it on things like insurance. Remember?'

Stuart made a gurgling noise down the telephone which Marianne took to be some kind of acquiescence. 'So, do you think it's worth fixing, Stu? The thermometer.'

'Well, I'd better take a look, hadn't I? See what sort of state he's in.'

'Thank you, Stu. I'll be in my office all morning if you've got time to drop round today.'

Marianne pulled her knees up under her chin and stared out of the study window at the clear April sky. She knew that having the thermometer fall over was the least of her worries. It was much more of a problem that the thermometer had hardly moved during the previous six months. As far as she could see there was nothing for it. The patient would have to be subjected to some radical treatment.

The train arrived one minute and fourteen seconds late. Robin and Noel stood either side of the barrier staring down the platform at the stream of people spewing out from the line of carriages.

'Remember,' said Noel. 'We'll only know him once he's gone past.'

Robin looked quizzical. 'Nothing on his front at all?' he asked. 'No tell-tale signs?'

'None. From the front you wouldn't know him from Adam,' said Noel.

'Except that Adam only wore a fig leaf,' said Robin.

'What?'

'Nothing. Here they come.'

The first passengers were now hurrying past them. As every man wearing a dark blue overcoat passed by – and there were many of them – Noel's and Robin's eyes followed the figure until they could see his back. Then they turned back to watch the rest of the approaching crowd.

'My money's on him,' Noel whispered, nodding emphatically in the direction of a bald, rotund man in his fifties who was waddling towards them with the gait of a penguin.

'You see? Coat's too big.' Noel paused before adding, 'And he looks embarrassed.'

Robin fixed his eyes on the ruddy cheeks of the man who now seemed to have increased the pace of his waddle to the point where he was becoming breathless. Noel and Robin adopted suitably innocent and carefree looks as the blue overcoated man approached within a few yards of where they were loitering. Even so, they both felt that the man gave them suspicious sidelong glances as he hurried by.

'Yessss!' hissed Noel as soon as the man's back was towards them. 'It's him!'

And, sure enough, it was. As Noel and Robin attempted to melt into the crowd whilst following the man at a discreet distance, they could see clearly the words on the back of his coat, picked out in a clear, gold weave:

## Buckingham Palace
### Make the most of it

'Come on,' said Noel. 'Let's follow him.'

Whether or not the quarry was conscious of being tracked, or just concerned to see who might be reading the words on his back, he turned his head several times over the next few minutes, causing Noel and Robin to adopt the sort of obviously disinterested poses they had seen in countless spy and detective films. One way or another, however, the man in the blue overcoat seemed to regard his followers as no more unnatural than everyone else who was caught up in the early morning melée, and he pursued his course with a certain intense vigour.

Turning right at the front of the station, he began to waddle along Victoria Street in a southerly direction. After a few hundred yards, he gave a quick and nervous look over his shoulder, and made a dash to cross the busy road. The movement was quick enough to avoid the red double-decker that was accelerating away from a bus-stop, but served only to precipitate him into the path of a black London taxicab.

Looking on the bright side – as Noel was later to do – the man in the blue overcoat could not have known much about it.

'He's broke,' said Stuart.

'You mean *we're* broke,' said Marianne, conscious of the dire financial circumstances that surrounded her on every side. Stuart looked puzzled.

'No. I mean *he's* broke. *Him*. The thermometer thing.'

'Oh, *him*!' said Marianne, rolling her eyes heavenwards and sighing deeply. The telephone rang and Marianne uncurled herself from the swivel chair before answering it.

'St Thomas's Vicarage. The Reverend Marianne Maddeley speaking.'

She pulled a distressed face for a moment or two and waved Stuart into the seat on the other side of the study, as she burrowed into the pile of papers on the desk in search of her diary. Once she had uncovered a well-thumbed Filofax, she settled back into her seat and started to flick through the pages in response to a request that was clearly being made by the caller.

She looked younger than her 32 years, largely due to her pink cheeks and plaited hair. In her smock, blue jeans and sandals, she looked more like an artist than a vicar. Only her crucifix earrings betrayed anything of her profession. Stuart, one of the churchwardens of St Thomas's, and a retired naval petty officer, twisted his tweed cap in his large, red fingers. He stared at his heavy, mud-spattered brogues, not wanting to look as if he were listening to the conversation.

'Mrs Murch,' said Marianne unenthusiastically, replacing the receiver with quiet precision. 'She's organizing another coffee morning, I fear.'

'Well, that's good, isn't it?' said Stuart innocently. Stuart devoted most of his time to the fabric of the church building, and managed to keep himself blissfully ignorant of the foibles of most of its acolytes. 'We could do with a bit more money.' Stuart was also a master of the understatement.

Marianne simply sighed once more. 'The last one made a loss of £12,' she said, managing something of a weak smile. 'Have you ever known such a thing? A coffee morning that made a loss! There's got to be a better way, Stu. There really has. I mean to say . . . Heaven help us all!'

Stuart appeared slightly embarrassed by the whole affair, and stared resolutely at his brogues.

The third man was waiting.

'Dead!' said Dominic Tredwell in exasperation. He pushed his long fingers languidly through his lank, flaxen locks. 'Dead? I don't believe it! For crying out loud!'

Robin grunted something under his breath and shrugged his shoulders. Noel breathed heavily, drained his coffee cup, and leaned forward with a look of blankness on his face. Dominic took off a pair of small, gold-rimmed glasses and laid them delicately in front of him.

'Dead,' he continued. 'Run over by a taxi! Your only exponent of a scheme that looked decidedly dodgy from the word go, and you get him killed off within minutes of the thing going public! I think even you have to admit, Noel, this whole thing has disaster written all over it.'

Robin sat back in his chair and gazed through the wide window at what was now a bright spring sky. Noel cleared his throat and fiddled with a teaspoon. It was nearly a year, but he was still missing his cigarettes.

'Look,' he breathed with an air of resignation. 'We've

been through this a hundred times already. I still think it's the beginning of something really big. A whole new concept in advertising. Using the one medium that is clearly not in short supply. People. Paying people to carry advertising has just got to be the biggest idea we've had for a long time.'

'Just so long as they don't fall under the wheels of a black cab and end up with tyre marks all over the bloody copy!' said Dominic through quivering, thin lips. 'I mean, it's not even as if the idea is new. It's simply sandwich-board men revisited – except without the rudimentary charm of a sandwich board. It's regressive – that's what it is. It sends out completely the wrong sort of message about an advertising agency that's supposed to be state of the art when it comes to new forms of communication. And as if that wasn't bad enough, we've now got to persuade the press that it wasn't actually our maniacal scheme that sent some poor commuter to an early grave!'

Dominic waved his hands about in a ritual of languid resignation before continuing. 'Come on. Come on! I thought we agreed we would be ground-breakers. That we would put an end to outdated styles of advertising. Instead of which we seem to have put an end to the one bloke who was fool enough to sign up for the new age of enlightenment! Can you imagine, can you just imagine, what the newspaper headlines are going to say? Oh, God!'

Dominic hid his face in his hands for a few seconds. When the face re-emerged it looked haggard and strangely pink. 'Robin,' he continued, rather more calmly. 'Robin, you're going to have to talk to the press. They'll believe you. That it was an accident, I mean. And that we are all – *all* – very deeply shocked and upset. And that our thoughts are with Mrs . . . Mrs . . .'

'Goodyear,' prompted Noel.

'. . . with Mrs Goodyear,' continued Dominic with a pained look, 'at this difficult time.'

Robin had been nervous about the initiative from the beginning. He felt sure that Mr Goodyear's death was not a

8

direct result of the now infamous overcoat, but he couldn't help thinking that the scheme had somehow always been doomed to failure. He was also fairly sure that the press would not let slip the chance to make the most of the situation. Whether or not they 'believed' him (as Dominic was inclined to think), Robin knew there would be some newspapers that would revel in the agency's apparent comeuppance. He briefly allowed himself to speculate about stories along the lines of 'Advertising Can Kill'. Even he, however, did not anticipate the 'Angel of Death' spin.

'I think we shouldn't overlook the positives,' said Robin, trying desperately to clutch at straws. 'Winning Buckingham Palace in the first place was something of a coup – no pun intended – and that was largely due to Noel's idea of not using traditional media: TV, radio, posters, and so on.'

'That's right,' added Noel, buoyed up by Robin's support. 'We won the pitch precisely because we were seen to be breaking the mould – but in a highly personalized way.'

'Oh, yes! Very highly personalized,' said Dominic. 'One man, in fact! Now deceased! Not exactly what you would call a mass movement, is it? Hardly likely to get the rest of the world beating a path to our door, is it?'

'Little acorns,' said Robin almost to himself.

'What?' said Dominic, pulling a face and leaning forward.

'Mighty oaks,' added Noel. 'Mighty oaks. Remember?'

Stuart did what he could to patch up the thermometer, but it looked to be on its last legs. It was a mainly wooden construction, about ten feet high, braced against the outside wall of St Thomas's Parish Church. It had been made by the Scouts at the suggestion of some parish worthy who had seen a similar device used effectively at an unspecified church a few miles away. The gradations up the side of the thermometer were calibrated as thousands of pounds: from one up to twenty at the top. At the base of the device was the bulge of the bulb or reservoir (a red plastic upturned bowl), from which protruded a capillary tube (or rather, a length of guttering) which extended up the middle of the thermometer. The idea was that more and more of the capillary would be painted red to reflect the increasing total of funds that had been raised for the maintenance and general running costs of the church building. It would be a 'sign to the gentiles' (the local people) of how well things were going in reinforcing the state of the building at the heart of their community.

That was the intention. The thermometer had been erected six months before with a flourish of pomp and circumstance at the end of the quarterly church parade. Someone had suggested that raising £20,000 before Easter was really 'not an issue'. The someone was right. Six months on and the figure of £1,246.38p had been raised. The red paint had barely passed the first mark on the side of the thermometer. What was more significant was that the mark had not moved at all during the dark and dismal months that followed Christmas.

As Marianne walked past the partially mended device on her way from the vicarage into the church grounds she reflected that there was really now no alternative. Having exploited all the traditional stratagems open to the Church of England (coffee mornings, jumble sales, bring-and-buy sales, and so on) without any noticeable success, there was only one thing left to try. She was going to have to pray for something different. For something *completely* different.

Robin sat in his office reflecting on the events that had brought him to this point. Angel, Fear & Tredwell had been formed two years before, when its three founders broke away from one of London's top advertising agencies to set themselves up as a new independent business. Calling itself a 'Communications Consultancy', this new company had consciously positioned itself as an innovative phenomenon in the marketing world: a business that would concern itself with all new forms of communications. That was the aim, but two years later it was still regarded by most observers as an advertising agency – albeit one with pretensions.

Dominic Tredwell was the agency's Managing Director and, to clients and potential clients, the most public face of the business. His slightly offhand manner (sometimes interpreted as arrogance) was excused on the basis of his undisputed effectiveness as a sharp businessman who understood clients' needs. Noel Fear was the Creative Director, and a bear of a man whose sideways perspective on most things was regarded as either creatively inspired or infuriating, depending on your point of view. Robin Angel was the least assuming of the three and, as Planning Director, was generally regarded as the thinker of the business. This was not so much due to any colossal brain – Dominic was probably more naturally intellectual – but rather to a degree of genuine insight and sensitivity that was considered rare in the industry. It was for this reason that Dominic tended to regard Robin as the agency's conscience.

The Buckingham Palace account had been acquired as part of the agency's strategy of targeting high-profile, ground-breaking clients. Yes, of course, argued Dominic, the agency should have its car account, its airline, its washing powder, and well-known brand of margarine – but it should also have 'new new clients' and provide them with 'new new communications opportunities'.

Dominic's original aim had been to acquire the Queen as a client, and – in case that didn't work – he had drawn up a target list of other Royals, their exes (former paramours), and general hangers-on with claims to regal connections. When he had suggested a policy that would see the agency working down the list until it found a 'taker', he had been pressed on 'how low the business should be prepared to go'. Noel had, indeed, asked whether a burnt-out marquis's son with a drugs problem, for example, would be considered sufficiently 'ground-breaking' as a client, or simply just bloody daft.

On this first occasion, Dominic had looked at Noel over the top of his glasses and said tartly, 'Mighty oaks from little acorns grow'. As it was, acquiring the Buckingham Palace account had satisfied several of the agency's short-term objectives. Until such time as the Queen *did* decide to start advertising, so Dominic reasoned, having the job of publicizing one of the nation's most eminent royal buildings was probably a good compromise.

The Palace project had also given Noel the chance to try out what he called his 'standard bearer' campaign. It was, he insisted, tailor-made for the opportunity – in more ways than one. It worked on the basis of choosing respectable individuals who commuted into the busy area close to Buckingham Palace. Those individuals would be paid a sum of money to advertise – or rather *communicate* – the benefits of the Palace to a wide range of people who travelled in from places such as Sevenoaks, Hertford and Woking on a daily basis, but who would not normally have considered paying to visit the newly installed simulated regal ride ('The Royal Rumble') which had recently opened at the Palace.

What is more, the 'communication' would be via a free, and uniquely personalized blue overcoat with gold lettering on the back. Perhaps, thought Robin, as he stared once more at the blue sky which filled the wide windows of the agency's Covent Garden offices, perhaps the 'how low should the business be prepared to go?' question of a few weeks previous had within it a clue for how such ground-breaking ideas could be tested. Were there perhaps ways in which really new ideas for potentially high-profile clients could be tested in small, low-risk ways? How might the temperature of an idea be taken without it costing the earth – and without giving the game away to competitors keen on a piece of the action?

Robin looked down at his pad, and wrote on it a single word: 'Thermometer'.

As he did so, the telephone rang. It was the agency's press officer asking if Robin would be prepared to give another interview regarding the lamentable case of the blue over-coat.

Several weeks later. The month of May.

Covent Garden was waking up and blinking its eyes. There was a thinness in the light, and a fleeting cleanness in the air. People moved purposefully as if shifting themselves into their positions for a play. It was the time of day when, for a few transient moments, thoughts of other existences might glide in and out of the imagination. It was possible to glimpse how, by turning up one street rather than another, one might be led to a whole new day, and a whole new way of life. But somehow those thoughts were rarely sufficient to override the various pressures that prompted people into their designated places.

Robin felt drawn along by an invisible thread. As he strode away from the tube station, he glanced at the sky. The thought of a walk by the river suddenly seemed the most appealing thing in the world. He could keep on going – through the marketplace, down to the Strand, and on to the river. He might even change his mind again before arriving there. Why not cut away to the right and wander through St James's Park? Why not simply walk – and then decide? Why not . . .?

The thread tugged and he turned into the street where the offices of Angel, Fear & Tredwell had been for the last two years. Not that this turning had necessarily closed down other possibilities, Robin reasoned to himself. He could keep going even now – ignoring the glass revolving door and moving on towards Charing Cross Road. He could dis-appear into a bookshop for an hour.

As he approached the tall, thin building that was home to his place of work, he winced at the knot of people he saw huddled around the entrance. Visitors? A welcoming committee? No. The smokers. The group known as 'The Last Gaspers'. Angel, Fear & Tredwell had introduced a no-smoking policy almost a year before – partly as a way of helping Noel in his efforts to give up. Those who wanted to smoke now had to go outside, and tended to stand only a few feet from the entrance as they inhaled in a hunched and single-minded way. As Robin neared the entrance he began to imagine a situation where the police would be called to move the smokers on, in the same way that vagrants were moved on. He opened his mouth to make some comment by way of remonstrance or warning, but instead found himself simply mouthing 'Good morning' as he was drawn finally into the angular and overtly artistic reception area.

On the second floor the agency appeared to be in turmoil – but then this was its natural state. Robin weaved his way along a corridor which opened into rooms on both sides. He was overtaken by a man running with a videotape in each hand. He was confronted by a woman balancing four plastic cups of coffee on a book. His progress was interrupted by bodies emerging quickly from one side only to disappear into a room opposite. The air was filled with the noise of hustle, and fraught with what Robin liked to think was 'creative tension'.

A man with a ponytail and a large nose, who was listing from side to side like a ship in choppy waters, smiled and said 'We've cracked it!' before squeezing past both Robin and a woman carrying a life-size cardboard cut-out of a man in a blue overcoat.

'What have you and Luke cracked?' Robin said, looking through a doorway into a room where a man with a pinched face and cropped hair was juggling with three magic markers.

'We've got the line,' said Keith. 'What do you think of this?' He put the magic markers down on what looked like a kitchen table, and picked up a whiteboard on which were scrawled the words: 'Leave a little love in your lav'. Robin looked unsure. 'Or how about this one?' added Keith. 'It's rather more focused on the product's functional benefit.' Robin stared at another board on which were the words: 'Flush with success'.

'I'm sorry, Keith,' he said, turning to go, 'but I'm due in the boardroom right this minute.'

St Thomas's Parish Church was on its knees – and so was Marianne Maddeley.

'Look, Lord, I know that, in the great wide vista of things, the fate of St Thomas's doesn't add up to a hill of beans. And I know we only ever get about 20 people turning up on a Sunday morning. But, even so . . . Would it really be asking too much for you to send us something to get us out of this hole? I mean, after all, I'm not asking for a visit from the Archangel Gabriel. A few thousand pounds to sort out the worst of the gaps in the roof would be enough. Well, at least in the short term. After that's been sorted, of course, we've got the problem of the bits falling off the spire, the collapsing pews, the broken windows, the recalcitrant heating, the unpredictable electrics, and the fence – or rather the lack of one. Then there's the flooring in the vestry, the hymn books, the broken lock on the west-end door, the crumbling wall along the south aisle, and something to stop the water leaking out of the font. Come to think of it, this might be a job for the Archangel after all. What's he like at plastering?'

Compared to the rest of the agency, there was relative peace in the boardroom. Noel was pouring himself a coffee. Dominic had not yet arrived.

'Keith just showed me some ideas for the new toilet cleaner campaign,' said Robin.

'San Pan,' said Noel slowly, enjoying the sound of the brand name. 'It's a blend of fine fragrance and enzymatic efficiency – not a toilet cleaner, if you don't mind. My vision for the product launch is an airship in the shape of the bottle, dropping perfumed parcels into the Thames. What do you think?'

Robin was spared the effort of an answer because, at that moment, Dominic Tredwell strode into the room and sat down at the head of the table.

'I've not got long. The new business pitch for those micro-waveable petfoods is in 20 minutes, so let's get straight to the point.'

'Which is . . . ?' said Noel vaguely.

'Don't you ever read your e-mails, Noel?' grunted Dominic. 'Charity. Ethics. Worthy clients. Yes? Something to regain us a little sympathy and credibility with the Great British public after that Buckingham Palace fiasco.'

'As it was my suggestion, perhaps I could just outline the idea again,' said Robin, anxious that his two colleagues should not fall out quite so early in the morning – and especially over a subject in which he felt a keen personal interest. 'Quite apart from the need to regain lost ground in terms of our public relations, it seemed to me to represent a real opportunity,' he continued. 'In a business environment that appears increasingly to be adopting something of an ethical dimension, we should perhaps try to make sure that some of our work at least is used to support a charity or another worthy, non-profit-making organization. It wouldn't be simply a matter of damage-limitation, salving our conscience, or philanthropy. I can see it very much as contributing to the sort of approach we've been adopting elsewhere. It would be different, potentially ground-breaking – and newsworthy in the best possible way. We would be seen to be in step with the trend towards a more caring kind of commercialism, and it would also demonstrate how versatile and adaptable our techniques and tools were. On balance, I think Mr Goodyear's death was finally seen for what it was – an unfortunate accident. But there's no doubt that we could do more to emphasize the point that our approach is essentially about creativity rather than destruction. Hence my e-mail, and this meeting.'

'OK,' said Dominic sternly, taking off his glasses. 'Charity client. Does that mean that we do the work out of a sense of charity? That we do it for love, as it were, and not for money?'

'Well, I'm not sure about "love",' said Robin, interlacing his fingers and speaking in a very deliberate way. 'What I had in mind was something of a virtuous circle.'

'Virtuous what?' grunted Noel, who seemed to slip in and out of conversations as various words engaged or lost his attention.

'Circle,' continued Robin, leaning forward with the first signs of animation spreading across his face. 'A way in which any activity would largely pay for itself by being based around some kind of sponsorship deal. We would dedicate a relatively small amount of creative resource to coming up with the ideas, and then various commercial businesses would invest in an enterprise that would be seen to be in everyone's interest.'

'I don't understand,' said Noel, pulling on his puffy face with his podgy fingers. 'Give us an example.'

'Well,' said Robin, 'let's imagine our charity is a special hospital of some kind. The hospital needs money, and we come up with some creative ways in which leading businesses and brands can advertise in and around the hospital in return for providing sponsorship money. Now, I'm sure, Noel, that you could come up with some better ideas than this – but bear with me. We could get a leading pantyhose brand to provide money and merchandise, so that the nurses – at least the female ones – could wear some chic black tights that displayed the brand name prominently. The hospital gets finance and goods from the deal. The pantyhose business gets branded exposure in a very worthy environment. And *we* get the favourable publicity of having set the whole deal up in the first place. You see? That's why I call it a virtuous circle. No one loses.'

'After all, what have we got to lose?' said Marianne, looking resignedly at the few faces around her.

'Desperate times call for desperate men,' said Stuart.

'I think it's desperate measures, Stu,' said Marianne. 'Not men.'

'And women,' said Gladys Wheeler, who appeared to have missed the point completely. It was a meeting of the rather depleted St Thomas's Parochial Church Council, convened to discuss the worsening situation of the parish finances. The vicar had painted a picture that was only too clear for those assembled. In the last six months the only thing that had been fixed at the church was the thermometer that now proudly showed how bad the situation had become.

Mrs Murch had asked if the bishop might be approached. Indeed, she offered to make tea in the event of an episcopal visitation. 'Surely *he* would appreciate our predicament and put everything right?'

In the face of such misguided optimism Marianne had realized that there was nothing for it. She would have to tell them. Yes, she had contacted the bishop's office. No, she hadn't spoken to the bishop in person – but she had spoken to the archdeacon. His analysis of the position had been bleak. He had revealed that a working party had been looking at the possibility of amalgamating the parish of St Thomas's with the neighbouring team ministry. However, this would not be a lifeline for St Thomas's Parish Church. Quite the opposite, in fact. It would almost certainly signal the closure of St Thomas's for good. The archdeacon had been, Marianne felt, very frank and very honest with her. St Thomas's would be given another six months to show some signs of 'recovery'. If no such signs were apparent, then the first steps would be taken to achieve what was now being described as a more 'strategic' solution. St Thomas's would cease to function as a place of worship, and the church's small flock would be invited to make the one-mile journey to the somewhat more prosperous environs of the next church along.

'But what about you?' Mrs Murch had enquired of Marianne.

'Oh, I'm sure they'd find another job for me. There are all sorts of new and exciting challenges awaiting the Church. Don't you worry about me.'

It was at this point that Stuart had chimed in with: 'You could take some time off to get married and have babies.'

'Yes, well, thank you, Stu, for that helpful suggestion,' Marianne had replied sourly. 'So, can I now please bring us back to the matter in hand and suggest that we really now have no option. We have to go for it.'

'Go for it?' asked Gladys Wheeler. 'Where are we going?'

'We're not going anywhere, Mrs Wheeler,' said Stuart.

Gladys looked reassured, and Marianne continued. 'We have to make one last effort. I know we've tried a whole host of things, but clearly none of them has worked. We now have about six months to have one last go. That means it's all or nothing. We've got to think of much more radical options. We've got to be different. Let's take a leaf out of Jesus' book.'

'You mean the Bible?' said Gladys Wheeler.

'Well, not exactly, Gladys,' said Marianne, pursing her lips patiently. 'I meant that we need to do the sort of thing that he did.'

'Like what?' said Stuart, who was nothing if not practical. 'I'm not sure I can do half the things he did.'

'No, Stu. I'm not asking you to do any miracles. I'm asking you to think radically. Jesus was always challenging conventional wisdom. He was always turning things upside down.'

'And that's what you want *us* to do?' asked Mrs Murch.

'You want us to turn the church upside down?' said Gladys Wheeler.

Marianne sighed and looked at the earnest, elderly faces around her. 'Er . . . possibly,' she said.

'But what if it doesn't work?' said Dominic, his brow furrowed with lines.

'If it doesn't work?' echoed Robin.

'If we choose some high-profile hospital or children's charity or whatever it happens to be,' continued Dominic, 'and the thing is either a damp squib or, worse, is seen as being in rather bad taste – what then? It will just confirm everyone's worst suspicions about us – especially after . . . Well, you know what I mean. I think we may simply be asking for trouble if we do anything other than keep a very low profile for some time to come.'

'It doesn't have to be high profile,' Robin countered. 'We could choose a small charity of some kind and just see how it goes. If it works, we can move on to something bigger.'

'So why would any self-respecting business want to get involved with a small charity?'

Dominic's greatest asset – but also the thing that most grated on his colleagues – was his relentless critical reasoning.

'A *local* charity?' hazarded Noel vaguely. 'Sponsored by *local* businesses? They'd share some kind of local purpose, I suppose.'

'Local?' Dominic almost barked at him. '*Local*? We're supposed to be a business of big ideas. Where does "local" fit into our strategy?'

'Well,' Noel continued, 'at least it would then all be to scale – if you see what I mean. Local businesses probably wouldn't want – and, anyway, couldn't afford – anything bigger. We could do a scaled-down test of what Robin's suggesting on a small, low-risk local basis. And then, if it worked, we could scale up gradually. Acorns to oaks again, as it were.'

Robin was nodding. Dominic did not immediately respond. He started to fiddle with his glasses. 'Except,' he said at last. 'Except we couldn't just scale it up if it was a hospital. We'd have to do separate deals with every different hospital. It would be a nightmare. And we'd have no single client.'

'OK,' said Noel, who was beginning to get interested in the idea. 'What about charity shops? The major charities have a shop in every shopping centre. We could start with one shop, and then work out from there.'

Dominic looked at his watch. 'But why would any local business want to sponsor one shop among many?' he said. 'Look, Robin, I'm sorry. I was never warm on this idea to start with. And, frankly, I'm getting cooler by the minute.'

As Dominic prepared to leave the room, Robin looked down at his pad and at the word he had written there some time before. *Thermometer.*

'Hold on!' he said excitedly. Noel and Dominic were taken aback by this sudden outburst of assertiveness. 'Hold on,' said Robin again, remembering the thing he had noticed every day as he walked from his flat to the tube station. 'I've got it! I've got it!'

'Bubonic plague? St Vitus's dance? What exactly is it that you've got?' said Dominic sardonically.

'Listen,' said Robin. 'Would you call the Church of England a charity?'

'Well, it's certainly not a business,' said Noel.

'And it's an organization that only seems to survive because people give it money,' added Dominic, 'if that's what you mean.'

'Exactly!' said Robin. 'It's a high-profile organization – and yet, for most of the time, people ignore it. It's a national organization – yet it's made up of thousands of very small local units. It's got lots and lots of valuable fixed assets – and yet it always seems to be in some kind of financial trouble. It's constantly seen as being out of touch – and yet no public figure ever wants to be seen to be at odds with it. At the same time it's both the most visible *and* the most irrelevant of our national institutions.'

'I think I see what you're driving at,' said Noel.

'But is it a charity?' said Dominic, who was now chewing the end of his glasses in a thoughtful way.

'Well,' said Robin, smiling at last. 'My impression is that the Church of England is whatever anyone wants it to be.'

St Thomas's parish 'surgery' took place in the vestry every Wednesday evening between seven and eight o'clock. Robin arrived at five to eight. Marianne was seated behind an old desk preparing to clear away and lock up for the night. The surgery had been an uneventful one: two couples had been in to collect banns certificates, and a man who was new to the neighbourhood had enquired whether he could have his new baby daughter christened at the church. Marianne looked up when she heard a knock on the already open door, and felt a slight flush in her cheeks as the slim, dark figure of Robin advanced across the floor with hand outstretched.

'Reverend Maddeley?' he said softly. 'I hope I'm not too late. You remember? I phoned yesterday to ask if I might see you.'

'Mr Angel?' murmured Marianne, standing up and walking around the desk to grasp Robin's hand. She laughed nervously. 'I'm sorry,' she said by way of excuse. 'I don't get many angels around here. Well, not at parish surgery that is!'

'Of course,' said Robin betraying no trace of a smile, and

suddenly finding himself at a loss for words. 'I'm sorry. About the angels.'

'Well,' she said hesitantly. 'At least we've got *that* in common.'

Robin looked puzzled.

'We're both sorry,' Marianne continued, putting her hands together, and moving her weight backwards and forwards from one foot to the other. 'So, what was it you wanted to discuss, Mr Angel?'

'Robin,' said Robin, clearing his throat. 'Please call me Robin, Reverend.'

'Marianne,' said Marianne, also clearing her throat. 'When you phoned, you said something about church finances – a subject dear to my heart!'

'Your heart. Yes,' said Robin. 'Indeed. That is . . . I mean . . . I was wondering if you . . . That is . . . If you would be interested in . . . a *plan*. Yes. A plan. A way, perhaps, of getting some more money into the church.'

There seemed to be quite a long silence before Marianne replied. 'More money into the church?' Her voice was quiet and non-committal.

'Perhaps we could discuss it?' Robin suggested, shrugging slightly, before once more clearing his throat and looking nervously around the room. 'I was just about to pop down to Luigi's for something to eat. I don't suppose you'd like to discuss it over a bowl of pasta, would you?'

'Discuss what?' said Marianne in a voice that sounded just a little bit long ago and far away.

'The plan,' said Robin.

'Oh, yes,' said Marianne. 'The plan.' She then paused before saying, 'I don't normally do this, you know.'

'This?'

'Go out with perfect strangers,' she added. Robin smiled for almost the first time since he had entered the church.

'How could you have known so quickly that I was perfect?' he said. It was such a little joke, but it served to break the ice at last, and the two of them chortled slyly like

23

schoolchildren who laugh at a grown-up joke about which they understand nothing except that it is something adult.

June.

The huge sheath had been placed over the church spire, but the fabric had snagged about halfway down. The crane began to move once again, and the cradle carrying the two men started to edge slowly away from the highest point of St Thomas's. Dave, the steeplejack, leaned out of the cradle.

'It's just a bit caught up on itself as far as I can see. Shouldn't be much of a problem. We just need to lift it away from the stonework and let it drop back again.'

'*We*?' said Robin. 'I only came along for the ride.'

Dave was very matter-of-fact. 'Yep. I reckon it'll take the two of us. Shouldn't be a problem, though. Just so long as Sean can keep the cradle from swinging about.'

Sean was the crane driver. Robin swallowed hard and looked out over the edge of the cradle. He could just make out the top of the apartment block where he lived, nearly half a mile away. Dave spoke to Sean on his walkie-talkie, and seconds later the cradle swung back towards the church spire. Robin hung on to the rail around the top of the cradle.

'Whoa!' called Dave, as the contraption jerked to a halt about three feet away from the stonework. The giant sheath, which had been created to fit the spire perfectly, was made of a light, off-white canvas material. Large red letters from top to bottom spelled out the word 'SPIRES'. Due to the snagging, however, it looked more like 'SPIP'.

'Right,' said Dave. 'If you can catch hold of that edge – yep, that one – then I should be able to lean round and pull the thing loose where it's doubled back on itself.'

Robin looked dubious. 'You want me to catch hold of the sheath?' he said in a voice that was somewhat smaller than the occasion seemed to demand.

'That's it,' said Dave, not even looking at him.

'Right,' said Robin. He swallowed again and looked down briefly. It was not a good idea. Below him he could see that a large crowd had now gathered to enjoy the spectacle, and the sight filled him with foreboding. With one hand gripping the rail tightly, he leaned across in an attempt to grab hold of the edge that Dave had indicated to him. It was just beyond his reach, and he had to strain to make the last few inches. Unfortunately, it was just as his fingers were closing around the canvas that he felt the cradle slipping back, just enough to tip the whole of his upper body into an almost horizontal position.

'Da-a-a-a-a-a-a-a-ve!!!'

It was more a strangulated cry than a recognizable name, but it clearly had the desired effect as Robin felt his legs suddenly gripped strongly by the steeplejack's hands.

'It's all right,' called Dave. 'I've got you!'

If Robin had had any breath left in his lungs he might have called back 'No, it's bloody well *not* all right!' As it was, he just grimaced and tried to think about anything other than the prospect of imminent death. His train of thought was interrupted by Dave, who – far from regarding the situation as anything like a crisis – was calmly relaying instructions to him.

'Right,' called Dave. 'Seeing as I've got your legs, you can let go of the rail altogether and use both hands to shake the whole thing free. All right?'

'Let go of the rail!?'

Robin's words issued forth as something of a squeak, and were probably lost in the light wind that was now causing the cradle to wobble slightly from side to side. He stared up at the letters spelling the word 'SPIP' and wondered how on earth he could have ended up in this situation.

It was partly Luigi's fault, Robin was later to reflect. Luigi had recognized Marianne as the local vicar, even though he had never spoken to her nor seen her in his restaurant. As part of the local Roman Catholic community, however, he had found the arrival of a woman priest in the Anglican parish church something of an intriguing curiosity.

'But surely you're against women priests,' said Robin, as Luigi insisted on pulling back the chair for Marianne to sit down.

'I'ma never againsta women anything,' said Luigi, his florid face managing to express nothing other than sincere egalitarianism. 'I'ma sure thata one day we'll hava Popess.'

'A Popess?' repeated Marianne, certain that Luigi was baiting her. The restaurateur, however, maintained his aura of seriousness.

'Si, signora. A Popess.'

In fact, Luigi seemed so impressed by Marianne's presence in his restaurant that he insisted on supplying a free extra bottle of wine with their meal – 'to celebrate the future of the one Church'.

'So,' said Marianne, once she and Robin were alone. 'You have a cunning plan. To assist with the finances of St Thomas's.'

'A plan,' repeated Robin. 'Yes, indeed. A plan.' He tried to stop himself from gazing so obviously into Marianne's eyes, and instead started folding his napkin into various shapes. 'A plan. Yes,' he said again. 'I call it my virtuous circle. It's an idea I thought might help attract some money into St Thomas's.'

'But why would you be interested in St Thomas's?' asked Marianne.

'Why indeed?' muttered Robin, trying to concentrate once more on the napkin, rather than on the face that glowed in the light of a candle just a few inches away. 'Because,' he said, 'because I'm in communications. Well, advertising, actually. And I'm very keen to try out an idea which is all about introducing direct sponsorship into something like the Church. You see, I live in the parish and, even though I don't come to church, I'm aware of how much potential St Thomas's has – as a building, that is. It is, after all, something of a prime site.'

'Prime site or not, you're presumably aware that the building is in a state of considerable disrepair, and that there really is no money to put things right.'

'Well,' said Robin, looking up again, 'I've seen the thermometer. Outside the church. I walk past it every day on my way to the station. I know the red bit hasn't moved very much.'

Marianne pulled a face as if to say 'it's even worse than that'. 'So what's so virtuous about your circle?' she said.

'Basically,' replied Robin, 'as far as I can see, no one should lose out. Although, clearly, I wouldn't expect *every*-one at your church necessarily to go for it. The idea, I mean.'

Marianne made a gesture that invited Robin to keep talking.

'As I say,' he continued. 'It works on the basis of sponsorship. My colleagues and I at the agency would come up with some specific ideas for using your church facilities to advertise one or more local businesses. We'd then contact those businesses, let them know our ideas, and invite them to pay for the publicity. The money would all come to the church, of course, rather than to us.'

'You'd be doing this for nothing?' asked Marianne suspiciously.

'Well, not exactly,' said Robin. 'The sponsorship ideas themselves would come only from us – and we'd try to make sure that each one of them was especially creative and in some way ground-breaking. It would therefore be a way for us to test out some slightly off-the-wall ideas – and, if it all worked, of course, we'd get the credit for the ideas, and for providing "free" help to a worthy and deserving client.'

In the ensuing pause they both sipped their wine thoughtfully.

'So you're not exactly doing this out of love, then?' she said.

Robin spluttered, misunderstanding for a moment what she had meant. 'Out of love? Well, no. It's very much in line with the agency's business objectives. We're not a charity after all.'

'No,' said Marianne thoughtfully. 'And perhaps the church shouldn't be a charity either.'

The Parochial Church Council was now meeting on an almost weekly basis, although most meetings seemed only to attract a handful of those who were entitled to attend. Stuart, the churchwarden, was there as usual, with Mrs Murch and Gladys Wheeler. Also in attendance on this particular occasion were Wilfred Maybury, the part-time verger, and Terry Webb. Terry was looking disappointed. His long body, which was usually cloaked in an overly large and wildly colourful, hand-knitted sweater, sagged on its chair. His long face, which was prone to random sproutings of facial hair, seeped with chagrin. The council had just rejected his suggestion for turning St Thomas's into a hostel, so that the local authority would be responsible for the upkeep of the building.

Wilfred's suggestion met with about as much enthusiasm. Even Wilfred Maybury's friends admitted that he looked like a ghoul. It was one of the things they liked about him. He always seemed to get served quickly in pubs. The suggestion was that St Thomas's should start charging an entrance fee at the door on Sunday mornings – 'just like some of the museums did'. Marianne probably captured the feelings of the rest of those present when she opined that this would probably have the effect of reducing attendances from the heady figure of twenty to something nearer five. Wilfred curled a lip in disappointment, and receded into the shadows in a ghoulish manner.

'Which probably leaves us,' added Marianne, 'with only the sponsorship idea left on the table. The virtuous circle.'

'I'm not sure,' said Mrs Murch, placing her head first on one side and then on the other. 'I'd be a bit worried that it was all something of a stunt.'

'A stunt?' prompted Marianne.

'Yes,' continued Mrs Murch. 'You know. A bit of a flash in the pan. Perhaps I'm being too suspicious, but I can see more benefit in it for these advertising people than for us.'

'I think I know what Mrs Murch is driving at,' chipped in Stuart. '*Any* kind of publicity is probably all right for *them*. But for *us*,' Stuart paused, 'for *us* there's got to be more in it. We've got more at stake, so to speak.'

It was at this point that Gladys Wheeler entered the debate. 'Why is it a circle?' she said.

'Why is what a circle?' countered Marianne.

'The virtuous circle,' persisted Gladys. 'Why is it a circle?'

Mrs Murch leaned over to her friend and whispered loudly that she would tell her later. That simply meant that Gladys took on the look of someone who had inadvertently asked a delicate and inappropriate question. For the rest of the meeting she sat chastened and resolutely mute.

'So,' said Marianne, sensing she should make the most of the ensuing silence, 'we're agreed then. We will go ahead with a pilot scheme to find out whether this approach will help us to raise some money.'

'Who's the pilot, then?' asked Stuart.

Marianne just stopped herself from correcting Stuart. His 'who', of course, meant 'what'.

'Well, Stu,' she said, 'I don't know all the details just yet, but I gather it's something to do with putting some advertising on the church spire.'

'But that's been done before, hasn't it?' said Mrs Murch, surprised at her own sense of disappointment. 'I think I remember reading about a church that had some advert or something on its spire.'

'You may be right, Mrs Murch,' replied Marianne. 'But

I get the idea that this is likely to be something a bit different.'

'A *what*?' Dominic's voice betrayed his exasperation.

'A sheath,' repeated Noel.

'A contraceptive?' Dominic's exasperation was now more akin to incredulity.

'No, of course not!' Now it was Noel's turn to be exasperated. 'When I use the word sheath,' continued Noel, calming himself with a mouthful of coffee, 'I'm talking about a tight-fitting, made-to-measure cover for the church spire. Something semi-permanent that will look very much as though it has been designed for the job.'

Dominic stood up and walked up and down in front of the large window that looked down on the busy street below. 'Look,' he said through thin lips. 'I'm not saying it's wrong. All I'm saying is . . . it all seems a bit . . . well, a bit . . . marginal.'

'Marginal?'

It was Robin's first contribution to the discussion.

'Yes. Marginal,' continued Dominic, looking at Noel. 'I mean, first there was your Buckingham Palace campaign. Sandwich-board men – without the sandwich boards. Now it's a sheath, for God's sake, on a church! You've got to admit, it's hardly the sort of ground-breaking work that's likely to make history, is it?'

'But there's more,' added Robin, feeling that Noel should not have to take all the blame – or the credit – for the creative idea. 'There's a combination of things here that's bound to ensure that the whole thing attracts a lot of media interest.'

'Like what?' growled Dominic, sitting down again.

'Like the name,' said Robin. 'The name of the advertiser.'

'It's Spires,' said Noel, searching in his pocket for a

packet of mints. 'Spires. The name of one of the local estate agents.'

'I saw the name the day after I met Marianne,' asserted Robin, who was keen to show that it had originally been *his* suggestion.

'Marianne?' said Dominic over the top of his glasses.

'The vicar,' said Robin, clearing his throat. 'The day after I met her I realized that Spires, the local estate agent, might be a candidate for some kind of pilot scheme. It just seemed too good a chance to turn down. That's when I got Noel on the job.'

'The sheath was my idea,' said Noel proudly. 'You remember some years ago those people who wrapped up the Reichstag like a parcel – as a work of art? Well, I thought that dropping a giant sheath over a church spire would be a great symbol of an antiquated institution embracing modern culture.'

Dominic pulled a face. 'Noel,' he said. 'Just stick to writing jingles, will you? And leave the social commentary to me.'

'But you haven't heard it all,' interrupted Robin, keen that Dominic should be made aware of the full potential impact of the sheath idea.

'There's more?' said Dominic, with just a hint of sarcasm. 'Don't tell me. It changes colour with the temperature.'

'Not quite,' said Noel seriously, wishing that he had thought of that idea himself. 'But it *will* glow in the dark.'

'At night you'll be able to see it for miles around,' added Robin. It might have been the last straw for Dominic. Had his mood been different, this last statement might finally have tipped him over the edge into an outright condemnation of the initiative. As it was, it was just enough to push him the other way. His immediate silence showed that he was considering the prospect carefully.

'I suppose it might be enough,' he said at last. 'It might be just enough to generate some real media interest. When does it go up? Or on? The sheath, that is.'

Noel smiled at Robin. He knew when he had Dominic's interest. 'It's being made next week,' he said.

'And I've arranged to be there when it's fitted,' added Robin, allowing himself to think of Marianne. 'I thought it was probably an occasion that deserved something of a hands-on approach.'

Whether it was an act of faith, desperation or blind panic, Robin wasn't really sure. All he knew was that he had let go of the rail, and was now clutching hold of the canvas sheath with both hands. Meanwhile his legs were still being held in a vice-like grip by Dave, who was bracing himself against the edge of the cradle that dangled from the crane.

'Don't panic,' called Dave. And then, in an effort to bring a relaxed note of levity to his voice, he added, 'You'll be OK – just so long as your trousers don't come off!'

Down below, Robin's movements were receiving a mixed reaction.

'Tell me again,' said Gladys Wheeler slowly. 'What does SPIP mean?'

'I just hope that cradle doesn't move any further away,' said Stuart helpfully. 'Otherwise that poor Mr Angel's going to be left dangling from the spire.'

'Yes, thank you, Stu,' said Marianne, catching her breath and trying to stay calm. 'I'm sure he knows what he's doing.'

'I knew it would be a stunt,' added Mrs Murch, oblivious to the evident concern in the vicar's voice. 'Look at them. All those people from the newspapers and the television. This is all being done for *their* benefit.'

And sure enough, by now, there was a considerable crowd gathered in the grounds around St Thomas's. That crowd was being added to by the minute, and even the traffic had stopped to watch what was going on.

'Stu,' said Marianne, picking nervously at her fingers.

'Call the police. Call the fire brigade! Call an ambulance!!'

'Why?' said Stuart, looking as vacant as it was possible to look in the circumstances.

'I don't know!' Marianne almost screamed. 'Just call *some*one!'

There was no need to call anyone, however. Everyone seemed to be there already – including several representatives of the emergency services. Most of them were staring up at the top of the church, although Noel (who had arrived late) was giving an interview to a television team. Suddenly a great shout went up all around the church, and Noel turned to see what had happened. Had his colleague finally lost his grip on reality and fallen to earth? No. The shout was a cheer – because Robin had managed to loosen the sheath, which had now fallen into place, revealing the full splendour of the large red letters spelling the word SPIRES. A second cheer went up when Robin, who had now been safely hauled back into the cradle by Dave, turned to wave to the crowd.

'Did you get that?' Noel was beside himself with excitement as he harangued the television crew. 'Did you get that? I do hope you got that!'

As the crane started to lower the cradle, the crowd began to disperse. Several people took the opportunity to make a comment of some kind to the vicar as they passed her.

'Very brave,' said one local dignitary as he clasped her hand in his.

'Yes, he is, isn't he?' replied Marianne, turning to watch Robin finally descending to ground level. The dignitary hesitated for a moment before saying, 'No, I'm sorry. You misunderstand. I meant it's very brave of *you*. Taking on something like this.'

'Oh,' said Marianne in something of a daze.

'Are you all right?' asked Stuart, who was now glowing with a sense of new-found celebrity.

'I think so,' said Marianne. 'I think so. Thank God it's all over!'

# II

## ANGEL SPEAKS

**With the growth of new commercial schemes now evident in several parts of the country, *The Church Times* asked Robin Angel, Planning Director of the main agency involved, to share some thoughts on the ways the various initiatives have developed. First, was he surprised by the extent of the activity?**

'Most certainly. By the extent, yes. But also by the speed. I don't think any of us anticipated the urgency with which other churches would take up the challenge. It's only four weeks since we put the sheath on the spire at St Thomas's, and yet reports are coming in daily of other churches launching local advertising and sponsorship deals.'

Were those 'deals' all being set up via Mr Angel's own agency?

'Not necessarily. In several cases, vicars have adopted copycat strategies, and formed alliances with local agencies and businesses. Many of these arrangements appear to be working on a fairly straightforward advertising basis, with each commercial interest paying the parish to use the outside of the church building for display purposes. Increasingly, though, calls are coming through to our agency for some kind of consultancy.'

Why did Mr Angel think this was?

'There are probably two main reasons. First and most important is the fact that a lot of the churches seem to want to be overtly associated with the approach being used at St Thomas's. The placing of the sheath over the spire attracted far more television coverage than we expected, and the vicar – the Reverend Marianne Maddeley – has become something of a minor TV celebrity. Because of that, the name of Angel, Fear & Tredwell has also become fairly well known in church circles – and, given that vicars on the whole are not used to dealing with advertising agencies, I think most of them would rather be talking to the one that they've heard about.'

And the second reason?

'Additionally, my colleagues and I went on record soon after the first coverage of the St Thomas's situation to say that our schemes would be both innovative and without cost. How? Well, in a nutshell, we decided that we wanted to associate ourselves very publicly with what we saw as a win-win situation. From the agency's point of view, an association with the Church guarantees us a large – and apparently growing – shop-window for a range of marketing initiatives which go well beyond the realms of the more everyday forms of advertising. From the local churches' point of view, they are guaranteed new ideas – by which I mean something more than just another sheath-on-a-spire campaign – without it costing them a penny. Any specific agency costs in all cases come out of the money that local business interests are prepared to invest.'

Mr Angel's smile was bemused as well as broad, as if even he could not quite grasp the way it was working. For, whilst it was clearly possible for churches to approach any local agency for marketing help of this kind, so long as Angel, Fear & Tredwell promised 'genuine innovation' free of charge, there was no great reason to go anywhere else. And with the number of churches in need of extra funds growing every week, it seems that Mr Angel and his colleagues may well have cornered the market, as they say.

But what of the Church authorities? Are there no plans to regulate this outbreak of localized commercialism? Well, apparently not – at least for the time being. Indeed, informed sources suggest that the Church may be 'over a barrel' on this issue. Whilst it may not exactly like the idea of creeping commercialization, the Church's parlous economic state at a local level means that no one seems willing to denounce an approach that is certain to raise not only funds, but also local interest and support – whilst also improving the Church's image and sense of relevance for the twenty-first century. It may yet be early days, but this writer for one feels that the signs are set fair for a whole new chapter in the history of the Church of England.

It was the first time Robin had ever picked up *The Church Times*, and when he put it down again it was with a great sense of satisfaction. They had not even mentioned the man in the blue overcoat. But then, of what importance was the past, he mused, when the future clearly offered so much more?

They had just emerged from the tube.

'Weren't you even just a *little* bit worried?'

'Of course not,' replied Marianne. 'It *is* your job, after all.'

'Not climbing bloody church steeples, it isn't,' said Robin warmly. He hesitated. He wasn't sure that using the adjective 'bloody' in such close conjunction with the word 'church' had been a good move. He was also not sure as to whether he hadn't used a double negative in the sentence.

'That is to say . . .' he continued at last. 'My job does not normally include doing things quite as hazardous as that. And I have to say that it was most definitely the first time I have been quite so high – and certainly the first time I have been quite so close to the top of a church building.'

'Mrs Murch maintains it was a publicity stunt, and that you purposely arranged to be hung out of that crane thing by your legs. She says that's why the television cameras were there.'

'And who, might I ask, is Mrs Murch?'

'Mrs Murch,' said Marianne, stopping and looking Robin full in the face, 'Mrs Murch happens to be a very eminent member of the PCC.'

'PCC?'

'The St Thomas's Parochial Church Council,' continued Marianne. 'An important local body which you should meet face to face, given the role you and your agency seem to have taken in the life of our local community.'

Robin was staring mutely back at her face, apparently lost for words.

'Of course,' he mumbled at last. 'Indeed,' he added, unsure exactly what he was saying.

'So,' said Marianne, 'I'll take that as a "yes", shall I? As an assurance that you'll come to the next PCC meeting.'

'Next PCC meeting,' repeated Robin weakly, turning his head and beginning once more to walk towards the agency office. Since the episode of the sheath on the spire, Robin and Marianne had met on a few occasions to discuss ways to continue the 'virtuous circle' initiative at St Thomas's. Most of the meetings had taken place in the church itself, or in Luigi's place – which had become something of an accepted rendezvous. In the eight weeks that had elapsed since their original meeting in the church vestry, however, Marianne had so far not visited the premises of Angel, Fear & Tredwell. In some respects, this was unusual. Robin would normally have wanted a new client to see the agency set-up at close quarters. But for some reason he had stopped himself from inviting the Reverend Maddeley to

Covent Garden. The omission had not passed without notice. Noel for one had made a few comments to the effect that Robin appeared to be 'keeping the vicar to himself'. It was partly because of this perception, and partly in response to Marianne's own enquiries, that Robin decided the time had finally arrived for her to see the inside of the organization that had already started to turn her church upside down.

By arrangement he had called at the vicarage on his way to the station, and they had travelled into town together.

'It may not be what you expect,' he said as they turned the corner – immediately berating himself for being so unnecessarily apologetic.

'Why?' said Marianne, rather more sharply than she had intended. 'What do you think I'm expecting?'

'Well,' said Robin, noting with some satisfaction that there appeared to be only two of 'The Last Gaspers' loitering outside the front door. 'You might have been expecting something . . . something overtly *creative* . . .'

He let the sentence drift into nothingness. No, he reflected, this was not going well at all.

'Whereas?' prompted Marianne, turning to look at him with apparently wide and innocent eyes.

'Whereas,' said Robin, coughing slightly, 'it's pretty much like any office really. You know . . . rooms, corridors, telephones ringing all the time, people rushing about, photocopiers. That sort of thing.'

'Surely not,' simpered Marianne, enjoying the debilitating effect she seemed to be having on Robin. 'You'll be telling me next that the copywriters have given up using quill pens. Do you honestly think I'm that naïve? Even if I had been, remember that, thanks to you, I've now also met Noel. Whilst you were doing your dangling and daring bit. Remember? Well, believe me, after listening to his graphic explanation of why a giant condom was "the best bloody thing the church could hope for", I'm not expecting your agency to be an oasis of pure craft and artistry!'

38

Robin did not smile. As he led Marianne into the building he felt a sudden urge to reinforce his position in the eyes
of this, his most recent client.

'Well, whatever Noel may have said or not said, can I
suggest that you continue to regard *me* as your primary
contact as far as agency business is concerned?'

Marianne couldn't help smiling as they took the lift to
the second floor.

**Continuing our look at the various commercial
schemes that have been started up by churches over
the summer, we sent Clifford Pugh to report on
activities in the Midlands. Clifford's first stop was
just outside Coventry.**

'St Peter's has embraced the new sense of enterprise
in a way that is modest by any standards – but a way
that is also likely to be copied quite quickly, I would
imagine, across the country. Why? Because it's about
hassocks. St Peter's has 30 new hassocks – or kneelers –
all lovingly embroidered by the ladies of the parish.
Nothing new about that, you may say. Except that the
embroidered design on each hassock is, in fact, a piece
of advertising for a local business. Accountants, solici-
tors, plumbers, even the local pest exterminator.
They're all represented – and, at prayer time, you can
find yourself kneeling on some of the most august
names from the local Chamber of Commerce. And
Betty Bobbit, local convenor of the Mothers' Union,
says they've only just begun, with the church's aim to
have 100 hassocks fully paid for by the end of the year.

'Just a few miles away, however, I found an example
of church advertising that's already taken on something
of an epic scale. The vicar of St Paul's, the Reverend
Quentin Bloworthy, had always been sorry that his

Victorian antecedents had run out of money before they could give the building the stained-glass windows that, he says, were always intended. Now, however, he has been able to do what the building's founders were unable to achieve. He is in the process of installing a grand set of windows along the south side of the church, all of which proclaim the delights of the local shopping mall.

'Not all the schemes I witnessed in and around Coventry were quite so linked to the church fabric, however. Several of the smaller churches have moved quickly to initiate ways of trying to attract more people to their services. Two ideas in particular, which I came across more than once, involved games of chance. The first idea is based around providing people with numbered tear-off counterfoils on their Sunday morning notice sheets. When the collection plate comes around, anyone contributing at least one pound is able to put his or her counterfoil into a box for a free draw. The vicar makes the draw at the end of the service – with half the collection money then being handed back to the holder of the winning number. The scheme has already proved so popular that the churches I spoke to claimed that their net takings from the Sunday collection had trebled.

'At another church the vicar has embraced the spirit of the National Lottery through a joint venture with a local turf accountant. Members of the congregation, on arriving for the main Sunday service, are given a piece of paper on which they can – again, for a pound – write down any number between one and three hundred. Then, as the service progresses, the hymn numbers are drawn from a box with the winner being the first person to have a chosen number. If no one wins then the money is simply held for a "roll-over" the following week. Defending the introduction of a lottery into his worship, the vicar asserts that the scheme has had many benefits – not least of which has been the creation of a sense of excitement and spontaneity around the choice of hymns!'

Next week Clifford visits Wolverhampton.

'Who is he again?' said Gladys Wheeler.

'He's from an advertising company,' said Mrs Murch. 'He's the man who put the notice up on the church steeple. You remember.'

Gladys looked as if she didn't remember anything. 'What's he advertising?' she said after a thoughtful pause.

Mrs Murch scowled. 'Himself, I think,' she said, looking sternly at Robin who had just taken his seat beside Marianne in the church hall for the latest meeting of the PCC.

'Is he on the television?' persisted Gladys Wheeler.

'He'd like to be, I'm sure,' said Mrs Murch, who couldn't help thinking that Mr Angel was being rather too familiar with the vicar. On entering the hall he had kissed the Reverend Maddeley on both cheeks. Mrs Murch could not decide whether this was a sign of foreignness, or simple lasciviousness – and she didn't know which was worse. When it came to a vote, however, at the end of the evening, she gave her support to Robin and 'the new way', as the vicar kept calling it. Well, what, after all – as she put it to Gladys Wheeler – was the alternative? There really was no choice in the matter. Gladys was really rather pleased. She always found choices somewhat arduous. Church was always much better, she felt, without choices.

The room was heavy with the smell of damp wool and stale cigar smoke. The only illumination was from two heavily draped lamps, which exuded a grainy, orange light across four leather armchairs. The chairs were arranged around a fireplace, but the fire was now no more than a small pile of softly glowing embers. In three of the chairs slumped elderly men with dark faces and clothes to match. Large crosses around their necks glinted weakly in the spare light. In the shadowy corner of the room a door closed and a fourth figure emerged from the gloom. He wore the same uniform as his colleagues, and he took his place amongst them.

'The call was from Conan,' said the man who had just sat down. 'Arch is expressing some concerns. He welcomes the energy, apparently, and embraces the sense of opportunity – but he's concerned about where it will lead. He's saying something about integrity and purpose – or so I gather.'

The other three began to murmur to each other, nodding large and heavy grey heads like slow-moving birds of prey. The mention of Arch – the Archbishop of Canterbury – had brought a small ripple of animation into their state of near somnolence. Arch would not, of course, have known that they were meeting together. Certainly not that they were meeting so close to home, as it were. The darkened room, in a dark house, in a dark square of Westminster, lay only just across the river from the Archbishop's palace at Lambeth. But he did not know that four of his most senior bishops were meeting so close by, nor that they had met in similar circumstances every four weeks for the last three months.

'I hope he's not going to be difficult,' said one. Knowing looks were exchanged. 'Any sagacity or sensitivity at this stage could stop the whole thing in its tracks before it's even started.'

'Did Conan make any suggestion?' remarked another one of the four, shifting himself uneasily in the chair. The dinner had been rich, and he felt a familiar tightness in his lower abdomen.

'He feels it's probably time to give Catchpole his head,' answered the first speaker. The comment brought forth several more weighty nods and assenting grunts. The general air of agreement was marked by a refilling of glasses. The port was unusually fine.

'But what of the current round of activities?'

The words were spoken by a new voice that was barely more than a hoarse whisper. 'Given Arch's . . . reserve, would it not be prudent to provide some kind of additional stimulus amongst those who are currently carrying forward the local schemes?'

'I agree,' said another. 'With no support or endorsement from himself at this stage, it is incumbent upon *us* to provide something in the way of tacit approval. There needs to be some sort of unofficial episcopal nudge, as it were. The sort of thing we can very easily deny, but which encourages those in the thick of it to carry on with their good work until such time as Arch can be . . . persuaded.'

There was a general nodding and murmuring of the word 'persuaded'.

'Do you have something in mind?' asked the hoarse whisperer. There was a pause, and then the first speaker – he who had spoken to Conan – made a suggestion.

'I think we need to mobilize one of our brother bishops. Someone who would be adept at communicating innocent enthusiasm.'

'An innocent enthusiast,' echoed another voice.

'Simple Simon,' came the sibilant suggestion from his whispering colleague. The heavy nodding heads seemed to issue forth something akin to the sound of sniggering, but it may simply have been the creaking of leather amidst the exhalations of air.

The large Turkish man gave no sign to indicate he was aware of what was being said. He simply ground his fist into Dominic's shoulder, while Dominic gritted his teeth and breathed heavily through his nose.

'She clearly liked your sheath,' Dominic said. 'This vicar

lady. As innovative sheaths go, it was probably one of the best. So what have you been following it up with?'

He blinked across at the marble slab which was parallel to the one on which he was lying, and was just able to make out the almost lifeless body of Robin.

'Flowers,' grunted Robin.

'Flowers?' said Dominic. 'Seems a bit tame after the sheath. What are you doing with flowers?'

Robin was now being pummelled by someone who looked as if he might be the Turkish man's brother.

'We've done a deal with one of the local florists. St Thomas's is now full of big floral displays, each of which has been supplied free of charge.'

'And what does the florist get out of this?'

'All the displays,' continued Robin, wincing as his arm was nearly wrenched off by the Turkish man's brother, 'carry very prominent notices showing the florist's name, address and telephone number. And then there's our special "rites of passage" deal.'

'Rites of passage?' grimaced Dominic.

'In effect,' continued Robin, 'we've made St Thomas's a closed shop. Anyone wanting to have flowers at a wedding or funeral that's being held in the church has to buy them from the nominated florist. That's the beauty of having displays permanently on show. St Thomas's operates as something of a shop-front. Rites-of-passage consumers can see what's on offer, and then they have to make a deposit on the cost of the flowers before the vicar confirms the booking for the service.'

'But can she really turn people away from the church if they don't want to buy their flowers from your florist?' asked Dominic.

'Well, not officially . . . no,' replied Robin. 'But there are other factors she can bring into play. Churches do it all the time.'

'It?'

'Choose . . . their own . . . selective policies . . . on so-called . . . rites of passage,' Robin gasped between exertions. The Turkish brother stopped his attentions, allowing Robin to finish his point. 'The Church of England might appear to have national policies on things such as baptism and marriage, but what happens in fact is that local vicars make up the rules for themselves. If you live in the parish, but the vicar doesn't want to marry or baptize you – or even if you *don't* live in the parish and the vicar *does* want to marry or baptize you – then he or she bends the rules. That's all Marianne's doing.'

'And she's happy to do that?' said Dominic, sitting up on his marble slab.

'I don't know that "happy" is the word,' responded Robin. 'It's more a question of survival. If St Thomas's closes, then *no one* will be baptized, married or buried at the church. Under this scheme, Marianne – that is St Thomas's – gets a weekly retainer fee from the florist, plus a percentage of all the orders for flowers that come via the church. Over a full year it'll add up to a not insignificant sum of money.'

'Noel's idea?' asked Dominic.

'Noel's idea,' echoed Robin, remembering how uncomfortable he had felt when first outlining the proposal to Marianne. He recalled the initial look of indecision on her face, as she wrestled with the principles involved. She had clearly been torn between concern at the implications of such a commercially based scheme, and the evident opportunities for building a sustainable Christian community at St Thomas's.

'Talking of Noel,' continued Dominic, looking round, 'it's not like him to miss out on a Turkish bath. Do you know where he went this afternoon?'

'Noel? I think he said something about finding "a new angle on bathing" – and then he tapped the side of his nose in that knowing way he has.'

At the beginning of September Marianne decided it was time for her to start taking the initiative. There were challenges and some contradictions for the church in this 'virtuous circle', she well knew – but there was also the chance to develop a new sense of mission. So far the various schemes were tapping into something that had appeal and interest for more diverse groups of people than would normally have associated themselves with the church. It was not simply that St Thomas's had started to put itself on a more secure footing, both in terms of finances and bums on pews – although that in itself was clearly significant. It was also that the whole approach promised something more in terms of ministry and outreach. If commercialization was a way to link the church to the wider community in the twenty-first century, reasoned Marianne, should she not grab that opportunity with both hands?

The meeting with Fiona Faulks was therefore Marianne's own idea and, initially at least, something she intended keeping to herself. Fiona was Customer Services Manager at the local, and very large, branch of Testway that had opened just a few miles from the church. This, the biggest grocery retail store in the area, was not technically within St Thomas's parish – but, if Marianne had learned anything from her brief liaison with Robin, it was that creativity knows no bounds. This was not the time for reserve and temerity – and, anyway, Marianne had decided that Testway's own local vicar would probably be one of the very last clergymen in the country to wake up to the potential that was almost quite literally on his own doorstep.

Marianne's first approach to Testway had been low-key. She had suggested that St Thomas's take the lead in organizing some sort of ecumenical presence in the superstore every day over the busiest part of the next Christmas season, which was still a few months away. Carol-singing, nativity scenes, even some form of basic 'service' – all her ideas had met with interest, if not outright approval. So much so that she felt increasingly confident in suggesting new ways in which the church's mission might be extended. Shoppers, she argued persuasively, would be more likely to visit a store that was taking steps to keep the *real* Christmas tradition alive. That first contact had put her in touch with Fiona, and the follow-up meeting in Marianne's office was intended to explore how the relationship might be accelerated.

'I've always been a great admirer of the Church,' said Fiona, sitting down at the table and carefully arranging her selection of personal brands in front of her: Nokia, Palm, Mont Blanc. 'After all, *you* were into Sunday opening a long time before we were!'

Marianne laughed politely, and decided to leave her scruffy Filofax and biro on the desk. 'But now you've caught us up – at least in that respect,' she said. 'Although it may be that we can still offer you something more that you'd find of interest.'

'More visits to our store? An *Easter* programme perhaps to build on what we all hope will be a successful Yuletide?'

Marianne took a deep breath. 'Well,' she said, 'I was thinking that you might even come to *us* – before we come to you as planned at Christmas.'

Fiona looked puzzled. 'I'm sorry. I don't understand. You're suggesting that we at Testway come to church? Here? Yes? That we come *here*? Sometime *soon*?'

'I had Harvest Festival in mind,' said Marianne, deciding that she might as well 'go for it'. 'It's only a few weeks away,' she added, 'but I'm sure such a tight timetable wouldn't be a problem for a business like Testway. And anyway, what I have in mind could happen at almost *any* time. Harvest, that is. I mean, after all, it's all about how we choose to define that word – "Harvest" – isn't it?'

Fiona continued to look blank. She began to fiddle nervously with her personal brands. 'I'm sorry,' she said. 'I'm getting confused. Harvest Festival. Testway coming to church. I'm not sure I catch your drift, as they say. Could we go back just a tinsy-winsy little bit and start again?'

Marianne felt a nervous giggle welling up inside her. She felt a bit out of her depth, but excited nevertheless.

'You're right. It's me who should be sorry,' she said, trying to stay calm. 'You see, I've managed to get myself rather hyped-up about this whole Harvest thing. I think it's such a good idea. And I'm hoping you will as well.'

'What do you mean, there's a bishop here to see me!' said Robin anxiously, as he emerged from a meeting on dog food.

'I mean there's a bishop here to see you!' shouted back Dominic. 'I can't put it much clearer than that. Bishop. Bishop. Bishop! Purple shirt. Dog collar. No chin. He's a bishop, all right? And he's here to see *you*!'

'Oh, hell!' Robin muttered to himself. 'A bishop. I just knew we were overstepping the mark with all this church stuff. He'll be here to put a stop to the whole thing. Where's Noel?'

But Noel was nowhere to be found. 'Immersion tank,' said Keith helpfully. 'I think he's gone somewhere to see a man about an immersion tank.'

Robin just stopped himself from cursing Noel in front of the team, and stomped off to confront the bishop whom he had been told was waiting for him in his office. If it wasn't for Marianne, he thought to himself . . .

'Good morning, your . . . your . . . your . . .' he stammered, trying to think of the correct form of address for a bishop, before finally plumping for 'Good morning, bishop!'

'Good morning,' said a tall, spindly man, as he unwound himself from a low and colourful seat. Dominic had been right: the man looked every inch a bishop. To Robin's eyes he conveyed an air of episcopal limpness that suggested he might once have considered a career in chartered accountancy, only to dismiss it as being something likely to set the pulse dangerously racing.

'You are presumably Mr Angel, the Director of Planning?'

'Director. Yes. Planning. Yes,' Robin said in staccato fashion, whilst also indicating that the bishop should, please, resume his seat. 'Yes. I'm responsible. If that's what you mean.'

'Jolly good,' said the bishop.

'*Jolly good*?' repeated Robin. '*Jolly good*? You mean you're not here to give me – that is, us – a ticking off?'

The bishop looked perplexed. 'I'm sorry, Mr Angel,' he said. 'I'm not sure I follow you.'

Now it was Robin's turn to look confused. 'You *are* Marianne's boss, I take it,' he asked.

'Marianne?' squeaked the bishop, managing to look even more at a loss.

'Marianne Maddeley,' said Robin. 'The vicar of St Thomas's.'

The bishop opened his mouth in a fish-like manner to show his surprise at Robin's supposition.

'No, Mr Angel. Regrettably, I am *not* the Reverend Maddeley's boss, as you put it. That honour belongs to one of my esteemed colleagues. No. I am . . . I am . . . erm . . . *another* bishop. Bishop *Simon*. From . . . you know . . . over . . . erm . . .' He waved a limp hand towards the window to suggest somewhere – *any*where – other than the area around St Thomas's. 'Nothing at all to do with the current . . . erm, I'm afraid.'

'Then why the devil are you here?' asked Robin sharply, and somewhat inappropriately, before adding quickly, 'I'm sorry!'

'Well,' said the bishop, with just a hint of mauve beginning to suffuse his cheeks. 'To *thank* you. To show *enthusiasm*. And, yes, perhaps . . . erm . . . to *encourage* you further. And, yes, also to ask for some advice, actually. That is, if you don't mind.'

'Advice?' said Robin. 'Advice about what?'

The bishop chuckled in a self-conscious way. 'Advice about how to run the sort of . . . project you've been running at St Thomas's. And, . . . erm, . . . so on. So as to spread the word, as it were. To enthuse others. To persuade. Yes, that's it. To *persuade*.'

'You mean to say you think it's *good*?' said Robin. 'What we've been doing at Marianne's . . . I mean, at St Thomas's? You think it's good?'

'Oh, it's marvellous,' said the bishop. 'Quite marvellous! It's exactly what we want.'

'Quick,' said Marianne to Robin, as she grabbed his hand just outside the vestry. 'I want to show you my tank.'

'Your tank?' said Robin, suddenly imagining Marianne sitting astride a large piece of mobile field artillery. They walked out into the body of the church where Marianne revealed a large immersion tank, like a small swimming pool. It had been installed about halfway along the south aisle where an old bookstall used to be.

'What do you think?' she said proudly.

'Well,' said Robin, 'as tanks go, I think it's pretty damn fine. What's it for?'

'Baptisms, of course,' replied Marianne.

'Baptisms? I didn't think that was your style,' said Robin. 'I thought you were more into fonts. You know – a bit of a quick splash on the head, rather than a full under-the-water job.'

'We *have* been – in the past,' said Marianne. 'But this seemed such a great opportunity. A chance to relaunch the whole idea of baptism here at St Thomas's. We're getting so many more people along to church now, that I felt I should do everything possible to respond to the increased need for Christian initiation. Just imagine it! All those potential new members of our congregation – and St Thomas's being able to offer a range of baptismal rites! It really does feel like a new beginning.'

Robin was clearly very touched by Marianne's passionate enthusiasm – particularly as she was still holding his hand and squeezing it with joy.

'That's brilliant,' he said. 'I know you've been a bit worried that the virtuous circle has been only about money – so it's really great to see that it genuinely *is* helping to build the church in all the right ways. But the tank? Were you able to pay for it all from the proceeds of the other schemes? From the money from the florist and so on?'

Marianne suddenly looked a bit sheepish, and she started to stroke Robin's hand gently. 'I have to admit,' she said, smiling coyly, 'there is a bit of a commercial side to this as well. To the tank, I mean. But that just made the opportunity, well . . . that much more compelling. *And* I did have a bit of help.'

'Help?' Robin sensed something in Marianne that was partly embarrassment, but also partly triumph.

'Yes,' she continued. 'I had a bit of help from Noel. But it was *me* that did the deal,' she rushed on, not allowing Robin to express his surprise. 'It was actually me who finalized the agreement – the contract with the firm that makes those lovely bath oils.' She pointed to a row of coloured bottles on a shelf close by. 'They said they'd pay for the tank, and a bit more beside, if I publicize their oils every time I do a baptism. And they have a great slogan they want to use: "Anoint yourself. It'd be a sin not to."'

Marianne ignored Robin's grimace, which she attributed to sour grapes. The advertising line had clearly not been developed by Angel, Fear & Tredwell. She also tried to ignore the fact that he had pulled his hand away from her's.

'What do you mean exactly by an agreement? A contract?' His voice betrayed more than a hint of irritation. 'You're not supposed to be putting deals together,' he continued. 'That's the agency's job. You're supposed to be making sure that everything is in line with what you're try-ing to achieve here. I thought that's what we agreed. A clear division of labour – and responsibility.'

Marianne moved closer to him and put her arm through his. Following so closely on the hand-holding, it was the most sustained physical contact they had had. 'Now, you wouldn't be getting just a little bit jealous, would you?' she said. 'After all, I'm only doing what you taught me to do. I'm using my initiative. It all started with my thinking about growing the church, and Christian initiation. It didn't start with thoughts of money and "deals". The idea of the immersion tank felt like . . . well, something of an experi-ment. An adventure. A way to strike out on a new path of ministry. It was only *after* I'd had the idea that I asked Noel if he could help. Help me to translate a sense of mission into action.'

'But why Noel? Why ask Noel?' said Robin, barely con-cealing his displeasure, although this time not removing Marianne's arm. 'You know that I expressly asked you to regard *me* as your agency contact – and as your, well . . . *confidant.*'

'I know that,' said Marianne, conveying in her look far more than a simple level of trust. 'But I also knew you'd say "No" – and tell me not to worry my pretty little head about doing the deals. Or at least words to that effect. And, any-way, I wanted to *surprise* you.'

'Surprise me?'

'Yes, surprise you. You see, I'm very grateful for what you've done for St Thomas's. Things are going very well. The church is safe. We have a bigger regular worshipping community than we've ever had since I've been here. And we're beginning to forge all sorts of new links with the local community. But St Thomas's can't always be reliant on you. If we're going to continue to grow long term, we have to do it ourselves. We have to start finding ways to make the vision live in all sorts of practical ways.'

Robin looked thoughtful. 'Have you talked to anyone

else about this,' he said. 'Have you talked to your bishop, for example?'

'I don't think he'd understand,' replied Marianne. 'At least, not yet. I think he'd see the problems before he saw the opportunities. The archdeacon might be happier – if only because of the positive effect on the finances. But I don't suppose he's going to be in any hurry to see the virtuous circle put into practice *every*where. As you may have noticed, the Church is a somewhat conservative body. I think most of my clergy colleagues will now want to sit back and see what happens to St Thomas's and all those other experiments that are springing up around the country. What did you call them? Copycat strategies?'

'Hmmm,' mused Robin, thinking of Bishop Simon, and the copycat schemes to which Marianne had referred. He couldn't help thinking that there was already more momentum behind this new approach than most people realized. Moreover, the bishop's visit to the agency had suggested that certain parts of the Church were taking a far from conservative view of the affair.

Marianne still had her arm through his. He put his hand on it and squeezed gently, intimating some special closeness or confidence. 'I think we should talk,' he said.

'Talk?' said Marianne, pulling a bit of a face. 'I thought that's what we *were* doing. Already.'

Robin coughed uneasily. He felt suddenly more nervous than he had expected to be. Perhaps now was not the time.

By the next morning he had decided that things had gone far enough. He would go in and see Dominic and admit that his colleague's misgivings had been well founded. Yes, the virtuous circle had proved its worth – St Thomas's was now a viable commercial proposition – and, yes, Angel, Fear & Tredwell had gained a lot of publicity from the scheme. But it now seemed clear to Robin that there were also dangers inherent in the approach. He was particularly concerned that he would not be free to develop his relationship with Marianne so long as Noel was on hand to encourage more and more bizarre expressions of ecclesiastical commercialism. It looked as if Dominic had exactly the same thought in mind as he advanced across the boardroom floor to meet Robin.

'Robin,' said Dominic meaningfully through tight lips. 'I need to talk to you about this church business.'

'It's all right,' said Robin, inhaling deeply and managing a smile at the same time. 'It's all under control.'

'It *is*?' Dominic looked quizzical.

'I'm in talks with the, um, vicar of St Thomas's at the moment, and I feel sure that I should be able to withdraw from the relationship – um, withdraw the *agency* from its arrangement with the church, that is – without too much consternation.'

'*Withdraw*?' snapped Dominic. '*Consternation*? What on earth are you talking about? I don't want you to *withdraw* our support.'

'You *don't*?' Robin's voice was thin and unsure.

'*Of course* not,' continued Dominic. 'I want to *build* on it. I want to *extend* it. I want it to be a national campaign.'

'You *do*?'

'Yes, I do,' said Dominic, who was now the epitome of a good-natured companion. 'And, yes, I know I must have sounded a bit sceptical at first. But that's just the way I am. Now the thing's proved itself, I'm as keen as *you* are.'

'You *are*?'

'I certainly am. And I know Noel's over the moon about it as well. What's more, I can see that the rest of the Church of England is just dying to get a slice of the action too. Just look at all those other schemes we keep hearing about. You can't fool me, Robin, with all this talk about . . . what was it? Consternation? Consternation, my foot! I know what you were up to with that bishop the other day. You were plotting, weren't you? You were plotting ways for rolling out this whole virtuous circle thing across the rest of the country, weren't you?'

Dominic slapped Robin affectionately on the shoulder before continuing. 'You know Robin, you're really quite a sly one, aren't you? I get the impression that you managed to get this whole thing going by charming the socks off this lady Reverend of yours! I just hope she doesn't give you too hard a time when she realizes you've only been using her to get the scheme under way!'

Robin looked shocked, and Dominic rightly took it as a sign that the thought had never entered his colleague's head.

'So you just forge ahead,' said Dominic, picking up his glasses and preparing to leave the room. 'I want this thing to go from strength to strength. I want it to go right to the top. In fact . . .' He paused thoughtfully on his way out of the door. 'In fact, I don't think I'm going to be happy until we have the Archbishop of Canterbury himself sitting right here in the boardroom!'

Dominic's laughter could be heard ringing out along the corridor, as Robin slumped heavily against the boardroom table.

'Oh, God!' he muttered mournfully. '*Now* what?'

'No. *This* time we really do have to talk,' insisted Robin.

'But the service is due to begin in ten minutes' time,' said Marianne, walking into the vestry and taking her robes from a hanger. 'It's a special Eucharist. And the church is absolutely full of people. It's wonderful. So, I'm very sorry, but it's going to have to wait. The talk, I mean.'

'But there's something I need to say, Marianne. Something I need to tell you.'

Marianne tried her hardest to look understanding, and Robin took this as a sign to continue.

'I think we should stop all this business,' he said, swallowing hard and waiting for her reaction.

'All *what* business?' she replied after a pause, her lip quivering just slightly as she began to put on her robes for the coming Eucharist.

'This . . . this . . . virtuous circle thing. I think we should stop it.'

Marianne first looked relieved, and then confused. 'Why?' she said. 'Why would you want to stop it? It's going so well. Just look at tonight. *Another* new idea – and the church absolutely full. All those people coming to worship. People who would normally never have stepped foot in this place. And I'm beginning to feel now that I'm personally helping to create and build it. I'm not just on the receiving end. It's really not just about money any more. It's about how we invite people into the church. It's about ministry. It's about service. It's about this service tonight, for one thing. Which is a very good reason why we can't talk now.'

Robin looked around him blankly, as Marianne continued to dress herself. 'This service?' he said almost to himself, trying to remember what on earth was special about this service. *Another* new idea? *What* new idea? He looked at his watch, and decided that a direct approach would be more appropriate. There was now a note of slight desperation in his voice.

'You don't think I've used you, *do* you?' he said. 'You don't think I've used you to get this whole thing off the ground, *do* you?'

Even as he said the words, he was aware how blunt and unhelpful they sounded. He should wait. He should not rush this. Marianne looked as if she were trying to concentrate her thoughts away from the man who stood opposite her, and towards the coming service. She was now ready. Dressed. She made a move towards the door. Robin sensed that he had to say *some*thing. But was now really the time to say what he wanted to say? His need for self-expression triumphed over his instinct for what Marianne might want to hear at that moment – a token of support.

'Marianne,' he almost gasped. She turned to look at him. 'Marianne,' he said again. 'I have these feelings. For you, I mean. I need to talk to you about them.'

She smiled and bit her lower lip, fighting back the tears that were starting up behind her eyes.

'Good,' she said. 'I'm glad. Only not *now*. I need to concentrate on the service. It's another one of my own ideas. I hope you approve.'

And with that she disappeared out into the passage where the choir and servers were waiting for her. Robin found his way into the body of the church and took his seat in the congregation, his mind fizzing with thoughts of every kind. Indeed, so preoccupied was he with Marianne, that he seemed almost oblivious of the innovation that the service was introducing to a packed house. He seemed almost not to notice that he was present at the Church of England's first sponsored Eucharist. He seemed not to see the names of a local baker and a local wine shop emblazoned across the altar frontal.

'This Eucharist is brought to you by . . .' it said in big bright letters.

But then Robin had only one thought in his head, and that thought was focused entirely on the woman who was standing resplendent in white and gold robes at the front of the church, smiling beatifically at the many faces that thronged the once empty pews of St Thomas's.

The meeting was supposed to start at ten o'clock. It was almost a quarter past ten. Noel was doodling on a large pad. Robin was growing increasingly impatient.

'They're late,' he said, stating the obvious.

Noel looked up. 'They're creative,' he replied.

Robin sighed, and continued reading the file of corre-
spondence and press cuttings relating to the growth of the
'virtuous circle'. Five minutes later the door finally opened
and Luke and Keith stumbled into the room, holding mugs
of coffee and chocolate biscuits.

'You're late,' said Robin once again, but no one seemed
to share his sense of unease. Luke made a shrugging gesture
which might just have been an apology. Keith looked at the
clock on the wall as if seeing it for the very first time.

'We've got some goodies for you, though,' said Luke,
sitting down, stuffing a whole chocolate biscuit into his
mouth, and re-fixing his ponytail.

'Bloody good too,' said Keith supportively.

Robin, thin-lipped, looked from one creative face to the
other. 'I think that's for Noel and me to decide, don't you?'
he said.

Luke and Keith glanced quickly at one another as if to
say, 'Ooohh, dearie! So who got out of bed the wrong side
today then?'

'Come on then, guys,' added Noel, laying down his
pencil and trying to engage with the conversation. 'Let's see
what you've got.'

Luke looked across at Keith. 'Have you got the art bag?'

'I thought *you* had it,' replied Keith.

There was a brief interlude whilst Luke left the room to
fetch the required art bag, in which was the latest batch of
ideas from the agency's top two creative minds. Whilst he
was gone, Robin stared once again at his papers, seemingly
intent on maintaining his air of strained impatience.

'OK,' said Keith, as Luke returned and started spreading
pictures and pieces of copy across the boardroom table.
'The first idea is about using churches, or preferably cathedrals, for murder mystery weekends. You know, those
things where people pitch up and play at being amateur
sleuths for a couple of days.'

'We thought it'd be a bit of a spin on the old country
house thing,' added Luke. 'After all, there seem to be quite

a lot of murder stories set in and around churches and . . . things.'

'Abbeys,' chipped in Noel.

'And monasteries,' continued Keith. 'Lots of monkish murders.'

'Murder at the Vicarage,' mused Noel.

'Yes, yes, all right,' said Robin rather testily, and flicking through the various ideas which had been spread out in front of him. 'I think I get the message. What else?'

Luke and Keith seemed a little disappointed with Robin's reaction to what they had clearly considered to be a winning concept.

'Well, just a *small* thing,' said Luke, playing down any sense of anticipation about the second idea, 'is to have a game in church on Sunday mornings where people bet on the length of the sermon.'

'A bit like those tickets you buy at a football match that give you a time. Like 3.24pm. If you end up having the ticket with the time when the first goal is scored, you win a prize.'

So saying, Keith showed a few outline concepts for posters to sell the idea. 'There're already a few churches around the place lined up to test-market this one. Mind you, we've got to watch out for any insider dealing. You know, vicars with an eye to the main chance, deciding in advance how long the sermon's going to be, tipping someone off, and then splitting the winnings with the lucky punter.'

Robin pulled a face, and intimated to Noel that they should move on. Noel, realizing that his colleague had not so far been unduly impressed by the scale of these creative ideas, decided to let Robin have a peek at the early thinking for a completely new idea.

'It's all about turning the Church into something of a financial institution,' he said. 'After all, in many respects that is surely where all this activity is eventually leading. Wouldn't you say? C of E PLC!'

Noel laughed at his own comment. Robin didn't. But he did at least look up, his face showing real interest for the first time since the meeting had begun.

'What do you mean?' he asked.

'Go on, guys,' said Noel. 'Show Robin the basic idea to launch the Church's own brand of financial services.'

'We thought we'd lead with a range of savings accounts linked to church giving,' said Luke. 'We would then follow that with a series of investment opportunities.'

Keith dug around in the art bag and emerged with two large sheets of paper which he slid across to Robin. The first one showed a picture of a man with long hair, a beard, and dressed in a loincloth, below which were the words 'Jesus Saves'. The second one showed the same man in a suit with a mobile phone. The words read, 'Jesus Invests'.

Marianne sipped her wine and replaced the glass on the table with an air of studied concentration. She glanced to her left, to where Luigi was employing his charm on a pair of first-timers, before refocusing on Robin. 'Honestly,' she said. 'It's not that I'm not interested.'

Robin cleared his throat.

'No, I'm sorry,' she continued. 'Interested isn't the word. I mean I am . . . That is, I do have feelings for you.'

Robin was staring at his plate.

'But I'm worried,' Marianne went on. 'I'm worried that my feelings might get in the way.'

'In the way of what?' responded Robin, in a tone that was rather sharper than he had intended. Marianne decided at this point that she might be able to say more through touching Robin than she could through talking. She put down her fork and stretched her hand out so that it covered his. She squeezed his fingers and felt a tingling warmth flow through her. Her body seemed to be accusing her mind. For goodness' sake, it said, say what you mean. Or at least what you feel.

'In the way. In the way of all the good that we seem to be doing through the church – and through the virtuous circle,' she said at last, as her reason gained ascendancy over her emotions. Robin looked up and smiled.

'It's at this point,' he said, 'that someone usually says "But I do hope we can remain friends".'

'I think we're more than that,' replied Marianne.

'*Are* we? Isn't there a little bit of you that wishes I'd disappear now so that you can run St Thomas's on your own? After all, you seem to have become quite proficient at setting up your own deals.'

Marianne let go of Robin's hand and took another mouthful of wine before replying. 'That's unfair,' she said. 'And you know it is.'

The look on Robin's face could have been interpreted as something approaching remorse.

'Don't you think,' she continued, 'don't you think the press would hound us relentlessly if they thought there was anything going on between us? Wouldn't that detract from what we're doing?'

Robin smiled. 'I think they're already assuming quite a lot about our relationship,' he said. 'I just wish they had more evidence to go on!'

Marianne smiled. 'Let's have coffee back at the vicarage and talk some more,' she ventured at last.

'Coffee? Talk?' said Robin. 'I can still remember the days when those words were code for something else. But I suppose when a lady vicar says them, they mean exactly that. Coffee and talk.'

'Is that a "yes"?'

Robin adopted his most boyish and innocent look. 'I could never say no to you, Marianne.'

# MIRACLE MONEY!

**Who says you can't buy happiness? Not St Bede's for sure. The new-wave Christians at this local church are selling miracles. A sin? No way, Nigel Clark (38) told *The Sun*.**

'We're a healing church,' says Clark. 'Several people have been healed by the Holy Spirit in this place. We're just making sure we keep that going.'

And, at the end of the day, that means money. Blindness, lameness, even paralysis – they all have their price at St Bede's. But that seems to have made it more popular than ever. Demand is such that there is now a waiting list. Getting a miracle cure could take longer than getting an NHS bed! But that's good news all round as far as Nigel Clark is concerned. 'Everyone's a winner. People are healed. The church receives money which is given in thanks. And that helps us to heal more people.' Us? 'Well, God, really, I suppose,' he added, red-faced.

As Nigel Clark says, everyone's a winner. And *you* can be a winner too with *The Sun*'s miracle-worker competition. Just rewrite the story of a well-known miracle in the style of the new, modern Church. You know the sort of thing: Jesus feeding the five thousand – by ringing for a take-away! Just send us your ideas (marked 'Miracle') by the end of November, and we'll send the writers of the three best to Bethlehem for a fully funded Christmas (or give you £1000 to spend on presents for yourself). Difficult choice! So, come on. Start thinking miracles – and start making money!

Following Marianne's lead with Fiona Faulks, Noel had developed further the concept of the St Thomas's Supermarket Family Service.

'It has a Harvest Festival theme,' he'd explained. 'Just right for this particular season. But also something we can carry on throughout the year.'

'What do you mean, "throughout the year"?' Robin had asked. 'If I'm not mistaken, tradition suggests that harvest comes but once a year – like Christmas.'

'Well, there's no reason why we have to be bound by tradition,' Noel had replied. 'After all, it's tradition that has kept the Church so out of touch with modern culture.'

The first thing Robin noticed as he arrived at St Thomas's on the morning of the first Supermarket Family Service was the number of cars parked outside the church. The second thing he noticed was the large banner over the south door. It showed a logo and name he knew very well: Testway.

Testway had been very keen to translate the concept into reality. With the support of Marianne and the Parochial Church Council it had been agreed that there should be four sponsored Supermarket Family Services a year – one in each quarter – but that Testway should have a presence in the church on *every* Sunday morning. The necessary changes had been made very quickly. The last five pews at the back of the church had been removed under the watchful eye of Stuart and replaced with fixtures and shelving from one of Testway's stores. It had been agreed that no frozen, chilled or perishable produce should be used, but the shelves still boasted a wide range of cans, jars and dry food, as well as a full assortment of detergents and toiletries. One section was given over to drink, although – in order not to provoke adverse opinion – there was to be no alcohol on sale.

The plan was for the groceries to be available every Sunday morning between the hours of nine and twelve. People entering the church would be offered a wire basket along with the more usual prayer book and hymn sheet.

The Testway checkout (which was positioned fairly discreetly in the north aisle) provided the option of paying by debit or credit card, with the added advantage of allowing people to make their weekly offerings to church funds via the same electronic transactions.

This was now to be the regular routine for a Sunday morning, but the four quarterly Family Services had several extra dimensions. For one thing, Testway had agreed to provide children's entertainment within the context of the service theme. That theme was always to be the same: the theme of 'harvest', with the message being that – thanks to Testway – *every* day was a harvest festival. Within that context, people would be encouraged to make 'harvest contributions' from their own shopping baskets towards a central store of goodies which could then be distributed to the needy of the parish. The incentive for the churchgoers was that every pound's worth of groceries donated to the central store qualified the giver for a ticket in the Testway free draw which was made during the service – and provided cash prizes of up to £1000.

It was, Robin felt, an almost perfect example of his 'virtuous circle'. Testway gained a new rent-free Sunday-morning site, with the only outlay being the quarterly prize fund and the cost of providing the children's entertainers. The needy of the parish gained through the receipt of the goods which people gave eagerly in order to gain tickets for a free draw which had better odds than almost any other lottery around. The churchgoers gained through the chance to combine shopping and a bit of a flutter, with a sense of social and spiritual well-being. St Thomas's gained by a marked increase in the number of people attending the services, and through the added income from those prepared to 'round up' the sums they were paying out on their debit and credit cards.

As Robin took his seat towards the back of the church, just in front of the pasta and sauce fixture, Marianne was leading the congregation in an opening hymn sung to the tune of 'We plough the fields and scatter': 'We walk the aisles with baskets brim-full with all we need . . .'

January of 'Year Two', as Robin was later to call it. More than six months after his first meeting with Marianne.

It was a grey morning. The vicar of St Thomas's was alone in the vicarage when the doorbell rang. The caller was small and very dapper. He announced himself as 'Mr Tadd . . . representing the Archbishop of Canterbury', and Marianne immediately showed him into the study.

'I know what you're going to say,' she said, dropping on to a chair opposite him. Mr Tadd was sitting with a perfectly straight back, his small manicured hands laid out on his thighs as if for inspection.

'You do?' he said softly, with the merest hint of a Welsh accent.

'The changes,' continued Marianne. 'They've mostly been my ideas. At least the more recent ones. The sponsored Eucharists. The links with Testway. I take responsibility for all of that. You can't blame the advertising agency. It was my decision, after all. But you see, I did it for the best possible reasons. Well, at least I *think* I did. I wanted to draw attention to what the Eucharist is all about. And Harvest as well. I really do think that in those services we're getting across just a little bit of the holiness that's there in the most ordinary of God's gifts. And, yes, of course I'm sorry that some people were upset by it. And I'm also very sorry, of course, that the Archbishop should be concerned. Assuming he *is*, that is. Concerned. But, as I say, the aim was to awaken a sense of creativity and . . . and . . . thankfulness in people, as well as to raise funds.'

Marianne's little speech had been delivered in one breathless gasp, as if she feared interruption. She had therefore not fully registered Mr Tadd's look of subdued and controlled surprise, which showed itself in hardly more than a slight raising of an eyebrow. As Marianne's brief flow of words came to an end, Mr Tadd waited for a second or two then lifted one of his small hands to his mouth and coughed in a perfectly restrained way.

'Forgive me, Vicar,' said Mr Tadd, stressing Marianne's title as a word full of meaning and responsibility. 'I think you may have misunderstood my purpose.'

Marianne looked at him properly for the first time since he had announced himself at the front door, and was suddenly struck by the thought that he was clearly much younger than she had originally assumed.

'I am not here to enter into debate with you as to the merits, or otherwise, of your sponsored Eucharists or your alliance with a prominent trading organization,' he continued. 'Indeed, all I know of those activities is what I have read in my newspaper.'

Marianne looked perplexed. 'You're not here to remonstrate with me?'

'Madam,' said Mr Tadd, his air of decorum taking on something of an icy quality. 'When I said that I was here to represent the Archbishop, I did not wish to suggest that I should be understood to be a representative of his opinions. I am merely here to represent his instructions – to express, in a manner of speaking, his wishes. And his primary wish is that you should attend upon him at Lambeth Palace at eleven o'clock in the morning the day after tomorrow. Assuming that to be convenient, of course.'

So saying, Mr Tadd levered himself into an upright position and, with one or two neatly packaged pleasantries, took his formal leave of a nervous and dumbstruck Marianne.

66

# III

They had had one of their regular breakfast meetings. Toast and coffee, with a pile of newspaper reports in the vicarage lounge. Marianne was adjusting her dog collar and staring into the mirror at Robin who reclined on a sofa behind her. He had decided to invest more time in building a close personal relationship with this increasingly important agency client, and had rearranged his diary to allow him to spend at least two days a week with Marianne. 'It will help keep a focus on the planning of our creative contributions,' he had assured Noel, who had responded with a large wink and a toothy smile.

'So why didn't he simply phone?' said Robin, returning to the subject of Mr Tadd. 'Or write a letter? Even an e-mail? It seems a bit odd that he should just turn up on your doorstep like that. Almost as if he were delivering a summons.'

Marianne's face in the mirror conveyed nothing but worry. 'I had the feeling he had been sent to spy on me,' she said nervously.

'Spy on you?' said Robin, sitting up and drinking coffee from a garish mug. 'What do you mean? Why would the Archbishop want to spy on you?'

'I don't think it's the Archbishop.'

'But surely Mr Tadd said . . .'

'I know what Mr Tadd said,' continued Marianne. 'He was very careful in what he said. And in what he *didn't* say. "I am not here to represent the Archbishop's opinions – merely his instructions." As if somehow he was using the opportunity to seek me out for something else. For some-

*one* else. As if he had been asked to find out what I was like in . . . in an unguarded moment. How I looked, how I was dressed. That sort of thing. The summons, as you put it, to meet the Archbishop is, I'm sure, genuine. But, yes, it *could* have been a phone call. Whereas this . . . this visit . . . was . . .'

Marianne's shoulders began to shake slightly. Her face crumpled. Robin jumped up from the sofa and folded her gently in his arms. It was, he told himself, the response of a compassionate human being to someone who was obviously distressed. He would have done the same thing for anyone. Marianne seemed to relax noticeably as he hugged her, but she sobbed quietly for a few moments, before attempting to speak again.

'I didn't like the way he looked at me, Robin. I'm frightened. I don't mind being sacked, if that's what this is all leading to. I don't mind being summoned for a dressing-down. Even by the Archbishop. But I *do* mind being got at.'

She gazed up at his face just a few inches away from hers, and then quickly looked away again.

'It's all right,' said Robin soothingly. 'He wasn't getting at you. I guess he was just doing his job. Don't worry about him. Look, I'll come with you if you like. I'll come with you to Lambeth Palace. I'll drive you there. Go on, let me come with you. I've always wanted to see what it was like inside.'

Marianne disengaged herself and smiled as she caught sight of the two of them side by side in the mirror. 'Thank you,' she said, still looking at his reflection. 'But I thought this was one of the days when you were meant to go to the office.'

'It was,' Robin replied. 'But this is more important. After all, it's not *every* day that one of my clients is invited to a meeting with the country's official spiritual leader. Come on. We'll do this together.'

She looked at him closely, as if taking in every feature of his face, before saying 'Thank you' once again. 'You go and wait in the car then,' she continued. 'I'll be out in a few minutes.'

'You've taken off your dog collar,' said Robin as Marianne closed the front door behind her. 'I would have thought if there was ever an occasion that demanded a dog collar, this was it.'

Marianne now had a look of serene determination on her face. 'No,' she said. 'If the Archbishop wants to see me, then he can see the *real* me. Not the uniform I sometimes hide behind. The uniform we all hide behind – when it suits us.'

Robin simply nodded as Marianne climbed into the car with a renewed air of confidence. 'It may not be as bad as you imagine,' he said as they drove away from the vicarage. 'I was just thinking about it – whilst you were getting changed. If it were simply a dressing-down, then surely you would have heard something first from your own bishop – or at least from the archdeacon, if he's your primary contact. There's surely some significance in the fact that the summons has come from the very top – regardless of what we might think of Mr Tadd's way of delivering it.'

Robin was suddenly reminded of Dominic's comment about having the Archbishop of Canterbury in the agency boardroom. 'I mean,' he said, trying to think of something more encouraging to add, 'it's not as if we're the only ones doing this sort of thing now. Half the churches in England seem to be getting in on the act. And quite frankly, some of their schemes have been quite, quite bizarre. I mean, far less, well . . . *constructive* than ours have been. I don't think the Archbishop can really blame us for all those, can he?'

'He's not a man I would ever associate with apportioning blame,' she said. 'But then so much has changed . . . *is* changing still. I think I need more time to think. More time to reflect on what's really happening.'

Robin took the hint and drove in silence for the next ten minutes. Suddenly Marianne said 'Stop!'

'What?' said Robin, swerving to one side of a busy inner London road.

'I'm sorry,' said Marianne, forcing a smile. 'Nothing serious. It's just that church we passed. Can we go back and have a look?'

Robin nodded, glanced at his watch, and tried to find a side street where he could turn round. They had left plenty of time to get to Lambeth Palace. There was no rush, he decided. He parked the car near some dilapidated buildings, and walked with Marianne back in the direction of the church.

As soon as he saw it, it was clear what had sparked Marianne's interest. Over the door was a big neon sign that said 'The Sanctuary'. As it was still morning – albeit a dark one – the sign was not illuminated, but Robin could imagine how it might look, lit up in fluorescent magenta. Next to the door was a large noticeboard that promised a 'Chaos Arcade'.

'Come on,' said Marianne. 'Let's go and have a look.'

Nothing could have prepared them for the sight that met their eyes. The inside of the church building looked like a huge amusement arcade. The pews were still in place, the eye was still drawn ultimately towards the altar. But around the walls were various kinds of electronic games and gaming machines, most of which were being played on by youths of varying sizes and ages.

'Good morning, fellow travellers. How wonderful to see you here on this overcast, but lovely, day.'

Robin and Marianne, their mouths still open with shock, turned to confront the person who had spoken the words. Standing far too close to them was a long, thin man with thick, black, greasy hair hanging untidily over his grey, emaciated face. He was wearing a green clerical shirt which appeared not have been washed for some time.

'The Reverend Roger Ricketts,' the man continued, proffering a damp, grey hand. He stared at them with his head on one side, clearly knowing their faces from somewhere, and struggling to remember where he had seen them before. 'Of course,' he said at last. 'I think I was expecting to see you a bit later.'

Robin and Marianne looked suitably confused.

'Yes, indeed. To arrange the wedding, wasn't it?' said the Reverend Ricketts. 'I thought we'd said later. But no matter. It gives me a chance to show you around. To show you what changes we've made to the church over the last couple of months. How we've started attracting more people back to . . . to worship. Especially the young. It's all very exciting.'

Robin and Marianne tried to share in the sense of excitement. As the Reverend Ricketts began to take them on a tour of the building, Marianne was doubly glad that she had not worn her dog collar. Apart from the fact that the man in the green shirt would almost certainly have recognized her from the pictures that had appeared in the newspapers, it now seemed that this was definitely one of those occasions when she was very happy to be someone other than a clergy-person.

In the meantime, the oleaginous Reverend Ricketts was leading them along the south aisle, explaining how salvation had come to his church as soon as that place a few miles north – St Thomas's – had 'breached the dam' and started to introduce 'commercial arrangements' in order to stay open. That had cleared the way for people like himself – people with enterprise and a sense of community service – to create the kind of church that society wanted. The kind of church that society *deserved*. That was why he had created 'The Sanctuary'. It answered the needs of local young people by providing amusements. It also replicated the kind of superficial chaos that their lives revolved around. And when they wanted to escape from the chaos – even if only briefly – he, Roger, would be there, in the side chapel with his urn of coffee and his friendly chat.

As Marianne listened to his soothing words, she felt that perhaps she had been wrong to jump to conclusions about the place. Perhaps this *was* a right use of a church – a way to reach out to people who would otherwise never come near the place. It was certainly no worse than what had happened at St Thomas's. Better perhaps. But, even so, she also felt an overpowering sense of discomfort, and she sensed that Robin felt it too. Seeing him trying to look slyly at his watch, she decided to take the initiative.

'Mr Ricketts. Reverend. I'm sorry to stop you mid-flow – and you'll have to excuse us – but we really do have to go. Right now, in fact.'

So saying, she grabbed Robin's hand and pulled him away towards the door, leaving the man in the green shirt as open-mouthed as *they* had been when first entering 'The Sanctuary'.

On arriving at Lambeth Palace, they were greeted by a clergyman dressed all in black who introduced himself with a brisk nod, a cold handshake, and the words 'Dr Conan'. Robin and Marianne were then conducted to an ante-chamber where they were asked to take a seat. The man in black disappeared through a heavy door to where the visitors assumed the Archbishop of Canterbury would be waiting. Marianne was perched on the edge of an armchair, biting her lip and nervously smoothing the front of her skirt. Robin prowled up and down restlessly, glancing from time to time at the door that separated them from their fate.

'You'll have to go in alone, of course,' said Robin, trying to think of something encouraging to add, but failing.

'Of course,' said Marianne, trying to smile. 'Just like the dentist's.'

Robin walked over to where she was sitting, took her hand in his, and gave it a squeeze. It seemed as if physical contact between them was now an accepted part of their relationship. As both seemed to be on the point of acknowledging a new closeness between them, the man in black reappeared at the door and beckoned Marianne. She rose and, with a last nervous look at Robin, made her way across the room.

Robin continued to prowl, stopping occasionally to peruse the bookcases without interest. The room, he decided, felt timeless. He imagined other people waiting impatiently on the same carpet 10, 20, 30 years before. He conjured in his mind generations of men in black attending a succession of archbishops. For the first time since he had conceived of the virtuous circle, he felt a weight of history bearing down on him.

Only a few minutes could have passed before the door opened again. He looked up expecting to see a flush-faced Marianne, but instead was surprised to see another face he recognized. The face was large and heavy jowled, below a mane of grey hair. The large body was dressed in a boldly pinstriped suit. The face and body both belonged to Sir Victor Catchpole, one of the most noteworthy clients of Angel, Fear & Tredwell.

Sir Victor Catchpole – leading businessman and financier – caught sight of Robin and, as he registered where he knew him from, quickly looked to see if he could make his exit from the room without engaging in conversation. It was a vain hope. Robin was prowling back and forth in the centre of the room, effectively barring Sir Victor's only way out.

It was Robin who spoke first, overcoming his own sense of confusion. 'Sir Victor,' he said, rather more loudly than he had intended. 'What brings you here?' As he said the words, he was conscious of how indiscreet they might have appeared. In a flawed attempt to make amends, he quickly added, 'I didn't think you were religious.'

Sir Victor, clearly discomfited by the encounter, managed to keep his indignation under control. 'I'm not,' he said. 'Religious. That is, I mean I'm not an activist – or whatever it is you call it . . . or them. My family are – that is, *were* – Catholic.'

'Of course,' said Robin, trying to look understanding, and shuffling about uneasily on the carpet. There was a brief pause, whilst Sir Victor eyed his escape route over Robin's shoulder. 'Look here . . . er . . .'

'Robin,' added Robin helpfully.

'Look here, Robin,' continued Sir Victor, his voice softening just slightly. 'You haven't seen me here. Is that understood? As I said, I'm not . . . that is . . . not religious. So, you haven't seen me anywhere near this place. Understood? Otherwise,' he added, forcing something of a smile, 'my company might decide it needs a new advertising agency.'

He looked Robin directly in the eye. 'Understood?'

'Yes,' said Robin, his voice quaking slightly. 'Perfectly.'

Sir Victor smiled again, and then narrowed his eyes and looked deep into Robin's face. 'Excellent,' he said. 'In which case, I will bid you a very good day.'

So saying, the large man in the pinstriped suit brushed past Robin and marched meaningfully out of the room.

Robin slumped in a chair and replayed in his mind the conversation with Sir Victor Catchpole. After several minutes, however, he was still no clearer about what had really been said. Any further deliberations were cut short by Marianne's re-emergence into the ante-room, closely followed by the man in black. She was smiling, but in a tired way – and the smile could not disguise the slight air of panic in her features. Not a word was said as they both followed the man in black back along the corridor and out into the cool air of the courtyard. In fact, Marianne said nothing until they were in the car and heading northwards over Vauxhall Bridge. Even then, she spoke only to answer a direct question from Robin who had decided that this was not a time to beat about the bush.

'Well, I have to ask,' he said. 'Have you been sacked? Fired?'

Marianne managed a half-hearted laugh. 'Not exactly,' she said.

'Not exactly?' repeated Robin. 'What does that mean?'

'My days as vicar of St Thomas's are over,' she said flatly.

'Ah,' said Robin non-committally, waiting for her to go on.

'I've been offered a new job,' continued Marianne, turning to look at Robin for almost the first time since they had left the palace. 'The Archbishop wants me to be his representative in co-ordinating the virtuous circle campaign across the whole country.'

Robin braked suddenly and was hooted at by a taxi which narrowly avoided crashing into the back of him.

'I'm sorry,' said Robin, driving on self-consciously at a rather sedate pace. 'It was just a bit of a shock. Your news, I mean. Co-ordinating a national campaign! Jesus!'

'Quite!' said Marianne, laughing properly for the first time all morning. It was as if Robin's expression had taken the lid off the pressure cooker of her emotions.

'Jesus indeed! What would *he* make of all this!'

Robin joined in the laughter, before asking, 'Do you think the Archbishop has thought through fully what a co-ordinated national campaign might entail? After all, we've not discussed it at the agency. That is, not as such. We haven't actually been asked to create ideas for a national campaign.'

'I honestly don't know,' she said. 'He was very nice – very gentle, very supportive, very wise. But I'm sure I could see tension in his face, and worry in his eyes. When he asked me to help by taking on this new job . . . well, it was as if he really *were* asking for my help. As if . . . as if . . . the whole thing were bigger than . . . I don't know.'

Marianne thought for a while before continuing. 'Do you know that feeling,' she said at last, 'when things build up in such a way that you feel powerless to stop them? When even your friends think you should say something or do something – but where you feel trapped by the expectations of other people? I think it's often like that when someone is trying to discern the will of God. There's a kind of inertia.'

Robin was not sure at all what Marianne meant, but he made a murmuring noise intended to convey understanding. She went on.

'I know it's an absurd thing to say, but I felt a sense of this around the Archbishop. And I think someone is ganging up on him. That Mr Smith, for example. There was something about him that made me think he was a bully. *And* he smiled too much for my liking!'

Robin quickly looked across at Marianne, and then back at the road as a large group of tourists were led by their guide across the street in front of them.

'Mr Smith?' he said, puzzled. 'Who's Mr Smith?'

'That big man,' said Marianne. 'You must have seen him come out shortly after I went in. A big man in a pinstriped suit. The Archbishop was on the point of introducing him to me, when he cut across what the Archbishop was saying – quite rudely, I thought – and said "Smith. Mr Smith. An old friend of the Archbishop's."'

Robin opened his mouth to speak, but then closed it again.

'Well, I can tell you,' continued Marianne. 'They didn't look like friends to me.'

The tourists had now all crossed the road. Robin was perturbed. What was going on? And how did it involve Marianne? But he decided that, for the time being at least, he would keep his thoughts to himself. As he accelerated away from the crossing, he turned the conversation back to the new job that Marianne had been offered.

76

'Run that one past me again,' said Dominic, who was reclining on a large leather chair. Noel picked up a magic marker and strode towards the flipchart.

'Sorry I'm late,' said Robin, looking flushed as he almost fell into the boardroom. 'It's Marianne's first day in the new job, and we had something of a celebratory breakfast.'

The news that Marianne was to change jobs had had a knock-on effect as far as her relationship with Robin was concerned. Whilst they still continued as 'just friends', they were no longer constrained by the parish and its particular expectations. That was not to say that the new situation wouldn't provide its own challenges. It had already been made clear to Marianne that she would need to travel a great deal and spend increasing amounts of time away from her new home – a church flat in Battersea, considerably smaller than St Thomas's Vicarage. As she accustomed herself to the idea, she also developed an acute sense of enthusiasm – indeed, of 'mission' – which swept Robin along for most of the time. In many ways he loved her new sense of energy, but there was also a part of him that missed the rather cosier parochial set-up.

'Noel and I were just running through the latest ideas,' said Dominic, swivelling his chair to face the flipchart and putting on his glasses. 'Ways of keeping the momentum going on a national basis.'

'Cath, Park & Kingdom,' said Noel, looking at Robin. 'Yes, I know it sounds like the name of an advertising agency, but it's three related projects. Project Cath, Project Park, and Project Kingdom.'

'Cath? As in the name? Catherine?' said Robin. Noel rolled his eyes heavenwards.

'Cathedrals, of course,' replied Noel. 'Not Catherine. *Cathedrals*.'

With a flourish of the magic marker he drew two vertical lines on the flipchart, creating three columns. At the top of one he wrote in capital letters 'CATH', and underneath he added the words 'maximizing the potential of some of the country's greatest historical assets'. At the top of the second column he wrote 'PARK', and below he added 'creating *new* assets – and new experiences'. At the top of the third column he wrote 'KINGDOM', below which he scrawled 'the church of the future – on demand, and online'.

'OK,' said Robin, sitting down. 'So Cath's about cathedrals. Tell me more about Park and Kingdom.'

'Project Park is about a theme park,' interjected Dominic. 'A Bible theme park. Great idea, isn't it?'

Robin looked as if he wasn't sure. 'It seems quite a long way from the original concept,' he said. 'Quite a long way from the idea of the virtuous circle.'

'Ah, no – not at all!' said Noel, who had clearly been hatching this plan for some time. 'The three elements – Cath, Park & Kingdom – are all related, you see. Once you view them as being all of a piece, then you'll see that the whole thing is a *very* virtuous circle. A very virtuous circle indeed. Project Cath, you see, is all about utilizing the full earning power of the country's cathedrals – primarily so that the money can be used to preserve those particular buildings for ever. But a percentage of the revenue from each of the cathedrals can also be used to help fund the theme park scheme – Project Park. But even *that* scheme is not simply a commercial enterprise. The whole thing is . . . well . . . spiritual . . . or, to use *your* word . . . virtuous. The point is that, however you look at it, the Church grows. It doesn't decline ever again. It grows and it grows.'

Robin looked even more doubtful. 'You're honestly trying to tell me that the theme park will be more than a money-making exercise? Something spiritual? Come on! Are you really suggesting that a combination of Disney and Deity will in some way reawaken the country's spiritual consciousness?'

Noel looked thoughtful for a moment or two. There was clearly something about the 'Disney and Deity' line that appealed to him.

'Well, yes I am, actually,' he said at last. 'And I think

everything we've done so far supports that view. After all, nobody nowadays would build a *cathedral* to capture the imagination, or the spirituality, of the modern generation. So the question surely has to be "What is the twenty-first-century *equivalent* of the cathedral?" Now, if we answer that in an imaginative and stimulating way through a theme park, we ought to be able to stir up enormous public interest, whilst at the same time attracting large sums of additional money for the Church through sponsorship and advertising. All of which means that it surely has to be the ultimate expression of your virtuous circle, Robin.'

Robin realized that resistance was useless. The idea was now bigger than he was, and had generated its own energy and purpose. He took out his pen to make some notes. 'Right,' he said with an air of resignation. 'Fine. Which just leaves the third part of the plan – Project Kingdom. So what's that about then?'

Noel and Dominic smiled at each other, before Dominic answered. 'We were just talking this through when you arrived,' he said. 'Because *this* could well be the cherry on the cake. The ultimate expression of the whole new approach – if you see what I mean. It's about building a virtual Church. A Church that is truly universal. A Church that is never closed. A Church that is online.'

Robin must have looked puzzled, because Dominic immediately went on to explain further. 'I'm talking about making the Church of England itself – the whole of it – a truly virtual organization. In some ways, it already is. Virtual. I mean, it doesn't have any real organizational cohesiveness even now. But this would take it further, and start making the whole thing web-based, rather than buildings-based. Going to church would be more about logging on, than about turning up.'

'I'm sorry. I don't follow,' said Robin. 'I thought just a minute ago we were talking about preserving the cathedrals for ever. They're not virtual. In fact, they're surely just the opposite. The ultimate statement of touchable solidity.'

'Exactly,' said Dominic. 'We must maintain the cathedrals because they are the crown jewels, as it were. We're not going to throw them away lightly. But a very large proportion of the Church's buildings . . . Well . . .' He let the thought hang in the air for a moment or two. 'Well, that's another matter entirely. I mean, to be frank, they're more of a hindrance than a help. We can use them as poster sites, certainly. And we can lease them to Testway and the like. But buildings will always have their limitations. Which is why a *virtual* Church of England has to be the answer. As I say, as an organization the C of E is already a bit "virtual". You know what I mean . . . a bit nebulous even. For all that we'd like to think that it was one corporate body, it clearly shows every sign of acting in as fuzzy and disjointed a way as it's possible to do. Plus the fact that I would have thought some kind of virtual reality was an obvious solution for an outfit whose focus clearly lies beyond the physical world. And with the money that's generated from selling off hundreds of unnecessary church buildings, we can create a truly remarkable and enduring cyberspace C of E.'

Whilst Dominic was speaking, Noel's face had taken on the look of slightly manic advocacy that Robin knew only too well.

'It would be a long-term solution, of course,' Noel said. 'We don't want to rush our fences. But, as Dominic says, it has to be the answer – in the end. Linking people up through chat-rooms, providing all the current benefits of church – and a whole lot more, via a combination of comprehensive Internet coverage, plus access to a number of virtual reality experiences. You see? The whole thing really *is* a lot more, well . . . spiritual or, at the very least, *immaterial*, especially compared to the current set-up.'

'A virtual church,' mused Robin, his face showing nothing other than tiredness. I wonder, he thought, what Marianne will make of it.

'As Noel says,' continued Dominic, 'we're not talking about the immediate future. No. Assuming we can sell these ideas to the powers that be, Robin, then Project Cath clearly comes first, followed by Project Park. But we have to be upfront in making proposals for Project Kingdom as well. Its fulfilment may be a few years away, but we have to have it in our sights. That's why we want to start putting plans together for the new C of E website as soon as possible.'

'The website?' said Robin, who now had the distinct impression that he was himself already losing touch with reality.

'www.kingdom.com,' said Noel proudly. 'It'll be the first real tangible step – well, *virtual* step, I suppose – towards the Church of the future. And, yes, I can see what you're thinking. "Surely someone has already registered kingdom.com as a name." Well, quite possibly, yes. But this has just got to be so important that it's worth spending a deal of money to get the name for the Church of England.'

'If Paris is worth a Mass,' said Dominic, 'as Henri of Navarre, I think it was, said . . . then kingdom.com has got to be worth . . . well, a cathedral at least!'

The image of Dominic laughing was not a common sight, and Robin looked across at him with a mixture of surprise and anxiety.

'Go on, Noel,' said Dominic, as his laughter subsided. 'Tell Robin where the kingdom.com idea came from.'

Noel looked slightly coy. 'OK,' he said. 'Now I know you're going to laugh at me, but it was the other day, when I was trying to remember the 'Our Father'. You see, I thought we might be able to use it in a piece of advertising for the new "Pray as you go" text-messaging service. I tried reciting it, but couldn't get any further than "Our Father, who art in heaven, hallowed be thy name, thy kingdom.com . . .".'

Two weeks later, Marianne seemed even more enthusiastic and missionary than ever. 'What do you think of it?' she asked.

'It's lovely,' said Robin.

'Don't be so patronizing!' said Marianne. 'What do you *really* think of it?'

'Really,' replied Robin. 'I think it's really lovely. It's a really lovely white car. I'm just not sure about the writing on it. That's all.'

'I thought you'd approve,' said Marianne, stepping back to admire once again the big black lettering along the side of the car. The letters proclaimed 'The Church on the Move', and next to the message was the logo of a large chain of car dealers. It had been provided as a 'company car' for Marianne in her new job. It was the first time she had had a new car. Indeed, it was the first time she had ever had a car that was not in the throes of terminal decline, and she was clearly delighted by everything that it represented. Robin, by contrast, had become used to having an expensive car as part of his agency remuneration package and was less than impressed by the prospect of being driven around in what was literally the latest advertising vehicle to have been created as part of 'the great campaign'. Marianne was quick to point out to him the irony of the situation.

'You can try harder than that, I'm sure,' she said, seeing his half-hearted smile. 'I know it must hurt – having to be so closely associated with your own agency's handiwork. I can see how it's fine for other people to carry your advertising, just so long as you personally don't have to be tainted by it!'

Robin decided he would not rise to the bait. He bit his tongue, and climbed into the passenger seat determined to be as patient and supportive as he possibly could be. For all their public protestations about being only 'good friends', the tabloids had soon picked up on the fact that the two 'campaign chiefs' were spending a lot of their 'private' time in each other's company. Several dubious-looking characters had even camped outside their two flats at one time or another, hoping to take a photograph of the two of them in some kind of intimate embrace. Those photographers would be back, Robin reflected, as he strapped himself in. The car would take care of that.

It was not just Robin and Marianne's relationship, of course, that was driving press interest. That interest had already become very evident as the various money-making schemes around the country had grown wilder and more exotic in their nature. Nevertheless it was true that speculation about the basis of their alliance was adding a certain spice to the stories – although the tone overall was supportive rather than anything else.

After the initial jokes and pointed comments, the coverage quickly settled into a vocal, almost jingoistic, kind of encouragement. The words 'The Church on the Move' began to be taken up in a very positive sense. Expressions such as 'A breath of fresh air' were soon being used on a regular basis, and the idea quickly became accepted that this was a change that was long overdue – exemplified in headlines such as 'Church wakes up to what people want'. What's more, Robin's and Marianne's assumed partnership began to be seen as symbolizing the new approach. One particular newspaper captured it in the words 'New Adam and Eve turn over New Leaf for Church'. An altogether more serious publication trumpeted 'Today's Robin Hood and Maid Marianne – redistributing the nation's heritage'.

Far from being castigated, therefore, Robin and Marianne very quickly found themselves being held up as models for a new age. 'The Reverend Maddeley and Mr Angel,' suggested one normally reserved journal, 'have, in their own lives, demonstrated an open and honest alliance that has now been embraced by the Church of England. In the public joining of commercial and spiritual interests, we might finally begin to think in terms of bringing down the curtain on several centuries of ecclesiastical hypocrisy.'

Whatever the terms used to describe the phenomenon, there seemed to be no doubt that the initiative had captured the public imagination. Some commentators described it as 'the sort of clear shift of mood that one might expect so early in a new millennium'. Others simply voiced the view that here was 'an idea whose time had come'. The biggest single indicator of this change in the public consciousness was manifested in the marked increase in church attendances. After years of falling numbers, congregations began to grow – and quickly too. This was spurred on by the special deals and features – such as St Thomas's partnership with Testway – that were fast becoming an accepted part of the overall church offering.

Although Marianne's brief applied only to the C of E, it was clear that the public did not discriminate very much when it came to churches. For most people a church was a church, and so the free churches – notably the Methodists, the Baptists and the United Reformed Churches – also found their congregations growing, at least in those areas where the local pastors showed themselves willing to adopt elements of the new enterprise culture. One eminent Nonconformist justified his 'conversion to the new way' by claiming that it combined perfectly the drive of the egocentric '80s with the spirit of the caring '90s to create a basis for driving growth in the new century.

This change in perceptions was also demonstrating itself through the other 'organized' religions. Muslims, Hindus, Sikhs and Jews were all registering significant increases in interest and income – although some were inclined to explain this as a result of people fleeing 'the naked aggression of Christian commercialism'. Only one major group seemed relatively untouched by the new wave of thinking, and that was the Roman Catholic Church which, with its greater sense of hierarchy and organization, saw the chance to reinforce its position as the one true and unchanging expression of God's way.

It was in the face of this evident shift of public opinion that Robin decided it was no longer sufficient to rely on headline news and media reports. He resolved to commission some detailed consumer research in order to understand better what was really driving the changes in behaviour.

'We've parked Project Park. Only for the time being,' said Marianne, giving the pasta sauce a quick stir to stop it from burning. 'And Project Kingdom . . .' she added. 'Well, the long-term vision is obviously going to need some debate. I'm not sure I know what I think about it yet. But I do think it's right that we should try to acquire and protect the kingdom.com name as soon as we can. With the website up and running within a few months, if we're lucky, we can at least then start to explore what the concept might mean on a broader scale.'

Robin sat, drink in hand, wondering whether she would ever talk about anything else.

'I also get the impression there are discussions going on behind the scenes, as it were. Discussions with all those people who we now call "stakeholders" in the Church,' Marianne continued, reaching out for her glass of wine and adopting something of a knowing look. 'But there's a lot happening with Project Cath as well – and that's where Dr Conan has asked me to concentrate my efforts. So I'll have to get out in the field and see as much of it as I can at first hand.'

'That's going to mean more travelling then,' said Robin unenthusiastically. 'And, anyway, what's Conan got to do with this? I thought you were working for the Archbishop.'

'Well, I am,' replied Marianne. 'But it's understandable that he can't personally supervise it all.'

She hesitated for a moment and looked thoughtful, remembering the look she had seen in the Archbishop's eyes when they had met at Lambeth Palace. She had not met with him since then, and all communication had been via Dr Conan. She was brought back to the here and now by Robin's voice.

'So, does that mean you'll be visiting all the Anglican cathedrals in the country? How long is *that* going to take?'

It was a voice that carried a note of impatience, and Marianne turned to look at him. 'You rather wish I wasn't doing this, don't you?' she said.

Robin looked surprised. They had not discussed properly what either of them wanted. He felt caught off guard.

'No, that's not it,' he said, after taking a mouthful of his drink. 'It's not the job. It's just the way things have happened – are *still* happening – at such a speed. I thought I knew all about quick turnarounds in consumer thinking – but this beats everything I've ever come across. It's all moving at such a ridiculous pace. And at precisely the time when I would have liked us to step away from it all. At least for a bit. That's why I'm feeling so . . . so . . . half-hearted about the campaign. It seems to be getting in the way of any chance we might have had of . . . well . . . being normal.'

Marianne almost laughed – largely from nervousness – but realized that Robin would have been hurt by such levity. She tempered her response.

'Normal? Well, you surprise me, I have to say. Normality is not something I would have associated with you,' she said. 'I think you'd get bored after a few hours of being normal – whatever that means. Of course, if what you're really saying is that you can't live without me, and that you don't want me disappearing for days at a time, then that's different. But please don't talk about normality. Surely if this whole thing is worth anything at all, it's because it's *not* normal. And I know that's scary. Part of me is as . . . as . . . unsure about a lot of it as you are. But another part of me feels that it represents the best chance I'm ever likely to have to build something like a truly modern Christian society. It may be very naïve of me – but it's that thought that keeps me going.'

Robin said nothing but simply looked more thoughtful as he sipped his wine. He had been hoping that it was something else that was keeping Marianne going. And he longed to say that he really didn't want her to disappear for days at a time. But he couldn't quite bring himself to put it in those terms – to say the words. In many respects he knew that he did not want to live without her, but again he couldn't find a way of suggesting to her that their – or at least *his* – personal happiness might be more important than the enterprise in which they were both now so deeply involved. And, after all, as they kept telling each other, they were only really just good friends.

'OK,' said Marianne, seeing his air of despondency and not wanting the evening to drift into a mood of melancholy. 'Why don't you come *with* me?'

'With you?' said Robin. 'Where?'

'To the cathedrals. Or at least to some of them. I'm only going to do a few at any one time. The first trip's lined up for the week after next. Go on. I'm sure your diary could be sorted out to let you get away.' She looked at him coyly. 'If it was important to you.'

He had to smile. 'If you'd told me a year ago,' he said, 'that I'd be prepared to traipse around after a woman vicar, visiting bloody cathedrals, I would have said you were one can short of a six-pack.'

Marianne beamed back at him. 'Is that a "yes" then?'

Robin arrived at the viewing facility at six o'clock. The first of the focus groups was due to start at half-past. The plan was for the consumer research programme to begin with 12 representative focus groups spread around the country. Each group would consist of seven or eight 'consumers'

recruited on the basis of certain pre-arranged screening criteria. Over a period of about 90 minutes a professional researcher would lead the group through a structured discussion of the key factors that Robin had identified as being central to an understanding of what was happening in the country at large. The groups would therefore be used to explore some of the big issues, and to validate (or otherwise) some of Robin's main hypotheses. This learning would then help fashion a questionnaire which could be used to obtain a more robust response from a quantitatively significant cross-section of people.

He peered through the glass at the room beyond, where a group of men and women were settling into their seats. Most of them glanced up at the large mirror that ran along one side of the room. It was behind this mirror that Robin was sitting in a small darkened ante-room. Two-way mirrors were a common feature of focus groups such as this. Those who were to be observed would be told that there was someone behind the mirror: in most cases it didn't have much of an impact on what was then said in the ensuing one or two hours.

As the researcher asked the members of the group to introduce themselves, Robin began to make notes on the pad in front of him. He drew eight circles to indicate the eight people in the group, and then wrote their names in the circles. He knew that group discussions could be useful indicators of overall patterns of public opinion, but that they needed to be treated with caution. In many cases, the apparent opinions of the group could be unreasonably led or dominated by one or two strong personalities or loud voices. Such was the case on this particular evening. Robin had attended so many focus groups over the years that he had acquired a good feel for how the group dynamics would work out. On this occasion, he could tell from the way Mitchell introduced himself that he would be forthright to the point of bigotry. He was not mistaken.

Mitchell's view dominated proceedings, regardless of

what the researcher did to temper his outpourings and encourage the others. Mitchell, it seemed, had a lot to get off his chest. He would not have considered himself a Christian. He never had been. Well, not until recently, of course. Now everyone was, weren't they? And why not? Stood to reason, didn't it? The way it was before . . . well, the Church didn't offer nobody nothing, did it? Whereas now . . . *Now*, it had a lot to offer. Hardly surprising then, was it, that people were getting interested? He couldn't think why the Church hadn't done it all a long time before. But then the Church had always had all those funny ideas. What *were* they? You know, those *beliefs*. Well, how could anyone believe in all that stuff and still hold his head up in the pub? It weren't reasonable, was it? But now . . . *Now* it was different. You didn't have to believe all that business about virgins and people coming back to life, did you? Who *said* you didn't? The bloke down the church, that's who. He said it was all made up, anyway. He said the main thing was 'getting something out of it'. He said if no one was getting anything out of church, well, then it wasn't any wonder it was dead on its feet.

At one point Deirdre tried to suggest that there might be more to it than that – and Graham seemed to be in agreement with her. But Mitchell was quick to put them right. It was all very simple really, he said. Robin wrote it down on his pad, along with his other selection of verbatim quotes. It was all very simple really.

As winter gradually turned to spring, more and more seeds of change began to grow. Experiments were transformed into established practices. Bastions of conservatism embraced novelty. Never a day passed without new news of innovation. There seemed only one subject of conversation. And the channels of communication buzzed with the talk of the day.

From the dark corner of a damp, leathery room in Westminster, a hoarse, whispering voice slid slowly and secretively into an old-fashioned bakerlite telephone.

'Tadd has been tracking the woman, so we're fairly clear what she's up to. Meanwhile Simple Simon has seen the agency man on more than one occasion, and seems reasonably familiar with the modus operandi. He's also been out and about with several of our brother bishops. All appears to be well. With one possible exception.'

The whispering voice paused briefly. Clearly someone at the other end of the line had spoken.

'Yes,' agreed the hoarse whisperer at last. 'Saxonford,' he said, making the sound of the word extremely long and sibillant, before replacing the receiver slowly and heavily.

A couple of miles to the east, in Covent Garden, Dominic breathed into his mobile phone. 'I know what you're going to say, Noel. Robin's a friend as well as a colleague. We shouldn't have any secrets. I know all that. But I'm just a bit worried that his relationship with Marianne Maddeley is beginning to get in the way. No, I don't mean that. I'm sure he can handle his own emotional problems. But, let's face it, he hardly seems to be in the office for more than half the week. And we can't sit around waiting for him to be there when there's so much else we've got to get on and do. What am I suggesting? Well, just that we get on with some things without him, that's all. Like what? Well, like Project Park for a start. After all, we're only in the early stages of working up the idea. And, anyway, he's got his hands full with Project Cath. Or at least that's what he told me. I think he intends trailing round after his lady friend, visiting a load of bloody cathedrals all over the country. Which reminds me. I think *we* should do something on the cathedral front as well. Yes, me and you. What? No. No, I don't think we have to tell Robin about every bloody thing we do. Look, if he wants to cover half of England seeing what's going on, then I think we should feel free to do something in our own back yard, as it were. Where? Well, I was thinking about

St Paul's. I met the Bishop of London the other night at the "Pray as you go" launch party. I think he could be on for a deal. And come on, Noel, let's do this on our own – and then we can . . . *surprise* Robin. He'll love it, I know he will.'

A few miles away, on the south side of the River Thames, a clergyman dressed all in black sat hunched at a large desk, his frame only half illuminated by a sharp wedge of light from an angle-poise lamp. His long finger punched at the numbers of a telephone keypad, before he spoke with a crisp and impatient voice into a grey mouthpiece.

'Yes, yes. As I said yesterday, it's all going to plan. We've even convinced Tredwell that he needs to put some distance between the agency and the Angel man. So as long as the media continue to be obsessed with following our cute little lovebirds around, we can get on with the other things – away from the glare of any publicity. Believe me, there's no reason to worry. Sir V is on top of all that. And Arch is quietly tucked away. So, quite honestly, the lower the profile you can keep, the better. Just trust me. I'll call you when I have more news.'

Back in North London, Robin was walking about in his dressing-gown, a white cordless phone wedged under his chin, while he crammed a late-night slice of toast and Marmite into his mouth.

'So,' he said finally, having swallowed the toast. 'We're off to Oakminster Cathedral tomorrow then.'

He couldn't believe how excited he was by the prospect of spending yet another day with Marianne, and how it warmed his heart to hear her voice on the telephone, even though they had parted only a few hours before.

'Great! So I'll meet you then at half past eight.'

On a bright and breezy April morning, Robin and Marianne set off for Oakminster Cathedral. They arrived some hours later and parked the car close by the old wharf, which had evolved into something of a recreational park. It was a short walk to the cathedral itself and, as they neared the building, they could hear what sounded like gunfire. They exchanged concerned looks and quickened their pace towards the cathedral close, only to find their way blocked by a crowd of people, most of whom were straining to get a glimpse of what was happening on the green in front of the building.

Within a few seconds, several scenarios had suggested themselves to Marianne. It was a terrorist attack on the cathedral. Inflamed by the new fervour surrounding the Church of England, and aware of the enormous interest now at stake in the exploitation of the nation's most under-utilized and valuable fixed assets, fundamentalist terrorists had taken control of the building and a group of hostages. The gunfire was the sound of the SAS storming this most strategic of targets. Almost as soon as the thought entered Marianne's head, she dismissed it as unlikely. If terrorists were going to storm a cathedral, why would they choose Oakminster? Surely somewhere in London would draw more media coverage and provide the terrorists with easier access to a major airport.

It's a robbery, she decided. All the publicity about the commercial renaissance of the Church had simply drawn attention to the fact that the nation's cathedrals, which had been overlooked for far too long, were in fact unlocked treasure houses, stuffed with valuable items. After all, wasn't that exactly why so many business interests were now being drawn into the ecclesiastical world? Stories were freely circulating about how churches were using their treasures as collateral to attract new inward investment. Yes, it had to be a robbery. Except that it had obviously gone wrong, and even now the police and the villains were shooting it out in front of a mesmerized local crowd.

As Robin and Marianne struggled to see over the shoulders of the people massed in front of them, she gave expression to her thoughts as one man turned to see just who it was that was breathing so close to his ear.

'It's a robbery, isn't it?' said Marianne, knowledgeably. 'It's not a terrorist attack at all, is it? It's a robbery.'

'You what?' said the man in front of her, his face betraying a degree of vacant incomprehension rarely seen by Marianne.

'It's a robbery, isn't it?' repeated Marianne through tight lips, more than ever convinced that her instincts had been right. It was at this point that a tall man standing next to the first man turned round.

'Battle for sanctuary,' he said matter-of-factly.

Marianne clearly did not understand what he meant by these words and, as her mind raced from one possibility to another, she turned to seek out Robin's eyes. Robin was trapped between a wide woman in a saffron dress and a postman. A few seconds passed before Marianne was able to establish eye contact with him. When she did, she mouthed the words 'Battle for sanctuary' in a way that conveyed only too clearly that she had no idea at all what was going on.

'The idea came to us during a chapter meeting,' said one of the canons, refilling Marianne's glass with a fine Amontillado. An hour or so had passed since Robin's and Marianne's arrival on the scene of the gunfire, and both were now sitting in the drawing-room of the dean's house in the cathedral close. Intermittently gunshots could still be heard in the background.

'It seemed as if the Holy Spirit were inviting us to use our imagination to find ways in which we could bring more money into the cathedral. It was then that the idea came up of making a film. Of course, the idea was initially rather different to what's happening now. We originally envisaged it as a documentary about the cathedral, into which we might be able to weave some kind of sponsorship theme. Something to involve local businesses. We would then aim to get the film shown on commercial television in the hope that it would attract more visitors – and, of course, more business as well. We were just copying you really. You know – your idea of the virtuous circle, and all that.'

'But that was when the dean had his big idea,' said the other canon, looking admiringly across at the dean who was sitting quietly with an expression of beatific peace spread across his face.

'His big idea?' prompted Marianne.

'He told us to think big,' said the first canon, continuing to speak of the dean as if he had been on the other side of the globe rather than a few feet away, sitting on a leather armchair with his fingers interlaced.

'He said,' continued the canon, 'if we're going to make a film, we should do it properly. Why put all our efforts into doing something that only scratches the surface of the potential that we have in this great building of ours? Why not aim high?'

'And that's when you came up with the idea for a feature film?' added Robin, who by now was beginning to piece together enough of the comments to see what had happened.

'That was when I wrote to Marcus Bonaventura,' said the dean, speaking for the first time since greeting Marianne and Robin, and adding by way of explanation, 'He's a sort of cross between Tarantino and Spielberg. Blood and special effects. A bit like God really!'

'Yes,' said Robin, forcing a smile at the dean's little joke. 'We know who Bonaventura is. But why did he want to make a film in Oakminster Cathedral of all places? I mean, with all due respect, it's not the obvious location for a blend of gratuitous gore and computer graphics, is it?'

Both canons responded at exactly the same time with a single word. One said 'Economy'. The other said 'Aesthetics'. Marianne asked for clarification.

'Well, to be honest,' said the dean, holding an empty glass up to the light as if expecting it to be filled by divine providence, 'both factors came into play. And I suppose we were fortunate that Bonaventura also had a pet project in mind that suited our situation perfectly.'

'*Battle for Sanctuary*,' interrupted one of the canons, flushed with excitement and the effects of the Amontillado. 'It's set in the future and is all about this group of mutants who take up residence in an old abbey. Well, we managed to persuade Mr Bonaventura that the cathedral would provide the perfect set – and that we could allow access to the building and the grounds completely free of charge.'

'But I thought you were in this for the money,' said Robin.

'Oh, we are,' said the dean calmly, and with a broad smile spreading across his face once again. 'But we regard this as the investment phase. You see, we have done the deal, as they say, on the basis of having the rights to the merchandising operation for everything and anything connected to the film. Bonaventura gets his authentic film-set for free – but we get the lion's share of the cash generated by all the pictures, models, T-shirts, and toys that will flood the market as soon as *Battle for Sanctuary* goes on general release.'

Robin and Marianne glanced at each other. It was clear that they both felt that the dean and chapter had responded in a rather smart, if radical, way to the spirit of Project Cath. It was equally clear, however, that both seemed to feel that the balloon of the dean's evident smugness needed puncturing. Marianne did not wish to be condemnatory; after all, her role was surely to encourage enterprise, rather than to dampen the ardour of its converts. Nevertheless, she did not wish to sound too obviously supportive of an initiative on which she had not been consulted – and in which she was struggling to see any real sense of Christian mission. Not that the lack of consultation was in itself surprising. 'Commercial confidence' and plain jealousy had

already ensured a high degree of secrecy in the way cathedrals were addressing the opportunities of Project Cath.

'And you believe that this justifies turning the cathedral
over to . . . to . . . an excess of mutants and something
resembling a pitched battle for several weeks?'

'Well, I think Jesus was a great believer in the end justify-
ing the means,' said one of the canons, looking towards the
dean for some kind of approval. 'After all, isn't that basically the message of St John's Gospel? Who would have
thought that a barbaric execution could be a demonstration
of God's glory?'

For the first time since she had taken up the new job,
Marianne felt a real sense of shock and unease. She looked
quickly across at the dean, but his expression betrayed
nothing other than delight. He said not a word, but instead
appeared to be enthralled by the sound of gunshots explod-
ing all around the cathedral close.

'OK, I admit it,' said Marianne resignedly, as they drove
back to London. 'There are days when I miss being just a
vicar in a very anonymous church like St Thomas's. It's
sometimes very difficult to believe that only a few months
separate me from the quiet, humdrum days that I used to
spend in the parish. And then you came along with your
virtuous circle!'

Robin wasn't sure how to respond. He had never regret-
ted for one minute meeting Marianne. In fact, he had convinced himself that theirs was a friendship built to last in
one form or another. Nevertheless he was sorry that so
much else seemed to have changed in their lives in such a
short time – and that he had been the instigator of it all. He
was particularly conscious that Marianne had lost most of
the things that had given her life continuity over the
preceding years: her job as a parish priest, her home, the
people who lived and worked around her.

'Would you like to go back to St Thomas's?' he said at last.

'To visit?' replied Marianne, assuming that this was what Robin had meant. 'It would be good to see the people again. It's been almost two months now. They won't have a new vicar yet, of course. They're probably muddling along somehow, I suppose. But I do feel I rather left them in the lurch.'

She paused and looked pensive for a minute or so. Robin did not want to interrupt her thoughts.

'Yes,' she said finally. 'Let's do it. Why don't we go there on Sunday morning? I have to visit another cathedral on Monday – Southwark. You can come if you like . . . before you go to the office. And it'll be good to recharge the batteries with a bit of old St Thomas's before then.'

'It's not quite *old* St Thomas's,' said Robin gently. 'Even without a vicar to keep the momentum going, the Testway connection and the sponsored Eucharist are not likely to have passed away just yet. I think we have to be prepared to accept that the things we introduced will not have disappeared.'

'I wouldn't want them to,' said Marianne firmly, beginning to feel that Robin was perhaps treating her slightly too condescendingly. 'Let's not get sentimental about this. The fact is that, if we had not made the changes we did, St Thomas's would have closed. We stopped that happening. We moved things on. The church is open for business as usual. And that has to be right. We should be proud about it. It's open – and will stay open. Open for anyone to drop in whenever they like. And the more the merrier. Doesn't that make it worth it? Isn't that what church is all about?'

'Of course,' said Robin, who felt that it was the only thing he could say.

Unfortunately it wasn't quite as easy to drop in as they had imagined. On arriving at St Thomas's 15 minutes before the service was due to begin on Sunday morning, they found they had to join a queue of people moving slowly towards the main door.

'Well, this looks encouraging!' said Robin, trying to sound as positive as he could.

Marianne scowled. 'I don't want to have to queue to get into my own church,' she said.

'It's not your own church now,' said Robin archly.

'Well, I don't want to queue to get into *any* church!' said Marianne, rather more loudly than she had intended. Several faces in the queue ahead of her turned round to see who was making the fuss. She didn't recognize any of the faces.

'Why on earth not?' said Robin, keeping his voice down. 'Doesn't that show that you've succeeded? That the Church has succeeded?'

Marianne did not get a chance to answer. They were now nearing the door and, for the first time, they saw someone they knew. It was Stuart.

'Reverend!' he exclaimed, his ruddy face breaking into a wide smile. 'And Robin!'

'You make us sound like the follow-up to Batman and Robin,' said Marianne, planting a kiss on the church-warden's red cheek.

'Good to see you, Stuart,' said Robin. 'And to see that St Thomas's is doing so well. It seems to have changed a lot since the vicar left. Do you always get this many on a Sunday morning now?'

'She's been fuller since we've been doing the wine,' he said.

'She?' queried Robin.

'The church,' said Stuart.

'The wine?' asked Marianne, conscious that their conversation was holding up the queue behind them.

'The free bottle of wine,' said Stuart, with the look of a

man who couldn't imagine why Marianne and Robin would have not known about it. 'The wine shop,' he continued, 'the one that's been sponsoring the Eucharist. They've got this offer, see? Got it started up as soon as the vicar left. You collect tokens every time you come along, and then, when you've got four tokens, they give you a free bottle of wine. Well, it's *me*, in actual fact, that hands them over. The bottles, I mean. When the folk come up to the rail for their communion, they hands over their tokens, and I gives them their bottle. It's all very simple really.'

Robin and Marianne moved inside the church so that those queuing behind them could get through the door. As the people moved past Stuart, he handed them a service sheet, a hymn book and a wine token.

'No, I'm sorry, ma'am,' he said to a stern woman who was indicating that her daughter had not been given a token. 'The tokens are only for adults.'

The woman remonstrated, saying that her daughter had been confirmed, and that therefore surely their family was entitled to two tokens – but Stuart stood firm. After the woman had grudgingly moved on, Stuart turned to Marianne and Robin to explain that, of course, the rules were open to a certain amount of abuse. Whilst handing out more pieces of paper, he regaled them with the story of how a family of four adults two weeks before, rather than taking their seats immediately, had sneaked out through the west-end door before trying to come in again through the main entrance so as to collect more tokens. He smiled again with a look of innocence.

'It's all a bit of a game really!' he said, in a tone that suggested he was bemused by the predicament rather than being either for or against it. Marianne was looking decidedly concerned by this time.

'But you have no new vicar,' she said, somewhat perplexed. 'So who is actually celebrating the Eucharist for you? Is there a visiting priest? And doesn't he or she have something to say about this?'

Stuart chuckled. 'No,' he said, 'we've not been bothering with a visiting priest this last four weeks. We did, of course, to start with. After you left. But a few weeks later no one turned up, and so the man from the wine shop stepped in. He's done it since then. 'Course, not everyone was keen at first. Mrs Murch didn't like it too much. But he makes a good job of it. And he's got a good loud voice, so's everyone can hear him.'

Marianne's jaw had dropped open. 'Are you telling me that the Eucharist here at St Thomas's is now presided over by . . . the man from the wine shop?'

But before Stuart could say any more, Robin had started guiding Marianne back out of the church, past a line of people who were still squeezing into the already full building.

They were walking close by the River Thames.

'Guns at Oakminster, wine merchants at St Thomas's. I have to say I'm not finding it easy,' said Marianne. 'I'm not saying it's wrong. The money's pouring in. The churches are full. The Church of England has never been so popular. There's still something in me that says "yes, this *is* ministry – this *is* mission". And perhaps this is what it means to be part of the twenty-first century. We are, after all, touching the lives of so many more people. But . . . but . . .'

Robin looked across at her, but remained silent.

'But where do you draw the line?' she continued. 'When does it stop being a . . . fusion of cultures, and start being . . . something of a travesty?'

Robin squeezed her hand. 'It's not something I feel qualified to have a view about,' he said. 'Only *you* – well, you and the Archbishop perhaps – can answer a question like that.'

Marianne smiled. 'I don't expect you to know,' she said. 'I'm not sure I expect *any*one to know – at least, not yet. I think we probably have to live with the consequences of your virtuous circle for a while longer before we can start drawing any real conclusions. I just know it's not easy. And it's not simple.'

'But at least we're here now,' said Robin. 'The place where you keep telling me it all began!'

They had arrived in a small square opposite Southwark Cathedral. It was a Monday morning, and the sun was shining brightly.

'It wasn't the beginning really, I suppose. Of my calling, I mean,' said Marianne. 'That was longer ago than I care to remember. But, yes, this place is where I was ordained . . . and it's very dear to me. Just seven years ago. I wonder what I would have said if you'd told me then that so much would change in such a relatively short time?'

'It *is* a change for the better,' said Robin, putting his arm round Marianne and giving her a hug.

'I thought, dear friend, you just said you weren't qualified to have a view,' replied Marianne, kissing him playfully on the nose.

'I don't have a view about where you draw the line . . . theologically, or ecclesiastically, or whatever the word is,' Robin continued, trying to retain a note of seriousness in his voice. 'I can only speak as a layman – a nominal Christian, perhaps – and I still think that, on balance, and despite all the challenges, it *is* a change for the better. Simply because of the numbers involved. You surely have to believe that.'

'Do I?' mused Marianne. They were now standing in front of the door. 'Yes. I suppose I do. If *I* don't believe it . . .'

The sentence was left unfinished. She made as to enter the building, but Robin hesitated. 'Are you sure you want to go in?' he said.

'Sure? Of course I'm sure. Given what I've already said about the place, of *all* the cathedrals I'm due to visit, *this* is the one I want to see most. Other than St Thomas's it's probably the church building that has the biggest place in my memory.'

'That's exactly why I'm not sure it's a good idea to go inside,' Robin said. 'You know what a shock it was yesterday at St Thomas's. Well, we know the provost here has made some radical changes of his own. We already know that he's linked the cathedral with several local initiatives of one kind or another. Project Cath seems to be progressing pretty much under its own steam in Southwark right now. I'm just not sure that you really need to visit every cathedral where things are happening. And that includes this one.'

'I'm not a child, Robin,' said Marianne firmly. 'And you're surely not suggesting that, having come this far, we go back. Come on. This is now my *job*. I can't afford to shy away from how people are interpreting the vision. I need to experience as many expressions of the virtuous circle as possible, even if they're not exactly . . . to my taste. Remember . . . the Church of England is a broad church. It has always embraced the exotic as well as the mundane.'

The first surprise confronted them as soon as they entered through the cathedral door, when they found their way barred by a turnstile and ticket office. It prompted Marianne to recall the letter she had received two weeks before from the provost of Southwark Cathedral. The letter had been phrased very carefully. In seeking to keep Marianne and 'other interested parties' informed of progress regarding the implementation of the principles of Project Cath, it had spoken of 'entrepreneurial opportunities' and of how certain partnerships had been formed with 'local attractions'. It had all sounded so very positive at the time. But what the provost, and the letter, had failed to mention was that one of the 'local attractions' was the London Dungeon.

The London Dungeon was a museum of gruesome torture and execution located only a few hundred yards away from the cathedral at the south end of London Bridge. Housed under some damp and dank brick arches, the

London Dungeon had been forced to find new premises when plans were announced for a wholesale redevelopment of the area. The provost had immediately seen the potential for a 'deal' within the scope of Project Cath, and had moved quickly to secure the London Dungeon as a tenant of the cathedral. In little more than one weekend, the grisly exhibits (most of which were life-size wax figures, portrayed in scenes of death or dire despair) were moved into the various aisles, chapels and transepts of the cathedral, so that the building now resembled some nightmarish gallery of grotesque torture.

At the ticket office, Robin and Marianne found that the cost of entering the cathedral-cum-museum-cum-dungeon was unexpectedly high and used up almost all the cash they were carrying. Once inside the building, however, the shock occasioned by the high entrance fee soon gave way to real horror.

Passing below a large sign that declared 'Only through suffering comes salvation', they shifted hesitantly from tableau to tableau. Marianne was speechless, her face ashen, as they made a slow and sombre perambulation of the shadowy cathedral interior. At the end of their circuit they eagerly pushed their way back out into the daylight, past a throng of eager schoolchildren who were clamouring to be let in.

Sitting on a wall, holding hands tightly, they sucked in the fresh air in large draughts. Marianne was shaking visibly. 'Well,' she said after several minutes of silence. She exhaled loudly and said again in a tone that was falsely jolly, 'Well . . . I suppose I asked for that. But it can't be denied. Project Cath is certainly having an effect. I don't suppose there are too many places left untouched by it. Thank God for that!'

'But I also think we – you – may be getting closer,' said Robin quietly.

'Closer?' There was still a tremor in Marianne's voice.

'To knowing where to draw the line,' replied Robin.

'Ah,' was all Marianne could muster.

'It won't *all* be like this,' continued Robin. 'I think we should keep going. In every sense. And I think your – I mean, *our* – next visit should be to Saxonford Cathedral.'

'Saxonford Cathedral,' repeated Marianne dully. 'Why Saxonford?'

'Well, I think it will be different,' said Robin. 'And I think I heard someone at the office saying the other day that they're still doing it the old way there.'

'The old way?'

'Still doing services, I mean, in a sort of *traditional* way. No obvious shift away from worship to being . . . well, being a film-set or a museum. It's worth a look, don't you think?'

Marianne turned and gazed at the features of his face, as if she were studying them for a portrait. She then looked down at their interlocked hands as if they belonged to someone else.

'The old way, the traditional way,' she repeated faintly. 'But is that any better? The Church clearly can't stay where it is. It *has* to move. We're right to be moving it. But what's it moving *from*? And what's it moving *to*? There are so many big questions. And the biggest one of all is where is God in all this?'

'I don't know,' said Robin, rather wishing that he *did*, if only to be able to say something supportive to the woman who was quietly weeping by his side.

# IV

Four weeks later.

Robin had just appeared through the front door of Angel, Fear & Tredwell.

'Noel's looking for you,' said Charlotte the receptionist. 'He says it's "great news".'

'Oh, God,' muttered Robin despairingly as he made his way upstairs.

Noel intercepted him before he reached his office. 'Great news from Lambeth Palace,' he said. 'From someone at the Archbishop's office this morning. It's about a new prayer book.'

'Prayer book?' Robin sounded bemused. 'What's a prayer book got to do with us? Is this part of Project Cath or Project Park?'

'Neither,' continued Noel. 'It's a new project – completely new. We've been asked to create a new prayer book.'

Robin raised an eyebrow and continued along the corridor before turning into his room. Noel followed him in.

'This all sounds a bit odd,' said Robin. 'I didn't think we got involved in . . . well . . . the religious side of things.'

'Well, when I say create, I suppose I mean *design*, really. It's more about layout – and how best to include advertising.'

'That still makes it a bit odd,' said Robin. 'It's not obviously part of the current plan. Although, in terms of virtuous circles and the like, I suppose we *can* get it funded by whoever's going to take the advertising space.'

'Money's not a problem,' said Noel. 'Catchpole's paying. Well, not personally, of course. Although, I dare say he could probably afford it out of his small change. But no – it's his company. Or *one* of his companies at least. He's going to bank-roll the project precisely *because* of the ads that the prayer book's now going to carry.'

Robin sat down heavily and stared at Noel, before turning to fix his gaze on the world outside his window. He had told no one about seeing Sir Victor Catchpole at Lambeth Palace – not even Marianne. As far as she was concerned, the man in the pin-striped suit was still 'Mr Smith'. But a simple plan to include advertisements in a new edition of a prayer book . . . was this what Catchpole had been so secretive about? Curioser and curioser, thought Robin.

'These ads,' said Robin, slowly. 'They'll presumably be ads for Catchpole's companies.'

Noel was about to answer when Dominic burst into the room. 'Heard the news about Catchpole?' he said loudly.

'Yes, I have,' said Robin, rather wearily. He was feeling that Sir Victor had already assumed too great a role in his life, even though he didn't quite understand what that role was.

Dominic looked irritated. 'I thought it was hot news,' he said. 'Just in. When on earth did *you* hear?'

'Noel's just told me,' said Robin. 'About the prayer book, and how Catchpole's paying for it.'

Dominic's expression brightened. 'Not *that*,' he said with some exultation. 'Not the prayer book. That's *old* news. The *new* news is that Catchpole's buying Amalgam Newspapers. It means he'll become a press baron overnight. Now isn't *that* news!'

'Yes. Of course,' said Robin smiling and speaking almost to himself. 'He'll be able to keep the story going – and going, and going.'

'Story? *What* story?' said Dominic, annoyed that Robin had not immediately grasped the potential for the agency: that, if things went well, Catchpole was likely to award the advertising account for Amalgam Newspapers to Angel, Fear & Tredwell.

'The story that the virtuous circle really *is* virtuous – and in everyone's interest,' said Robin, gazing around him with the kind of smile that betrayed as much horror as satisfaction.

'What do you mean?' said Noel, who was confused beyond measure.

'And, of course, the prayer book will be just another way to deliver the story to the punters,' continued Robin, the eerie smile spreading across even more of his face. 'The prayer book will carry ads for the newspapers – and the newspapers will reinforce on a continuing basis the benefits of the Church's commercialization. It's brilliant! A real virtuous circle if ever I saw one!'

'I don't understand you,' said Dominic, whose patience was wearing thin. 'Robin, what's this all about? And what's going on?'

'What's going on?' repeated Robin, suddenly breaking into a fit of nervous giggles. 'What's going on! *I* don't know! You tell *me*!'

The following Sunday morning Robin and Marianne set off early to drive down to Saxonford in time for the main mid-morning Eucharist at the cathedral. They parked a few minutes' walk from the city centre, and made their way towards the building whose spire dominated the surrounding area for miles around. As they entered the cathedral nothing struck them as particularly unusual, other than the fact that the congregation – in line with everywhere else in the country – seemed to be much larger than it would have been in previous times. Robin and Marianne looked around nervously, but saw no immediate signs of the kind of naked commercialism that they had witnessed in their visits to Oakminster and Southwark.

'So far so good!' whispered Robin, as they slid into a couple of empty spaces about halfway along the nave.

Marianne dropped to her knees to pray, and Robin began to look at the various books and papers that had been given to them on their entry. There was a copy of the prayer book – the one, Robin reflected, that would presumably be replaced by the latest (Catchpole-financed) initiative. There was a hymn book. There was a photocopied sheet giving details of other services during the week. And there was a copy of a slim newspaper. It was called *The Free Newspaper* – and, as its name suggested, it was quite evidently 'free'. Below the name, in smaller letters, were printed the words 'The voice of Saxonford'.

Robin was prepared to ignore the newspaper altogether, except he noticed that the front-page stories appeared to be less than fully supportive of some of the schemes that had been introduced in other cathedrals over the last few weeks. In particular, there was a piece declaring that Southwark Cathedral 'in making a pact with a dungeon, has perhaps made itself a prisoner of the new world of commercial enterprise'. What was surprising was not the tone nor the implied criticism – both of which were fairly mild – but the fact that it had been published in a cathedral newspaper. Amidst the generally supportive popular press, there had been a few signs of unease at the speed and direction taken by Project Cath – but, without exception, the various cathedrals had formed a united front in supporting each other's commercial efforts. That did not necessarily mean that (for example) Oakminster actively endorsed Southwark's hosting of a series of ghoulish tableaux – but not to be at least superficially supportive was to suggest that its own money-making exploits might be called into question.

Marianne rose from her knees and resumed her seat – and Robin turned to show her the newspaper. Before he could do so, however, the organ began the first chords of the opening hymn, and the congregation stood up as the choir and sanctuary party processed into the main body of the cathedral church. As the assembled crowd chimed in with 'The Church's one foundation', Marianne turned to

Robin and whispered quickly, 'Still looking good!' By this she meant that, as far as could be seen, the service had begun without novelty or incident, and with no suggestion that the forthcoming Eucharist would be anything other than a 'normal' and 'traditional' act of worship.

As the hymn continued, the procession moved along the side aisle, turned into the central nave, and began to make its way between the serried rows of the congregation towards the sanctuary and the altar. Robin and Marianne glanced to one side to watch the procession pass by. First the crucifer, carrying the cross. Then the choir, in twos. Then various clergy and servers. And finally, at the back of the procession, the bishop himself. Everything seemed normal. Not a sign of outward commercialism. No sign of obvious advertising. Not, that is, until the bishop passed the row where Robin and Marianne were sitting. It was only then, as they were able to see his back for the first time, that they noticed the words emblazoned in gold across the dark green, floor-length cope that hung from his shoulders covering his vestments. The words immediately reminded Robin of the messages that had been embroidered on to the backs of dark blue overcoats as part of the campaign for Buckingham Palace.

The words simply said 'Keep Salisbury Free'.

The service progressed without incident and, as soon as it had finished, Robin and Marianne made their way to where they hoped they would find the bishop. They had not arranged to meet him but, once he knew who Marianne was, he was very keen to entertain them as guests. The tall, dark, distinguished-looking man invited them to follow him out of the cathedral to his office in a neighbouring building, where he sat them down with mugs of coffee and a plate of chocolate biscuits.

'Yes, I have to admit,' he said, with a look that combined

embarrassment and pride, 'that *The Free Newspaper* was my idea. It's not really a reaction against what you're trying to achieve. After all, it's paid for by the advertising that it carries – so it's very much in line with the spirit of your virtuous circle. The same source of revenue has allowed me to indulge in the cope.'

'But the freedom theme is about some kind of independence, isn't it?' prompted Marianne. ' "Keep Salisbury Free" sounds like a rallying cry. So what exactly is it that you want to be free of?'

The bishop sat back in his chair and munched his biscuit thoughtfully. When he finally spoke it was clear that he was neither overtly defensive nor aggressive in the way he expressed his views. His comments were phrased in a matter-of-fact way and communicated with a degree of serenity.

'The Church of England has always prided itself on being a broad church,' he began. 'A church embracing many styles and preferences. At the same time it has striven to be a true holy, catholic and apostolic church – a church with a unified identity and sense of united mission. Not simply a collection of different churches banded together under a flag of convenience. The challenge for its leaders has always been getting the balance right. Now, I'm all in favour of bringing the Church of England into a brave new world of economic reality. Many of our problems in the past have been due to our commercial and cultural ineptitude. However, in moving towards something better, we clearly don't want to get into bed with Mammon.'

The bishop sipped his coffee as if allowing time for the word 'Mammon' to sink in. 'I am sure that I don't want Saxonford to be left behind in the race towards a new role for the Church in society, but I think we have to be clear that the whole thing does indeed now appear to be a race. Races have winners and they have losers, and I can't help thinking that the speed with which all this activity is progressing is likely to create more losers than winners. You've already mentioned your visits to Oakminster and Southwark. But, of course, the same thing is happening everywhere. Some people will say that the plan to run the British Badminton Championships in York Minster is a fairly safe and innocuous use of a building with a high ceiling. But how long will it be before they convert the Lady Chapel into a squash court?'

Robin and Marianne couldn't help smiling. The bishop was making his point with more good humour than pique.

'Now you may feel I'm being old-fashioned,' he went on, 'but I don't think I am. As I said, I honestly don't want us to be left behind in this commercial revolution. But I *do* want the time for us all to consider the options – the pros and the cons. I certainly don't want this diocese and this cathedral simply to be swept along mindlessly by the momentum that has gathered pace across the rest of the country – and which seems to be encouraged every day by the sorts of stories and reports that I read in the national press. That's largely why I felt *The Free Newspaper* was a good idea. It is at least something of an antidote to the argument that all is for the best in the best of all possible worlds.'

The bishop put down his mug, as if signalling the end of his speech and inviting comment.

'I have a lot of sympathy with your views,' said Marianne immediately. 'My role is supposed to involve encouraging and co-ordinating the virtuous circle idea across the country – but I have to say that, from the moment the Archbishop asked me to do the job, the whole thing has moved forward at such a pace that I've been hardly more than a spectator. Certainly as far as Project Cath is concerned, the bishops and the cathedrals seem to have needed very little encouragement!'

'Hmmmm.'

The bishop's 'hmm' was full of meaning.

'Please forgive me, Marianne. I don't for one minute want to suggest that you are not a very talented and energetic person . . .' He paused just long enough for Marianne to indicate that she really did want to hear what he had to say. 'But,' he continued, 'have you ever wondered why the apparent co-ordination of such an enterprise should have been entrusted to someone with rather limited experience of Church politics?'

'You mean that if it was really what was wanted, they would have given the job to someone important,' said Marianne, more as a statement than a question.

'I'm not sure what I mean exactly,' said the bishop, 'but I suspect that any real management of this whole thing will have very little to do with your efforts – commendable though they might be.'

He looked about him and then leaned forward in his seat. Robin and Marianne glanced at each other.

'I'm not supposed to tell this to anyone,' said the bishop confidentially, 'but there is a meeting of bishops tomorrow in London. The meeting has been called to discuss "the way forward". At least that's how it was described to me during a short telephone call last week. "Embracing the Vision: The Way Forward" – to give it its full title. All the bishops, as far as I can gather, have been invited – and each has been asked to travel to the meeting separately, and not to wear clerical clothes.'

He leaned even further forward in his chair. 'And,' he continued, dropping his voice, 'there is a secret password. It's "Kingdom". If I don't use the password at the door, I won't be let in. Now, my friends, you are the instigators of the virtuous circle – and yet I have the feeling that you know nothing at all about this conference.'

Marianne and Robin looked at each other again.

'We know nothing about it,' confirmed Robin, speaking for almost the first time since they had arrived in the bishop's office. His mind was racing, especially as he couldn't help noticing that the password was the same as the name that Dominic and Noel were using to describe the third and final stage of the proposed plan for transforming the Church.

'Bishop,' asked Marianne, 'are you prepared to tell us –

in confidence, of course – where the meeting is taking place?'

'I've told you this much. I don't see why you shouldn't know the rest,' said the bishop immediately. 'It's being hosted by a leading businessman. I expect you've heard of him. Sir Victor Catchpole.'

'The name's familiar. I think I've read about him in the newspapers,' said Marianne vaguely, unaware of the thoughts that continued to race through Robin's mind as he sat bolt upright on his chair.

Sir Victor's head office was a grand terraced building along one side of a green and leafy central London square. Robin and Marianne sat on a bench together looking, for all the world, like a courting couple enjoying the morning sunshine. It was half past ten and they had an unimpeded view of the main entrance to the building. The meeting was due to begin at eleven o'clock. Over the next 15 minutes or so, about 10 people came out of the building, and about 30 went in. Of these, around 20 were men in their fifties or sixties, all of whom appeared to be dressed fairly anonymously in grey suits, white shirts and ties. The whole scene was extremely unexceptional by any standard.

'Would you recognize any of them?' said Robin without looking at Marianne.

'No. That is, I expect I'd recognize my own bishop – but perhaps not if he was going out of his way to assume an air of anonymity. Middle-aged men in suits all look so alike.'

Robin suddenly turned, took Marianne in his arms, and kissed her passionately on the mouth. It was the first time they had had such intimate contact.

'Sorry!' he said, finally breaking off after half a minute.

'Don't apologize,' said Marianne, catching her breath and suddenly wishing that they were somewhere slightly less public. 'It was just a bit sudden, that's all.'

'I'm sorry,' said Robin once again. 'But I had to do it. To make sure we weren't spotted, I mean.'

Marianne's face betrayed disappointment, and invited some further clarification.

'The man who just walked past us,' said Robin, who looked quite flushed. 'I think he's the bishop who's been to see me at the office. Mind you, I can't be sure. As you say, they do all look the same – like accountants – without their collars on.'

'So the kiss was just a way of avoiding detection, was it?' said Marianne. 'Just like in that film.'

Robin laughed, immediately recognizing the image that was in her mind. '*The Thirty-Nine Steps*,' he said. 'Yes, it *is* a bit like that, isn't it? Or perhaps I just made it up – the bit about the bishop – as an excuse to kiss you.'

'Well, bishop or no bishop, I'm not complaining.'

Robin looked deep into her eyes. 'But I thought you didn't want to get involved,' he said.

'I think I *am* involved,' said Marianne. 'I think we *both* are. Up to our necks. Don't you?'

He moved as if to kiss her again, but she stood up. 'Later,' she said, smiling at her own sense of self-control. 'Come on. We're supposed to be on duty. As spies. Remember?'

'OK, I'm sorry,' he said, standing up. He was conscious that it was his idea to mount this 'stakeout' of Catchpole's office. 'I agree it's not the most exciting way to spend the morning. Especially when there's so much else we could be doing.' He smiled and took Marianne's hand in his, before saying 'Shall we go and get a coffee somewhere?'

'Well, you have to admit,' said Marianne, 'this whole spying thing has been pretty inconclusive. For one thing, we've no idea if those men going into the building really are bishops. And even if they *are*, what does it prove?'

Robin nodded as they started to walk across the square and out on to the main street. He wasn't sure himself what he was hoping to see or find out. After crossing two more roads they arrived at a coffee shop and Marianne began to pull Robin towards it. She was surprised when he resisted.

'Not here,' he said, glancing quickly over his shoulder. 'Let's walk on a bit further. In case there's something better.'

Marianne was puzzled, but decided to indulge him. Robin then turned off the main road and led her on a rather circuitous route that, five minutes later, ended up back at the same coffee shop.

'No, I'm sorry,' said Robin, smiling. 'You were right first time. This is clearly the best one around here. Do you want to sit inside or out?'

'I don't mind,' she said, looking at him suspiciously as he led her inside. Nothing further was said until they were seated in a corner with their cappuccinos, and then she could wait no longer.

'So what was all *that* about then?' she asked. 'All that cloak and dagger stuff?' She dropped her voice and said in a mock serious tone, 'Do you think we're being followed? Just like in *The Thirty-Nine Steps*? Is this all part of a plan to get me ready for another kiss?'

She was surprised that Robin did not smile. 'So you saw him as well?' he said earnestly.

'Saw him?' said Marianne, just stopping herself from laughing out loud. 'Saw *who*?'

'The man in the black suit,' said Robin.

'What!?' said Marianne, sitting back in her chair and shaking her head. 'Are you serious? First we're watching men in grey suits. Now we're being watched by a man in a black suit. Tell me you're not serious.'

Robin sighed, smiled, and once more took her hand in his. 'You must think I'm getting a bit obsessed with this,' he said. 'But there *was* a man in a black suit and he was following us.'

'And I suppose he was wearing dark glasses as well!' said Marianne, smiling broadly.

'Well, yes,' said Robin. 'As a matter of fact he was!'

Despite his obvious discomfort, he could not help sharing in Marianne's laughter, which served to defuse the situation. As they finished their coffees, they made a concerted effort to speak about anything other than their spying escapade, and by the time they went back outside their minds had settled on other things entirely. In fact, they had resolved to return to Marianne's flat with a view to furthering the new dimension in their relationship. Which is probably why they did not notice the white-shirted man who was sitting outside with a coffee, enjoying the full glare of the sunshine, having taken off his black jacket and sunglasses.

Jonathan arrived at Marianne's flat at seven o'clock in the evening. Whilst Marianne and Robin savoured their wine, he sipped his orange juice and looked around furtively.

'Yes, I *was* surprised to be invited round,' he said in answer to Marianne's question. 'I've followed your progress in the newspapers, of course. But you and I were never really close. In the deanery, I mean.'

Jonathan was the vicar of an evangelical Anglican church in the same deanery as St Thomas's. Marianne had met him a number of times at local events, and had mixed feelings about him. On the one hand, she disliked the narrow view that Jonathan took of the Church. He had always regarded himself as pretty much a law unto himself. He had taken a conservative evangelical line on most issues, and had withheld parochial money from the diocese in protest at what he saw as unnecessary interference by the ecclesiastical authorities in the goings on of a local and thriving church.

On the other hand, Marianne admired the single-minded way in which Jonathan had built up his own congregation and church organization. St George's had been by far the most successful church in the neighbourhood in terms of 'bums on seats' and 'share of wallet' – and the gradual demise of St Thomas's was, in some sense, directly linked to the growth that had taken place only a couple of miles down the road.

It was Marianne's idea that Jonathan be invited to supper to discuss 'the situation'. Fresh from their trips around the country, Robin and Marianne were feeling somewhat depressed by the speed and direction of the cathedrals' response to the new challenge. Moreover, Robin in particular had been worrying about what he saw as a possible conspiracy between leading business interests and the Anglican bishops. Following the inconclusive 'stakeout' of the bishops' meeting in London, he had shared all these worries with Marianne – and he'd also told her about Catchpole's presence at Lambeth Palace on the morning of her interview with the Archbishop.

Marianne's response was to suggest a meeting with Jonathan Bigley. Jonathan, she reasoned, would clearly be having no truck with any of the new initiatives. Having declared something of a state of independence at St George's, he would presumably have some distinctive views on how the conservative evangelical wing of the Church of England would maintain its integrity in the face of the growing commercialism. Unfortunately, Jonathan proved to be yet another disappointment.

Over the risotto, and in a relentlessly humourless way, Jonathan suggested very little about his personal plans, but set out clearly the reasons why the current situation was, in fact, being welcomed by church communities such as his own.

'At one level, of course, the Evangelical Church has always been the great force for movement and innovation in the C of E. Where the traditionalists have grimly hung on to tired old liturgies and social structures, we have moved ahead and found new ways to bring people to Christ. Your own initiatives have gained a great deal of press coverage but, in some ways, they have all been less fundamental than the changes we've been building in the hearts and minds of people over the last few decades.'

Jonathan listlessly poked his fork at the food on his plate. He seemed not to be a man of great appetite. 'So, far from condemning your techniques, I quite admire them,' he continued. 'They will not succeed, of course, because the beliefs on which they are founded are false. But, as *techniques*, some of them have much to commend them. After all, our Lord was no slouch when it came to marketing.'

His comments were delivered in a dull, flat monotone, and carried no hint of uncertainty. Jonathan's whole approach seemed to imply that disaster was so imminent for most of the Church of England that it hardly warranted any debate. Only churches such as his, it appeared, would be saved. He had clearly accepted the invitation to supper with the sole intention of putting Marianne right on that score.

'And you see the collapse of the broader Anglican Church to be in your interest?' asked Robin, trying to make explicit what he understood Jonathan to be suggesting.

'In the interest of the faith,' said Jonathan, correcting him. 'It will enable communities such as the one at St George's to be liberated once and for all from the antiquated structure of the Anglican hierarchy. We will once again become free churches.'

'But what about Church and State?' said Marianne. 'The Church of England, in all its weird and wonderful forms, is the established Church in this country. Surely you're not suggesting that the Church of England will be *dis*established?'

Jonathan smiled slightly, or at least the corners of his mouth turned upwards. 'My dear Marianne,' he said rather patronizingly. 'I would have thought that if anything ever signalled the coming of disestablishment, this was it.'

'Disestablishment,' said Marianne once again, after she and Robin had collapsed in a crumpled heap on the sofa. Jonathan had left at half past ten to cycle home. 'I don't understand,' she continued. 'Why would the Government want to disestablish the Church of England, and relinquish control over it, when it's clearly growing now in all sorts of ways?'

Robin didn't answer immediately. He was staring into the distance, his brow furrowed with thought.

'I just hadn't considered it before,' he said at last. 'But now it's been mentioned, it seems so obvious. We must have been blind not to see the signs.'

'You mean you think it will happen?' asked Marianne.

'Not necessarily,' replied Robin. 'But I can see why some people might want to see it that way. And if that's what some people want, then encouraging them is a good strategy for making sure they don't rock the boat.'

'It's late. I'm tired and I've had too much to drink,' said Marianne. 'I'm not sure I follow.'

Robin stretched and put an arm around her. 'Well,' he said, 'I may, of course, just be imagining all of this. Just like the man in the black suit. But just suppose . . . Just suppose the people who had most to gain from the commercialization of the Church considered the conservative evangelicals to be the biggest obstacle to success. In such a case, it might be a clever move to suggest that the real momentum was towards disestablishment and, to use Jonathan's word, the "freeing" of the churches. For example, have you noticed how many politicians now seem to speak openly about the advantages of what's going on in the C of E? A few months ago you could hardly get one of them to open his or her mouth on the matter. They were all waiting to see which way the wind was blowing. But now . . . *Now* . . .'

'Now *what*?' said Marianne, who was getting sleepier by the second.

'Now they can see how it might become a big parliamentary issue. They can see how it might become a great *cause célèbre* for the Government. And they can see votes in it. Under the guise of supporting something of a moral crusade and a spiritual awakening, all the major political parties can start manoeuvring themselves into what they imagine will be a winning position.'

'But I thought you were suggesting just now that the whole disestablishment thing was something of a chimera. Simply an idea put about to win over the evangelicals. Now you're suggesting that it might be for real. I'm getting confused, Robin. Very confused.'

As she said the words, she drifted off into half-sleep. Robin looked down at her and said softly, 'I think that's what they want, my love. I think that's what they want.'

It was a Saturday morning. They had been shopping in Knightsbridge and were now walking through Kensington Gardens.

'Now, as I've said before, I know you think I'm getting obsessive,' said Robin, giving Marianne's hand a squeeze. 'But you know that man I thought was following us before? No, don't turn round!' They walked on in silence for a few yards before Robin continued, 'Well, I think he's back. And this time, he has a friend with him.'

They stopped at the next empty bench, sat down and tried to look as nonchalant as they could. Marianne turned her head slowly to take in the view. About 50 metres along the path to their right two men in black suits were approaching at a leisurely pace. Both wore sunglasses, although that in itself was not remarkable: the sun was by now high in a clear sky. The shorter of the two men was talking in a fairly animated way, and using his hands to express himself. The other man looked at his colleague intermittently, but seemed to be staring ahead in a fairly abstracted way.

Marianne and Robin said nothing to each other, but continued to gaze around at the various people enjoying themselves in the sunshine. The two men drew nearer and nearer, never once looking in the direction of the bench where Marianne and Robin were sitting. Seconds later they had passed by, their pace unchanged, the shorter one still speaking expressively.

'You really could be imagining it, you know,' said Marianne at last, when she was sure that the two men had shown no apparent interest in them.

'It was the smaller one,' said Robin as if he had not heard her. 'The smaller man followed us from Catchpole's office on the day of the bishops' meeting. I've not seen the other one before.'

Marianne decided not to take issue with Robin. She suggested they go back the way they had come, and they retraced their steps along the path before heading off towards South Kensington. Every so often Robin found a reason to stop and look around him, but finally he had to admit that there was no sign of the two men. Marianne wanted to say something along the lines of 'I told you so', but restrained herself. Robin did not look to be in the mood to have his leg pulled. Instead she decided to play along.

'Who do you think they are?' she ventured, as she and Robin passed by the Royal Albert Hall.

'I'm not sure,' said Robin. 'At first I thought they were Catchpole's men – making sure we didn't upset things.'

'Upset things?'

'The discussions with the bishops,' continued Robin.

'But you don't think that now?' pressed Marianne.

'I'm not sure. They *might* be Catchpole's men. But they might be working for someone else entirely.'

'Like who?'

'The Government perhaps?' he said with a straight face. Marianne could not help smiling.

'The Government? *Our* Government?' she said. 'But why?'

'You remember what we were saying about disestablishment? Well it had never occurred to me until then – but it's just possible that they want to make sure that nothing happens to slow the momentum.'

Marianne stopped and stood directly in front of Robin so that he had to look into her face. 'Robin,' she said tenderly. 'I do think you're getting just a little bit too one-track about this. That's not to say you're wrong. It's just that perhaps your fears and feelings are getting the better of the available evidence. I'm prepared to accept that perhaps those men were following us, but I also think there's very little basis for your latest speculation. Catchpole – yes. Possibly. Given the charade I now know he played out at Lambeth Palace, I can believe that he might be into all this spy stuff. But the *Government*! I'm sorry, Robin, but I just can't see it. After all, you and I are the ones who made this whole thing happen in the first place. We're hardly likely to want to stop it now, are we?'

Robin allowed a smile to soften the hard lines of his face. 'Aren't we?' he said quietly. 'I'm beginning to get the feeling that we're the only two people around with any real concerns about the way it's all working out. And what would happen, I wonder, if we were to go public with those concerns? Don't you think that might have some effect on the relentless populism that claims to have taken its lead from our small beginnings?'

Marianne looked doubtful. 'I'm not so sure,' she said. 'I think you may be overestimating the influence that we have on popular opinion. I think things have moved on a lot in the last couple of months.'

'Well, it may not be long before we find out,' replied Robin, stepping to one side and beginning to lead Marianne on again. 'The consumer research that we've been conducting is being debriefed on Thursday. That should give us a better idea of what people really think.'

Robin had been an observer at the first pilot focus groups back in February and March. Over the following two months a wider programme of consumer research had taken place at different locations around the country based on a common questionnaire. It was now time for the researchers to debrief the main findings of this work.

The boardroom at Angel, Fear & Tredwell was full. Dominic had invited what he considered to be a cross-section of bishops and other senior Church figures, and had been surprised at the number of acceptances. Noel had gathered together a collection of his key creative directors, keen to pick up as many hints as possible for future campaign ideas. Robin and Marianne were also both there, of course.

'There's Dr Conan,' whispered Marianne in Robin's ear as they took their seats.

'Yes,' said Robin. 'And talking to Dominic. I didn't realize they knew one another.'

'Perhaps they don't,' added Marianne, seeing the suspicion in Robin's face. 'Perhaps they've only just met. I know what you're thinking – but consider. I've only met Dominic once or twice in all the time you and I have been . . . Well, you know what I mean. But it would hardly be a surprise to find myself in conversation with him at a meeting like this. This is exactly the sort of occasion where someone like Dominic is going to go out of his way to talk to anyone and everyone, don't you think? Especially if they have the air of being important.'

Dominic must have felt the weight of Robin's and Marianne's gaze, because at that moment he turned round, before ushering Conan over to where they were standing. He nodded informally to Robin, before saying, 'Marianne, how nice to see you again. You both know Dr Conan, of course.'

'We've met once,' replied Robin.

'Yes, of course,' said Marianne, proffering her hand respectfully.

Conan grasped it briefly, and then shook Robin's hand stiffly.

'Dr Conan is here representing the Archbishop of Canterbury,' added Dominic with evident delight.

'Indeed,' said Robin tersely. He was saved the trouble of any extra conversational exertions, however, when one of the researchers announced that she was about to begin the debrief, and would everyone please take his or her seat.

Using a series of computer-generated charts as visual aids, the researcher spoke without interruption for 45 minutes, during which time her audience sat in stony silence. The main findings of the quantitative stage of the project, she stressed immediately, were absolutely consistent with the indications that had emerged in the focus groups. Overall the entire programme of research suggested a clear and straightforward story.

The story was that – to use the words of one of the interviewees – the Church of England 'was coming home'. Over a long period of time – possibly hundreds of years, in fact – the Church of England had become more and more remote from the people it was supposed to be serving. Those people had always had a deep longing to be part of the 'something greater' that the Church represented – but the Church had put up more barriers than it had 'issued invitations'. The result had been a seismic dislocation of people and Church, with alienation on a scale never before known.

That had all changed with the initiatives that the Church had undertaken over the recent months. The changes had themselves been dramatic – but their effect had been beyond anyone's imagining. This was because the people had been looking for almost any excuse to 'come back' to the Church that had abandoned them. Once the doors were opened, as it were, the flood of new and lapsed Christians had been both vast and fast. The commercialization of the Church had been the catalyst. In its various shapes and forms this liberation of the Church of England had put it back in touch with the aims and aspirations of the people. The Church had once represented the incarnation of everything that people could have hoped for – and now it was doing so again. Yes, the free gifts and extra incentives to come to church were all having their own impact on the pattern of church attendance, but these were only the most evident signs of a more deep-seated shift in public affiliations. Whilst it was still too early to declare the birth of a spiritual awakening as a direct result of the commercial exploitation, there were indeed signs that a real yearning was being met.

*However* . . .

Ah, noted Robin. 'However.' So how big would this 'however' be? It was to be, Marianne reflected later, a rather large and worrying 'however'.

*However*, the researcher had continued . . . there were some doctrinal issues that were still causing problems. The doors might be open in lots of new ways, but certain doctrines were still obstructing a genuine and full reconciliation of Church and people. What *sort* of doctrines? Well, the good news was that most of them were not to do with God. Overall those people questioned had come out broadly in support of God. There were a few worries about the high-handed attitude he had been apt to take on occasions – but overall, he was not regarded as being a major problem.

*However* . . .

Another 'however', thought Robin!

*However* . . . Jesus had not come out of it quite so well. Not *every*thing about him, of course, was seen as a problem. No one had anything *against* Jesus, as such. It was rather the uninviting doctrines that the Church had draped around him.

Like *what*?

Well, the virgin birth for one. That was considered to be an unhelpful fairy story. And then there were all those miracles. As one respondent had put it, 'They hardly fit with a modern world, do they?' But the problems with the miracles were as nothing compared to a general unease with the Resurrection. That really *was* seen as a major barrier. After all, it was straining credibility to the limit to imagine that anyone in this day and age could possibly believe in a man coming back to life. The researcher went on to add that the most positive feedback had come from those people whose churches had abandoned or moved away from the traditional doctrines – and it was on that basis that the research had led to the following three clear recommendations: first, that the Church of England should put less of an emphasis on Jesus; second, that, in its references to Jesus, it should play down explicit mention of the Resurrection; and third, that it should explore options for *new* doctrines to reflect the new kinds of interest being manifested in people. Not to do so would be to risk the early collapse of the growth that had been occasioned by the recent changes.

The researcher finished and sat down. The silence was deafening. Robin and Marianne dared not look at each other. No one else seemed able to speak, such was the evident shock that had engulfed the assembly. Finally, Dominic – unusually pale and open-mouthed – rose to his feet, thanked the researcher, stared around at the array of faces, and tentatively asked for questions or contributions. After a few strained coughs, and fidgeting movements, a crisp, sharp voice was heard cutting through the heavy mood of the room. It was Dr Conan.

'I'd like to add my thanks for a . . . a . . . a . . . very illuminating analysis of the situation,' he said. 'And to say that, as far as the matters of detail are concerned, I feel sure that the Church of England will want to take note of what has been said. After all, there's too much at stake for us not to do so. And there is no doubt that we would all benefit from some doctrinal clarification on the key issues.'

The words served to break the atmosphere of paralysis. Robin and Marianne turned for the first time to survey the other faces in the room. Around them, various bishops were nodding.

Robin and Marianne continued the discussion over breakfast at Robin's flat.

'Did you notice how the researcher at the debrief kept referring to "the people"?' said Robin. 'She kept talking about how the Church of England was "coming home to the people".'

'Is there something wrong with that?' replied Marianne. 'I would have thought that was a good thing. Perhaps this whole business can be justified just because, if nothing else, it reunites Church and people – even if that means divorcing Church and State through some kind of disestablishment.'

Robin frowned. 'Perhaps,' he murmured. 'Except I don't think it's about people at all. I think that's just another bit of the front.'

'The front?'

'Front, charade, conspiracy,' he continued. 'I know you think I've developed something of a conspiracy theory about this whole thing. Well, perhaps I have. And as far as I can see, it's nothing to do with people at all.'

Marianne buttered her toast and waited for Robin to develop his theory.

'It started to dawn on me,' he continued, 'when Jonathan kept going on about how the evangelical wing of the Church would welcome disestablishment. He said it would give them freedom. But freedom to do what? Freedom to go off, presumably, and run their own affairs without having to look over their shoulders at any kind of Government or episcopal authority.'

Robin looked towards Marianne for some sign of support, and she duly nodded whilst munching her toast.

'So the largest group of people opposed to the commercialization would effectively walk away from the Church of England,' Robin went on. 'And that is, of course, exactly what they want.'

'*They*?' said Marianne between mouthfuls.

'Whoever's behind all this,' added Robin. 'In the short-term they may want people to be attracted to the Church, because it increases the C of E's commercial value, but, in the longer term, they want all the evangelicals to leave.'

'Why would they want that?' said Marianne. 'Surely as long as the evangelicals don't actually cause any problems, the Church of England will want to hang on to all its people.'

Robin had a slightly manic gleam in his eye. 'But this really is not about people, you see!' he said, with the air of a man who had made something of a discovery. 'The evangelicals may go. Others may go. But the buildings and all the land will remain the property of the Church of England. And that's what this is all about. This is not about people. It's about property.'

Marianne smiled. 'You know, that's quite interesting,' she said. Robin looked hurt that his argument should be considered only 'quite interesting'. 'I was reading last week in one of those newspapers that your friend Catchpole now owns,' continued Marianne, 'an article that was comparing what we've done to what happened during the English Reformation under Henry VIII. Well, when you think about it, that Reformation was more about politics and economics than it was ever about people or theology. So you might just be right. But, come on, we'd better get moving. Remember that Noel would like to see us at nine-thirty to tell us about his ideas for Project Cath and St Paul's.'

Robin was just about to remonstrate about her reference to his 'friend' Catchpole, and to press home the argument that this was more than 'quite interesting', when they heard the clatter of the letter box.

'Postman's early today,' he muttered gruffly, as he padded out to the hallway in his bare feet. He bent down and picked up a buff envelope that was addressed simply to Mr Robin Angel and the Revd Marianne Maddeley. There was no other direction on the envelope, and Robin assumed it must have been delivered by hand. He opened the front door of the apartment and looked up and down the corridor, but there was no sign of anyone. He quickly walked through to the lounge and looked out of the window on to the street below. A white van drove past. An elderly woman was walking her dog on the other side of the road. There appeared to be no one else about. He walked back into the kitchen and handed the envelope to Marianne without a word. She glanced at him, puzzled, and then opened it. Inside was a letter. As she read it quickly to herself, Robin could see the colour draining from her face. She sat down again at the table, and he did likewise.

'Well?' he said anxiously after a few seconds. Marianne looked him squarely in the face, and then peered back at the letter, which she began to read aloud.

*Dear Marianne and Robin,*
*We know you must have noticed us – and we apologize for our lack of subtlety. Unfortunately, the various issues and interests involved make it difficult for us to be as open as we would like to be. Please believe us when we say we are entirely supportive of what you have done, and are continuing to do. The time is ripe for change – but it is important to guard against those who would pursue narrow goals. We should fear fragmentation. We should seek to preserve integrity. We must keep the Church in England whole, intact and united. Beware of dissolution masquerading as freedom – and be guided by the one true faith.*
*Yours in Christ.*

Robin waited, but it was clear there was no more to be read out.

'It's not signed?' he said enquiringly.

'It's not signed,' said Marianne, handing him the type-written sheet of paper, before adding, 'Is it your men in black?'

'I don't know,' Robin said truthfully. 'And who are they anyway?'

They were sitting around a table on which was a scale model of St Paul's Cathedral. Noel was just beginning to become really animated.

'You may remember,' he said, 'that a number of years ago St Paul's got itself mixed up in some advertising. The name and image of a chocolate bar were projected on to the dome one night. It all turned out rather badly, I think, because not everyone had agreed the scheme. *This* time, however, everyone is in agreement! The Church, the Government, business – even the Palace! In fact, HRH is even going to do the honours!'

Noel waved his arms about enthusiastically over the model which had been constructed by one of his studio teams.

'HRH?' said Robin, glancing sideways at Dominic who was looking half smug and half embarrassed.

'Do the honours?' said Marianne.

'All in good time,' Dominic assured them. 'Let's see Noel's creative concept before we get into the details about who might be coming or doing what. Over to you, Noel.'

'Right!' said Noel. 'Just wait till you see this!'

He walked to the side of the room, closed the blinds to shut out any natural light, and bent down to the switch at the electric socket. Marianne gripped the side of her chair, fearing that something was about to explode or at least make a loud sound. As it was, neither thing happened. As Noel flicked the switch, the model suddenly came to life in the form of a dazzling light show. Spotlights flashed on and off at various points across the scaled-down site, whilst snakes of electric bulbs around the main contours of the building created a sense of wave-like movement. The centrepiece, however, was the dome which was studded with hundreds of small lights. They turned on and off in such a sequence as to make it appear that the whole of the dome was in fact revolving. Marianne, Robin and Dominic stared at the model for some seconds, slightly mesmerized by the effect that was being created in the half-darkened room.

'Well?' prompted Noel, who was growing impatient at the silence. 'What do you think?'

Dominic had seen the model once before already, but was still clearly excited by everything it represented. 'It's fantastic!' he said. 'Well done, Noel! I think it's an absolutely fantastically creative interpretation of the brief. Sheer brilliance!'

In the shifting light that was bouncing off the walls, Noel's face clearly showed his pride and pleasure. Robin and Marianne nodded their agreement and made vague supportive noises.

'The brief,' added Robin. 'Can you just remind me again, Noel, what the brief was?'

Robin was aware that Marianne had mentioned in passing that the Bishop of London had met Dominic and discussed in outline a few ideas for St Paul's – but that had apparently been about celebrating mission and the gospel, and nothing (as far as he could remember) to do with a light show.

'The brief,' muttered Noel, shuffling some of his papers in the glow of the flashing lights. 'The brief. Ah, yes. Here it is. It came directly from the Bishop of London. He basically said "Project Cath. Celebration of mission for the City of London. Suggest a new interpretation of a well-known Gospel theme. Perhaps John chapter l." That's the one that starts "In the beginning was the Word".'

'Yes, I think I know it,' said Robin with just a hint of sarcasm.

'Well,' continued Noel, 'I didn't think there was much scope in that. After all, as I was saying a few minutes ago, the *last* time St Paul's got into advertising, they used a big word on the dome. So I decided to drop the idea of the word, and go for the light instead. There's a bit in John chapter 1 where it goes on about light coming into the world. That's where I got the idea.'

'But,' said Marianne tentatively, not wanting to deflate Noel's evident enthusiasm for the Gospel message, 'don't you feel the bishop might regard this as being a slightly extreme interpretation of his brief? I mean, don't you think he might have had in mind something a little more muted, perhaps?'

Noel's face lit up even more as he leaned forward over the model. 'No,' he almost shouted. 'He loves it! The bishop loves it!'

'You mean he's already seen this?' said Robin tersely. 'You showed it to him before showing *us*?!'

Noel seemed unaware of anything other than his own sense of excitement. 'Well, yes,' he squeaked. 'I showed it to him yesterday. He loves it. He absolutely loves it! He's convinced that it's just what he needs to get all the others on board.'

'The others?' said Marianne.

'The business sponsors, the Government – and, of course, HRH.'

'His Royal Highness the Prince of Wales,' added Dominic, who was now looking slightly embarrassed by the fact that Robin and Marianne had not been included in the deliberations. 'Royal patronage, you see,' he went on quickly, keen to lay out the magnitude of the opportunity as rapidly as he could. 'Hence the secrecy. Of course, normally we would have involved you more closely,' he simpered, smiling at Robin and Marianne, 'but you were out and about visiting the other cathedrals – and it didn't seem to be the sort of thing to blab about over the phone, or write lots of e-mails about. Plus the fact that Noel and I thought we could get it up and running without having to bother you – especially as it's almost literally on our doorstep. Noel concentrated on the creativity, and I set about putting together an alliance of sponsors to back the Bishop of London's plan to celebrate mission in the City. First, I was able to involve Sir Victor Catchpole who – with a view to making the most of the project within the Square Mile – was keen to put some money in "up front". Then, he and I managed to get the Government on board. I was aiming just at the Secretary of State for Culture and Heritage initially, but – for some reason – the Government seemed to be more excited by the scheme than any of us might have imagined. In the end, we were even able to line up the Prime Minister for the inauguration of what's now going to be called the London Festival of Light. And then, through the Prime Minister and through the contacts we made earlier on the Buckingham Palace account, we were able to secure the support of HRH. In fact, it will be the Prince who will be throwing the switch to turn on the lights.'

Dominic finally paused for breath. Robin and Marianne sat in a state of stunned silence as patterns of light continued to revolve around the walls. It was clear that Project Cath had now well and truly overtaken them. Whilst they had been touring the country seeing what the various cathedrals had been making of their new-found commercial independence, Dominic and Noel had put together the beginnings of a scheme that was likely to eclipse all the others in terms of its impact on public awareness.

Finally, shrugging off the hypnotic effects of the swirling lights, Robin found his voice. 'So when is all this due to happen? This Festival of Light.'

'Next month,' crowed Noel. 'The beginning of July. The contractors start work on Monday, and the last light bulb will be in place three weeks later. It really is going to be electric!'

'Do you think this is working?' asked Robin.

'This?' said Marianne. 'What do you mean? By "this" do you mean "us"?'

'Well, not exactly,' said Robin. 'That is, no. I don't mean us. I mean this arrangement we seem to have developed.'

'Arrangement?'

'The fact that I stay at your place for a few days, and then you stay at my place for a day or two,' added Robin. 'It feels a bit . . .'

'A bit . . .?' prompted Marianne.

'A bit makeshift. That's all,' said Robin.

'Meaning . . .?'

'Meaning that perhaps we should . . . live together. Properly, I mean.'

'And what does "properly" mean?' pressed Marianne.

'Well, you know,' said Robin.

'No I don't,' responded Marianne sharply.

Robin swallowed. 'I mean . . . in just one flat rather than two,' he said after a few seconds.

Marianne scowled at him. 'You're so romantic!' she said dryly. 'One flat rather than two. Think of the money we'll save!'

'No . . . That is . . . What I *really* mean is . . .' he stammered.

'Yes?'

'I love you,' he said quietly.

'Well, thank goodness for that!' said Marianne, still with a hint of dryness in her voice. '*And* . . .?'

'And?' repeated Robin, who now looked confused.

'Yes,' said Marianne wearily. 'And . . .'

'And . . . I think we should . . . live together,' said Robin hesitantly. 'In one flat. Not two.'

Marianne growled, stood up, and threw a cushion at Robin, whose face seemed to convey the words 'Was it something I said?'

134

With only one day to go before the lights were due to be turned on, St Paul's looked anything but ready. Scores of men were engaged in an effort to dismantle the large expanses of scaffolding that still covered much of the building. Many others were working away at ground level, pulling cables one way and then another. Loose wires dangled from clusters of light bulbs, and the air was heavy with the smell of frenzy.

At the top of the steps at the front of the cathedral a gang of men was at work erecting a large metal platform where the main switch would be housed, and from where the lights would be turned on. St Paul's had been closed to visitors and worshippers alike for most of the preceding three weeks, and the building was now ringed by barriers. Tourists and passers-by gathered in groups to stare at the frantic activity that seemed to have enveloped the cathedral. Noel stood in his raincoat staring up at the dome, his shoulders hunched against the unforeseen and unseasonal rain that was now making the final preparations even harder to complete. The beginning of Project Cath had signalled the end of Noel's period as a non-smoker. He was now smoking more than ever before and, as he crushed one cigarette under his foot, he fumbled in his coat pocket for another.

'It'll be all right on the night,' he said, forcing a smile.

'Of course it will,' Robin said supportively, although he wasn't at all sure that it would be. As the rain started to fall more heavily, Dominic arrived on the scene.

'Morning,' he croaked. 'Typical bloody English summer, eh? Well, I suppose we should have known better. Planning this for the same week as the Wimbledon finals. Anyway . . . how are things going?'

Noel and Robin both gave non-committal nods which Dominic decided to interpret as positive signs.

'Good,' he said, staring up at the dome. 'Well, I just hope everything stays on track.' He coughed and then paused, before adding, 'Because I've heard a rumour that HRH might not make it.'

'Might not make it?' said Noel, his face contorted into something between horror and anger. 'Might not make it! Who the hell does he think he is?'

'Well, the Prince of Wales, I think,' said Dominic sourly, indicating simultaneously that they should lower their voices and take cover from the rain.

'It is just a rumour,' he emphasized in a hushed tone as the three of them sat down around a small table in the corner of a nearby public house. 'It may be untrue. And, whatever the case, you're not to breathe a word. Apparently he was happy with the idea until he realized it might have Christian overtones. Well, as you can imagine, his advisers have made it clear to him that there's nothing very Christian at all about it – but I gather he's not convinced.'

'But why's that a problem?' asked Noel. 'After all, he's practically head of the Church of England, isn't he?'

'Well, quite,' replied Dominic. 'But that doesn't actually require you to be Christian. I think he's more of a multi-faith sort of bloke when it comes to matters spiritual. Anyway, as I say, it's only a rumour – so we shouldn't put too much store by it.'

'If he can't, or won't, do it,' said Robin, 'presumably the Prime Minister could step in and throw the switch.'

'Aaahh,' said Dominic knowingly. 'Not as straight-forward as it might appear, I'm afraid. He's very keen to be there, of course, but he doesn't want to be seen as the prime mover in the whole thing, if you catch my drift. Apparently he wants to be seen as acting objectively when it comes to disestablishment.'

'Disestablishment!' said Robin, finding it difficult to keep his voice down. It was the first time he had heard the word used by either of his agency colleagues.

'Shhh!' hissed Dominic. 'I'll tell you more later. We've got a meeting with a Government minister next week to discuss it.'

Noel's optimism seemed to have been justified. At seven o'clock the following evening St Paul's Cathedral appeared to be in complete readiness for the big occasion. Some concerns had been expressed about the speed with which the final lighting arrangements had been put in place, but those thoughts had now been forgotten amidst the swell of excitement. The summer rain, which had continued through into the afternoon, had now stopped, with only the puddles bearing witness to the dampness of the preceding 24 hours. Large crowds had arrived to see the spectacular event, and the police were out in force to keep people back behind the barriers. All road traffic around the building had been stopped, and Ludgate Hill and the Strand had also been closed to create a clear route for the cars that were expected from Clarence House and Downing Street.

It was shortly after seven that the loudspeakers announced, with much regret, that the Prince of Wales would not be able to attend the ceremony due to a stomach upset. Instead, the lights would be switched on by the Bishop of London. The hum of disappointment was palpable everywhere. Dominic turned to Noel, who was sitting beside him on the seats reserved for VIPs, and gave him a knowing look. Noel pulled a face and muttered a string of obscenities under his breath. In the row behind them, Robin squeezed Marianne's hand. He had told her about the rumour, but was now wary of imputing too much to Dominic's story.

'Well, perhaps it *is* a stomach upset,' he whispered in her ear. 'There's a lot of it about.'

'A lot of it about?' repeated Marianne. 'Well, there's certainly a lot of *something* about, and if you ask me . . .'

It sounded as if Marianne were about to offer some pronouncement on the events surrounding the Festival of Light, but her words were drowned by the din of the loudspeakers announcing the arrival of the Prime Minister.

After the various speeches, there was a hushed silence. At the foot of the main steps the invited guests sat on serried ranks of chairs. Behind and around them, pressing against the barriers, massed the expectant crowds. At the top of the steps, alone on the specially built platform, stood the Bishop of London, his hand poised over a large metal switch. Dark clouds rolled by in an overcast sky. The street-lamps and the lights of the adjacent buildings had been dimmed. The only bright light was the theatrical spot that was trained on the platform. The only noise was the sound of the bishop's voice.

'It now gives me great pleasure to begin this wonderful festival by repeating those words once used by God himself, "Let there be light!"'

With a large and dramatic gesture, the bishop brought his right hand down on the switch and initiated a massive power surge that rushed through the cables and his body with equal ferocity, rendering him 'live' a split second ahead of the building. As the electricity coursed through his frame, his skin started to glow, his hair stood up in tufts, and his eyes rolled wildly in their sockets. A few seconds later this remarkable sight was gone, as the Bishop of London exploded in a blaze of golden sparks with a tremendous bang like a giant firework.

The explosion was followed by a concerted 'Ooooohhhh!!!' from the crowd – although this was probably occasioned by the fact that the whole of St Paul's had suddenly been illuminated by thousands of swirling light bulbs. It was only as the dome of the cathedral began to flicker like some gigantic and gyrating spaceship, that several people started to move disbelievingly towards the pile of ash that marked the spot where the Bishop of London had met his maker only moments before.

# V

July 10th, year two.

The newspaper story was again headed 'Angel of Death'.

The difference this time was that no reference was made to Robin Angel. *This* time it was simply a convenient phrase to encapsulate the bizarre demise of the Bishop of London.

Robin read through the piece anxiously once more, to double-check that he had not been mentioned by name. As much as the bishop's passing had been a sad and tragic occasion, Robin was able to take some comfort from the fact that he had not been directly or personally responsible for what transpired. The national press also seemed to have lost interest in his role in developments. It was one more indication of the way the whole programme of Church commercialization had developed a life of its own. Angel, Fear & Tredwell were still, of course, deeply involved in a wide range of initiatives, but they were no longer seen by anyone to be directing or driving events. Other, more potent, forces seemed to be at work.

In some ways, Robin was glad. He tossed the Sunday newspaper to one side, and reclined on his sunbed in the glare of the Mediterranean sun. Four days had passed since the strange opening of the Festival of Light. Only four days – and yet it felt as if so much had changed. He and Marianne had left the summer rain of London behind them for a two-week holiday on a Greek island. Soon after arriving there, they had sat at a small taverna on the beach, and Robin had proposed marriage to a surprised, delighted and wet-eyed Marianne. As they were to recall for years to come, his somewhat dramatically romantic act of dropping to one knee – and almost precipitating a waiter and two moussakas into the sea – was met initially with a shriek from Marianne and an exclamation of 'At last! Now get up, for goodness' sake before you do some damage!'

For the next ten days or so it seemed to both of them as if they had escaped into a fantasy world where the only point for discussion was the way in which they would live the rest of their lives together. Towards the end of the two weeks, however, the realization dawned that they could not simply walk away from what was happening 'back home'. Both of them acknowledged the responsibility they still had for seeing through something which had been born out of their first conversations more than a year before.

'We've lost the ability to control it,' said Robin, as he packed a suitcase.

'I'm not sure we ever had that ability,' said Marianne. 'But that doesn't mean we can remove ourselves from what's happening. I'm still clinging to the hope that this will all build to something better – something right and true.'

'OK – not *remove* ourselves,' added Robin. 'But we should at least try to have some kind of existence that goes beyond it. We mustn't let it run our lives. Not now that we have so much more to look forward to. We have to be able to step away from it – even if only for short periods of time.'

Marianne smiled at him, as if to say that that was easier said than done. She could see that, with every item of clothing that Robin was putting into the case, he was also packing away his newly assumed sense of detachment. She could see, even now, that he would be reaching for his mobile phone as soon as his feet were once more on British soil. For all his talk of being relieved that the two of them were no longer the centre of attention, the St Paul's incident had reinforced Robin's sense of unease at being excluded by his colleagues from a key agency initiative. As the suitcase was finally closed and locked, Marianne resolved that she would have to take the lead in making sure that the sentiment Robin had expressed was carried through into action.

The newspapers continued to reflect on the death of the Bishop of London, and the state of the Church of England, right through August. It was, Dominic asserted, a sure sign that nothing else was happening in the world. The truth of the matter was, however, that the incident continued to intrigue and interest people of all persuasions. It had, more than anything else so far, caused people consciously to consider the implications of what was happening to one of Britain's oldest institutions. Some commentators reflected a common view that it was perhaps an act of God, and a condemnation of the wave of commercialism that was sweeping the Church. As the weeks went by, however, more people seemed inclined to see it as an unfortunate accident. Indeed, some sections of the Conservative press went so far as to proclaim the event as something of a deliverance.

'Were it not for his indisposition,' declared a leading broadsheet, 'we might have been lamenting the passing of our future king. By comparison with which, the martyrdom of the Bishop of London must be seen as a noble sacrifice – a sacrifice in the tradition of so many former Christian leaders.'

'Oh God,' murmured Robin, folding the newspaper carefully and placing it on the sofa beside him. They had been back in the UK for almost three weeks now. Their holiday escape was already no more than a sunny memory. Robin put his arm around Marianne and said softly, 'Marianne, you *are* going to marry me, aren't you?'

She looked at him and smiled. 'Of course I am,' she said. 'Why? Are you getting cold feet?'

Robin seemed suddenly to realize what he had said, and looked embarrassed.

'No. I'm sorry,' he replied. 'I just feel . . . I have to keep reminding myself, that's all. Reminding myself that we *will* have another life outside all this virtuous circle stuff.'

Marianne looked at him. Sometimes, she thought, he seemed so on top of whatever life threw at him – the quintessential quick-thinking, smooth-talking agency man. And, at other times . . .

'Robin,' she said, almost as if she were talking to a child, 'we have that *now*. We have it *already*. It's not something that's being put off until the day we both say "I do". We have our lives – our *life* together – we have it now. It's not *another* life. It's not an alternative to whatever else is going on around us. It's here, and it's now – and it's us. It's what we make of it once we realize we already have it.'

She paused, hoping he was listening to her words. He was staring at the wall.

'That sounds a bit deep,' he said.

'It is,' whispered Marianne, as she put her arms around him and held him hard. 'As deep as deep can be. And it lies at the heart of all love and all trust and all faith. But, if you like, we'll get married as soon as we can. It would certainly simplify quite a lot of things.'

'Simplify things?' said Robin. 'What do you mean?'

'Oh, you know,' she replied, looking coy and not wanting to say too much. 'Living together and all that stuff. After all, I *am* still a minister in a church that professes the sanctity of marriage. So far *that* at least has not changed.'

A misty September morning in London.

'You're probably wondering what this is all about,' said the man in the grey suit. 'I'm sorry we've had to appear so secretive. But, as you can imagine, there's a lot at stake.'

Robin and Dominic had arrived at the Cabinet Office shortly before ten o'clock. Noel had stayed at the agency to oversee some new developments on Project Park – the Bible theme park idea – which was now being accelerated in the wake of Project Cath's apparent success. The man in the grey suit – who introduced himself as 'Grimes: a mere official' – had met them and shown them into a small meeting room at the end of a long corridor. Robin was only there because he had invited himself when he found out that the meeting had been arranged directly with Dominic. He decided to take the initiative by speaking first on behalf of the agency.

'We're used to acting in confidence,' he said. 'Secrecy in itself is not a problem. But, now that we're here, who exactly are we due to be meeting?'

Dominic gave him a look as if to say, 'Just wait. I'm sure everything will be made clear in good time', but Robin was chafing with impatience and a degree of hurt pride. Could the fact that they were somewhere in the Cabinet Office mean that they were going to meet the Prime Minister himself? The man in the grey suit, as if reading Robin's thoughts, smiled at him knowingly.

'This morning,' he said, emphasizing the words in such a way as to imply that what he had to say could not be seen to apply to any other day ever. 'This morning you will be meeting the Minister without Portfolio.'

As if these words had been a cue, at that precise moment the door opened and the Minister hurriedly entered the room, quickly shook hands with both Dominic and Robin, waved them impatiently into a couple of chairs, and started to talk quickly, pausing only to push the hair away from his high forehead.

'I won't detain you long. You've signed the Official Secrets Act, I take it?' He looked across at the man in the grey suit who nodded. 'Good,' continued the Minister. 'Then I don't need to tell you how important it is that you say nothing at all about this before the public announcement. The PM's going to be making a statement in the House on Thursday, but we need you to be briefed up and ready ahead of that announcement. I dare say you know what I'm talking about.'

Robin was intrigued by how the Minister assumed that they knew what Grimes assumed they did not know. Dominic and Robin both managed to give discreet, non-committal responses, suggesting that it would be helpful if the Minister made the matter slightly more explicit.

'Disestablishment,' said the Minister immediately. 'It's about the disestablishment of the Church of England. I don't want to say too much now about *how* exactly it will happen. The PM doesn't want me stealing his thunder – even with you! But you need to know that it's going to happen – and pretty quickly too. The reason for telling you now is because the Government would like you to act as advertising consultants for the whole show – which means we want some initial ideas in place as soon as the PM makes the announcement.'

'On *Thursday*?' said Robin, stopping himself from making a comment to the effect that less than a week's notice hardly gave them a chance to have much of a plan in place.

'On Thursday indeed,' repeated the Minister, apparently unaware of any scepticism implied by Robin's remark. 'Of course, there'll be a proper brief prepared for you over the next few days – but I want you to start thinking about this straight away. If I speak frankly, from *our* point of view disestablishment offers the chance to kill two birds with one stone. On the one hand it will be the ultimate step towards a privatized, stakeholder society. On the other hand, it will be a way of taking a populist approach to matters moral and spiritual. Not that we want to say too much overtly about that. No – the theme must be "Freedom". That's what we want you to think about. Freedom.'

'Freedom,' repeated Dominic, writing it on his pad in big letters.

The Minister without Portfolio suddenly stood up and shook them once more by the hand. The meeting was clearly over. 'There is a confidential conference being held in two days' time to discuss some of the implications of the move. I'd like you and perhaps one or two of your colleagues to be there. Grimes will give you the details. Thank you for coming in.'

And with a last nod in their direction, the Minister swept out of the room with the same urgency with which he had entered it.

For the meeting two days later it was decided that the full agency team should be fielded. That meant Dominic, Noel, Robin – and Marianne as well, as now so much of her life seemed to be inseparable from the work of Angel, Fear & Tredwell. The location of the meeting was a conference suite in the middle of a large and labyrinthine building close to Smith Square in Westminster. The time was noon – 'high noon' as Robin kept referring to it. Marianne had seen an opportunity to combine the trip with a visit to an ecclesiastical outfitters nearby, and she met Robin for coffee in Victoria Street at eleven o'clock in the morning.

'You haven't looked,' she said as they made their way from the coffee house to the outfitters.

'At what?' said Robin.

'To see if we're being followed,' said Marianne. 'Have you changed your mind about the men in black?'

'I haven't seen them since that day in Kensington Gardens, if that's what you mean. But, no – I haven't changed my mind. I still think there's something going on – but I also get the feeling that we may be getting just a little bit closer to the truth. The fact that the Government seems to have taken us into their confidence probably means that I – that is, *we* – have less to worry about. Well, we'll see, won't we?'

They had arrived at the outfitters and, on entering down a flight of stairs, were greeted by a small, thin man who appeared to be dressed in the clothes of a much larger man. It was not an appearance that was likely to inspire confidence in a tailor – but Marianne seemed not to have noticed, and greeted him in a tone that combined her natural warmth with the kind of formality the establishment appeared to require.

'Mr Pettigrew,' she purred, her face beaming. 'How good to see you again.'

'Reverend Maddeley,' responded Mr Pettigrew, nodding sporadically like a bird pecking at seed. 'Good day, madam. Good day, sir.'

Robin nodded back, feeling that he had been caught in some kind of time warp.

'The cassock-alb, madam?'

'The cassock-alb, Mr Pettigrew,' confirmed Marianne, referring to the new robe which she had commissioned some weeks earlier to celebrate the first successes of Project Cath. Mr Pettigrew disappeared behind a curtain briefly, allowing Robin and Marianne to exchange sly smiles.

'I dare say you've been kept rather busy of late,' said Mr Pettigrew, emerging with the required garment. 'What with all the goings on.'

'Goings on?' said Marianne hesitantly.

'All the activity,' continued Mr Pettigrew, 'and the excitement. Not to mention . . . Well, there's never been anything like it before, has there, madam?' He helped her to slip on the cassock-alb over her blouse. 'And, of course, there was the lamentable passing of the Bishop of London. But I gather that's now considered in some quarters to have been suicide.'

'Suicide!' Marianne and Robin both exclaimed together.

'Oh, I'm terribly sorry,' said Mr Pettigrew, managing to look hardly sorry at all. 'I've obviously spoken out of turn and said too much.'

'No,' gasped Marianne, who was now standing looking pure and angelic in the new item of clothing. 'Do go on. Please.'

Mr Pettigrew looked towards Robin, who simply repeated the word 'please'.

'Well,' continued Mr Pettigrew, looking over his shoulder towards the curtain that marked the entrance to another, smaller room. Marianne and Robin both involuntarily glanced in that direction, concerned that the curtain concealed perhaps more than a store of ecclesiastical clothing.

'It may be that there is no truth in it at all, but there is a story going round in certain quarters that the bishop decided to take his own life – and that he couldn't resist the temptation to do it in a spectacular and quite literally electrifying way.'

Robin and Marianne remained silent and waited to see if Mr Pettigrew had more to say, but this seemed to be the full extent of his revelation.

'But why would he do that?' asked Robin at last. By way of reply Mr Pettigrew simply gave him something of a knowing look and made a quiet remark to the effect that particular information, had it come to light, might have portrayed diocesan affairs in an unfavourable way. The outfitter very quickly qualified his suggestion, however, with a much louder comment asserting that this was, after all, 'only hearsay, and certainly not something that anyone could have any real faith in'.

By now he had regained possession of the cassock-alb and was folding and wrapping it neatly. Robin caught Marianne's eye, and she gave her head a slight shake as if to imply that they should not pursue the subject any further. For his part, Mr Pettigrew continued to act as if he had been doing no more than passing the time of day with two anonymous customers. He smiled sweetly at them as they made their way towards the door, and offered some parting comments along the lines that 'People do love to speculate' and that 'No doubt, all was for the best after all'.

'What do you think he meant?' said Marianne, as she and Robin emerged back into the daylight.

'It's absurd,' said Robin. 'The suicide story. It's quite absurd. Everyone knows it was a mix-up in the wiring that killed the bishop. The contractors may escape direct liability, depending on what the investigation shows. But that just means it'll go down as accidental death or death by misadventure, or whatever it is they call it.'

'So where's the suicide story come from?'

'Who knows,' said Robin. 'Except that it seems to be very mischievous. You had an appointment to see Mr Pettigrew just then, didn't you? I mean, you had pre-arranged the visit. It wasn't just a casual, let's-see-if-the-cassock-alb's-ready sort of call, was it?'

'You know it wasn't,' said Marianne. 'I told you I would arrange to see him and pick up the cassock-alb as soon as we knew I was coming to this meeting with you.'

They had started walking back towards Smith Square and Robin was looking nervous.

'More of the conspiracy?' said Marianne, clutching at his hand.

'I'm not sure,' said Robin, slowing his pace and chewing his lip thoughtfully. 'There are several stories circulating at the moment about the bishop's death. The consensus seems to be that the contractors were at fault in the way the electrical connections had been made. It may even have had something to do with the amount of rainwater that was around. I don't know. Some people, however, are still hanging on to the idea that it was an act of God. So far, that view appears to have been on the decline, and the overall momentum behind the whole commercialization process has hardly slackened. But what would happen if the "act of God" story gained ground? You know, as some kind of popular myth. It would almost surely slow things down, don't you think? Divine disapproval and all that.'

'That must be unlikely though,' said Marianne. 'As far as I can see, just about everyone assumes that the problem *was* a serious electrical fault. It's surely only a matter of establishing what exactly went wrong, and who was responsible.'

'I'm sure you're right,' said Robin, smiling at last. 'But in the meantime, perhaps a bit of disinformation will serve to put some people off the scent.'

'Which scent is that then?' asked Marianne.

'Again, I'm afraid I don't know,' said Robin. 'I wouldn't make a very good detective, would I? I spend the whole time getting suspicious, and very little time finding any evidence. Perhaps I'd better just stick to advertising. Come on. Let's go and meet Dominic and Noel.'

They met Dominic and Noel at a discreet distance from the appointed place and, after exchanging a few words, split up again so as not to arrive together. The meeting itself was a surprise both in terms of how many people were there, and who they were. It appeared that the location had been chosen because it had several points of entry: different participants had obviously been briefed to arrive at different entrances at different times so as to dispel any impression of a major gathering or conference.

There were upwards of 50 people in the room. Some were politicians from all the major parties. Many were bishops and prominent Church of England figures whom Marianne had met over the previous weeks and months. The Archbishop of Canterbury was not present, but Dr Conan was very much in evidence as he moved between eminent personages, implanting a few words in the ear of each. Robin scoured the room for a sight of the Bishop of Saxonford. He was the one bishop who, so far, seemed to have taken something of an independent stand on what had been happening, and Robin was keen to find out what his views were on the current plan for disestablishment. There was, however, no sign of him.

At noon precisely a side door opened and in walked three men who were introduced as Mr Grimes, an official from the Cabinet Office, Sir Victor Catchpole, 'the Government's business adviser', and the Minister without Portfolio. Everyone sat down and, amidst an expectant hush, the Minister set out the plans for the disestablishment of the Church of England – to be known as Operation Kingdom.

Marianne and Robin quickly looked at each other. It was not possible to exchange any words, but the look in their eyes showed that they were sharing the same thoughts.

Kingdom. *Project* Kingdom – the third part of what Robin had been led to believe was the agency's creative plan for the transformation of the Church of England. Kingdom. The password for the secret meeting at Catchpole's head office that the Bishop of Saxonford had told them about. And now . . . *Operation* Kingdom – the Government's name to describe the countdown to disestablishment.

It was surely not a coincidence. But what was it exactly that linked everything together around this word?

The proposals for Operation Kingdom were announced in summary form the following day by the Prime Minister, speaking to a packed House of Commons. The Church of England would not 'simply' be disestablished. It had proved its commercial independence and value through a whole series of imaginative initiatives, and had quickly reached the point where it ought to be given the freedom to do even more, and go even further. The Government had therefore decided, after long and detailed consultation with 'leading figures' in the Church of England itself, that the spirit of the times demanded an imaginative response to the various initiatives. The Church of England as a whole would be incorporated as a Public Limited Company and floated on the stock exchange. This would provide it with an increased degree of commercial independence, and allow it to 'compete' more effectively in its pursuit of the hearts and minds of the British people. In preparation for its new modern incarnation, the Church of England would be embracing all available channels of communication, and developments could be followed through a special website – www. kingdom.com – that was being set up for the purpose.

'The aim is to build a Church of England that is more open and accessible than it has ever been in its entire history. To facilitate that, the Government will be bringing forward legislation as soon as possible,' declared the Prime Minister to loud cheering from both sides of the House, 'not simply to disestablish the Church of England, but to establish the Church of tomorrow – the Church of the twenty-first century!'

Robin and Marianne were married a few days later. It was a small affair, conducted in a London church in the early evening by one of Marianne's clergy colleagues, and attended by the bare minimum of witnesses and guests, including Dominic and Noel. The happy couple had promised themselves a 'proper' wedding and honeymoon just as soon as 'this whole business' was over. For the time being, however, they had decided to celebrate in simple style with dinner for two at one of their favourite restaurants. Even on such a night, however, soon after they arrived home, the conversation turned once more to the events of the preceding days and weeks.

'I spoke yesterday afternoon to a colleague at St Paul's,' said Marianne. 'About the contractors for the lights. There were a lot of different ones involved – just like we expected. None of them seems to have been directly responsible to the overall project manager. Instead, they all reported through a facilities management company called RC Intercom Limited.'

'Should I have heard of them?' asked Robin.

'Probably not. The name certainly meant nothing to me. So, I did some digging,' continued Marianne. 'RC Intercom is a subsidiary of Crossway Communications . . .'

'Which is itself a subsidiary of one of Catchpole's holding companies,' added Robin.

'You're not surprised?' she said.

'No more than I suspect you were when you found out,' he said, smiling. 'I think we would have both been surprised if he *hadn't* been involved, don't you? I get the impression that his role in a lot of this is much more than just financial backing or business advice.'

Marianne agreed, but thought that Robin might have been a bit more enthusiastic about her own piece of detective work.

'And as for the suicide story,' she continued. 'I also took the opportunity to pick that up – and everyone I spoke to thinks the whole idea is completely mad. Until the last moment, of course, the bishop didn't even know he was going to switch the lights on.'

'Quite,' said Robin. 'I was thinking about that as well – and I decided that perhaps everyone, including the bishop, knew all along that HRH was not going to be there.' He paused. 'Either that,' he continued, 'or . . .'

'Or what?' prompted Marianne.

'Well,' said Robin quietly, 'perhaps the thunderbolt was meant for the Prince.'

Marianne sat up straight. 'Murder?' she said. 'Of the heir to the throne? You don't really think that, do you?'

'Well, no, I don't,' replied Robin, putting his arm around her and pulling her towards him. 'At least I don't *think* I do. But it just goes to show how these ideas can develop. At least in the imagination. I'm inclined to think, like you and most other people, that the bishop's death really was an accident. But I still can't help feeling that the complex mix of events and motivations that lie behind this whole enterprise goes much further than we know. And I'm also concerned that we might be sucked into it more than we would like. Which is why I don't think we should wait until our postponed honeymoon before we get away again. We should try to take a break as soon as possible. Not like our holiday. Something shorter. But a nice quiet break away from it all.'

'What sort of "away from it all"?' asked Marianne. 'Paris? Rome? New York? Where are you thinking of taking me *this* time, oh man of much money and air miles?'

'Well, I was thinking of Norfolk actually,' said Robin, looking slightly embarrassed. 'Near where I grew up. A bit of country air. Getting back to the roots. It just feels like the sort of thing to do. You know, after getting married and all that. A way of getting back in touch.'

Marianne smiled broadly and then kissed him full on the lips. '*Anywhere* would be wonderful with you, my darling husband,' she said. 'Especially Norfolk!'

She stood up and started to walk towards the kitchen, adding as she left the room, 'Just so long as you don't make me visit Norwich Cathedral – or any other cathedral for that matter! I'm just about cathedralled-out!'

The announcement of the flotation plans marked something of a watershed in the overall process of commercialization. At about the same time the momentum behind Project Cath began to slow. The illumination of St Paul's had been a crescendo in the efforts of the various cathedrals to outdo each other in raising their profiles. But at the same time, of course, it had also served as something of a warning. By now, most cathedrals had adopted some kind of ongoing commercial activity, and the newsworthiness of the diverse schemes had begun to fade.

General interest was now concentrated on the impending flotation of the Church of England. This required fresh energy and impetus, and so, at Angel, Fear & Tredwell, Project Park began to be talked about as the new focus for capturing and maintaining the public's imagination. Where Project Cath had been about utilizing some of the C of E's biggest existing assets, Project Park would be about creating a completely *new* one – the Bible theme park.

For Robin and Marianne, of course, the transition marked by the flotation announcement and the re-emergence of Project Park was also reflected in their personal lives. Very shortly after they were married, Marianne received confirmation of what she had suspected a few weeks before – that she was pregnant. The news was greeted with rapturous incoherence by Robin, who very quickly started encouraging his wife to lay aside her church responsibilities so as to prepare for the coming event. Marianne was inclined to think that his protectiveness was certainly premature and just a little bit old-fashioned, although she had to admit that she now felt noticeably less motivated in her church co-ordination role.

It was in this state of mind that she phoned Dr Conan one morning in October to ask for a meeting to discuss the future, and to understand whether her terms of employment made any provisions for maternity leave. Dr Conan invited her once again to Lambeth Palace, and when she arrived she was taken aback both by what she saw and by what she heard.

The first thing that surprised her was that Dr Conan's office and the surrounding rooms were littered with half-full packing cases. When Marianne asked if he were leaving, she received a rather offhand reply to the effect that 'we all have to move on when duty calls'. Dr Conan was similarly dismissive when she raised the subject of maternity leave.

'There have been a great many developments since your appointment,' he said. 'Co-ordination of the various schemes is now not really the issue. It is more a question of – how can I put it? – *execution*. Or perhaps I should say implementation. "Execution" has such a final air about it, don't you think?'

It was at this point, Marianne remembered, that Dr Conan laughed. It was the first time she had heard him laugh. It sounded, she thought, like someone insistently trying to clear his throat. The laugh did not last long, and Dr Conan quickly resumed his serious demeanour. Using words that should have been comforting, but which managed only to sound threatening, he outlined a process that would see Marianne ceasing employment with immediate effect, but that would provide her with what he described as 'an allowance' for a further year.

At one level Marianne was pleased that the terms appeared to be better than she might have expected: 'maternity leave' was not an expression with much of a history in Church circles. At another level, however, she had the distinct impression that she had, in fact, been summarily dismissed and was being paid over-generously to ensure that she stayed well out of the way as regards the forthcoming flotation. Her marriage to Robin, of course, meant that she would continue to be in touch with the programme of events – but her change of circumstances would deny her any direct influence on the presentation of that programme.

As she was about to leave she decided to take a chance. 'Is the Archbishop here today?' she enquired. 'Only, if he is, I would appreciate the opportunity to say a few words to him.'

Dr Conan's brow furrowed. 'I regret that the Archbishop is not available,' he said. 'Indeed, he is not even here. But please do not worry about him. He is being taken care of very well.'

Marianne was aghast. She had not been worried about the Archbishop at all before Dr Conan had spoken – but now she was very worried. 'Being taken care of'. Her mind was racing as she left the building. Outside a large lorry was unloading more packing cases. It looked as if more things were 'on the move' than simply Dr Conan and his belongings. Going out through the front gate, she turned right and walked towards Westminster Bridge. She tried to see things in as positive a way as possible. She tried to focus on the future – on life together with Robin and their baby, and on a whole new start. Nevertheless, she felt – for the first time since the visit to Southwark Cathedral – a profound sense of unease and personal disappointment.

'Resurrection,' said Noel excitedly. 'Resurrection. What do you think about *that* as a campaign theme?'

'Well, it's hardly original, is it?' said Dominic.

The first manifestations of Angel, Fear & Tredwell's flotation campaign had appeared within days of the Prime Minister's announcement in the House of Commons. Taking the word 'freedom' as the keynote for the campaign, large posters had appeared in all major cities proclaiming Freedom Day – the day when the Church of England would be floated on the stock market. This was soon abbreviated to 'F-Day'.

'"F-Day. A Day of *Resurrection* for the Church of England"! Don't you think that has a certain ring to it?' said Noel, his enthusiasm still evident despite the look on Dominic's face.

'I don't think so,' said his colleague crisply. Noel looked hurt. 'It's the word "Resurrection",' continued Dominic. 'It's likely to give people the wrong impression.'

Noel now looked as if he were about to take issue with this, and so Robin decided to enter the debate.

'The basis of the idea is good, Noel,' said Robin. 'It's just the use of the word "Resurrection". Remember what the consumer research said. The word "Resurrection" doesn't really connect with many of the new churchgoers. Whereas for many of the old-style Christians, it's such a central word and concept that *our* use of it might suggest we were trivializing matters.'

Noel had started nodding. 'I certainly don't want to *trivialize* things,' he said. 'In fact, I thought the word "Resurrection" might actually do quite the opposite. I thought it might set up a real sense of *expectation*.'

'That's what I'm worried about,' added Dominic. 'That's *exactly* what I'm worried about. It's certainly nothing to do with your concern about trivializing, Robin. Quite frankly, I think we're already well past the point where Christian sensitivities need get in the way of this. This is now an issue of the people. The Church of England is the people's Church – and we are liberating it. In that respect, I think "Resurrection" is a *good* word. What we're doing may well be the most important thing since . . . well, you know. No, *my* concern is that Resurrection implies death – and, mainly thanks to our efforts, the Church of England is certainly not dead. I think I'd be happier with something that was more about "New Birth" rather than "Resurrection". Something that focused on a completely new beginning – rather than carrying any hints of coming back from the dead. The key-note has to be about a continuing transformation, rather than a one-off resuscitation.'

'New Birth . . . New Birth,' Noel began muttering to himself. 'Yes. I think that has real possibilities. After all, that conjures up Christmas feelings more than Easter feelings, if you know what I mean.'

'I'm not sure I do,' said Robin.

'Yes you do,' insisted Noel. 'Easter's always so miserable. At least it always was when I was a kid. Yes, of course you've got the eggs and all that coming back to life stuff. But only *after* you've had all the doom and gloom of Good Friday. It's almost as if Christians can only cheer themselves up after they've made themselves bloody miserable in the first place.'

'Whereas *Christmas*,' said Dominic, looking at his watch and prompting Noel to finish his theological thesis.

'Whereas Christmas,' continued Noel, who looked as if he could have gone on for some time with his critique of Easter. 'Whereas Christmas is all about happy things. You know . . . babies, presents, all that jazz. Personally I've always thought it was something of a strategic master-stroke that Jesus got himself born at Christmas. So, if we take *Birth* as our theme, we can tap into all those nice, cuddly things about babies. Perhaps we could even link the whole campaign to the Christmas story.'

'With ourselves as the three wise men presumably,' said Dominic, looking first at Robin and then back at Noel.

'I don't know about "wise",' said Robin. 'I think we'd have to be more like magicians or even conjurors. F-Day is next *April*. Not Christmas.'

'Exactly,' said Dominic. 'Spring. What better time for a new beginning? And if we can link it to Christmas *as well* . . . so much the better!'

Robin and Marianne were walking hand in hand through Kenwood Park in North London. From their high vantage point they could see the metropolis spread out below them, glinting in the sunshine. They sat down on a bench and stared at the blue sky against which floated the odd, fluffy white cloud.

'The sky was like this the day we met,' said Robin.

'You see? You *are* a romantic,' laughed Marianne. 'You don't remember at all what the weather was like then.'

'Yes, I do,' insisted Robin. 'I remember the weather was fine for a week or more. That's when I first noticed your thing.'

'I beg your pardon!'

'Your thermometer thing,' added Robin. 'Outside the church.'

There was a pause in the conversation before Marianne said, 'I wonder how he is.'

'He? The thermometer?'

Marianne laughed again at Robin's unintentionally appropriate remark.

'It wasn't *that* funny,' he said, smiling.

'Oh, but it was. I was thinking of Stuart. You remember the churchwarden at St Thomas's? He always referred to the thermometer as if it were a person. I was just wondering how Stuart was – and what the new vicar was like. Assuming they found one, of course.'

Marianne put her arm through Robin's and drew herself nearer to him. 'Sometimes I can't believe how it's all happened so fast,' she said. 'I know that you're used to change and things happening so quickly. But people like Stuart and Mrs Murch – well, they're not used to it at all. And yet they seem to be going along with it.'

'Going along with it?'

'Well, being swept along really,' continued Marianne. 'As if they had no power to do anything about it. Everyone has decided that things will change. The bishops, the business world, the Government – *you*. But that doesn't make it right, does it? And what will happen when the Stuarts and the Mrs Murches all wake up one morning and find they've been left with nothing of their old world – nothing at all?'

Marianne paused before continuing. 'Every morning when I wake up I tell myself that it will be all right. Every night before I go to sleep I pray that it will be all right. But I'm not sure it will be any more. I'm not sure of anything any more.'

Robin squeezed Marianne's arm. He wanted to be as supportive as he could be. 'Remember, Marianne, you're the one who always saw the great possibilities in all this,' he said. 'The potential for building the Church into what it could and should be – a major focus at the centre of a community's life and aspirations. And, let's be fair – not *every*one is, as you put it, simply "going along with it". There are those like Jonathan and his evangelical friends who have their own priorities. And then there's the Bishop of Saxonford. When we met him, he seemed to be standing up for something different – with his freedom rallying cry.'

'Yes,' said Marianne, 'except that even *that's* been appropriated by you and the Government as the watchword for the new advertising campaign. A very clever move, I must say, Mr Angel!'

'And what's that supposed to mean?'

'Well, I know we've never actually spoken about it as such,' continued Marianne, 'but you're surely not suggesting it's an accident that the Bishop of Saxonford's key word is now synonymous with the Government's own initiative for the Church of England. Without even lifting a finger against the bishop, you've managed to make his protest invisible. As I say, Mr Planning Director – it was very clever.'

'Now you know that's unfair,' said Robin, who couldn't keep the smile off his face. 'The idea of Freedom was a specific part of the Government brief. And it was also a theme that emerged clearly from the consumer research. People saw it as the biggest single motivating factor in the whole business.'

'Hmm,' mused Marianne, partly to herself. 'Even so . . . Another one of your coincidences, perhaps?'

'Coincidence? Freedom?' Robin said the words as if the idea had honestly not occurred to him before. 'Well, I have to say that it does appear to be a rather common word in this context. And I'm certainly not claiming any copyright for it. But to suggest it was stolen, as it were, from the Bishop of Saxonford? Well, I don't know about that.'

'Indeed,' said Marianne, who now seemed rather melancholy. 'Freedom is, after all, one of those words that belong to everyone and to no one. Like Love. If I were to create an advertising campaign for God, I'd probably base it on Love. So would lots of other people. That's how it *should* be. Sometimes the obvious word is the right word – the kind of word that unites people because they all have some basic understanding of what it means. But, by the same token, it's dangerous. Words like Freedom and Love hide too much. They too easily become a shorthand for something that needs a lot more exploration and explanation.'

'Wow!' said Robin, squeezing Marianne again, and trying to lift the mood of the conversation. 'I'm going to have to ponder on that for a bit!'

Marianne pulled a face. 'Don't make fun of me,' she said. 'I've had a lot of time to think since I stopped dashing from one cathedral to another – and there are a lot of big issues that are simply being overlooked at the moment.'

Robin looked suitably penitent. 'I'm sorry,' he said. 'I didn't mean to sound patronizing. Perhaps I just don't want to face all those issues yet. Perhaps I'm not ready to. Perhaps I *do* want to hide behind words like Freedom and Love. I know I do when it comes to *us*.'

'Robin,' said Marianne softly. 'I know that "us" is the most important thing – especially now that there's another little bit of "us" growing inside me. But I can't let go of what brought "us" together in the first place – and that was a genuine attempt to blend traditions, and embrace new opportunities. The pursuit of that vision has given rise to a whole raft of new and difficult challenges. We can't simply let those questions go unanswered – no matter how much we may personally want to escape from what looks more like madness every day.'

'You're right,' said Robin. 'But we need to find a balance. A balance that keeps us close to the way the bigger picture is developing – but that also gives us some space for ourselves.'

If there was one thing that really brought home to Robin the gap that was opening up between his own life and the life of 'the great campaign', it was Project Park. In the early months, after the creation of the initial outline plan for a Bible theme park, there had been little visible activity around the subject. Most of Robin's and Marianne's efforts and energy had been channelled into Project Cath – to the extent that neither of them had thought much at all about the theme park idea.

What they hadn't been aware of, however, was that Noel and his team had quietly been putting together their ideas for Project Park with a view to having a whole 'package' available for implementation as soon as the official go-ahead was given. As soon as Robin realized this he took the issue up with Dominic and Noel and was astounded to find how much things had moved on. He was also aware of how sheepish his two colleagues looked when it became clear that there had been a concerted effort to keep certain information from both himself and Marianne. At one level Robin knew he should be furious at this behaviour. At another level, however, he found – oddly, he thought – that it didn't surprise him very much. Indeed, when his colleagues finally 'came clean' he found that he felt sorry for them more than he felt any real anger. It did, however, strengthen his resolve to deal with matters on his own terms.

It had all come to light during a regular board meeting. Dominic's and Noel's awkward looks had increased as Robin had asked them more and more questions about Project Park. Finally Dominic had suggested that they all go for lunch. It was only twelve noon, and so Robin knew that something was 'up'.

'No, not there,' said Dominic, as Robin began to walk towards their usual haunt. 'Let's stroll for a while.'

The idea of a 'stroll' with Dominic was bizarre enough to prepare Robin for some pretty unusual revelations – which is exactly what he received. The time had come, Dominic admitted, for frankness. It was a sad indictment of the way business now operated, but one had to be open to the possibility that the agency's offices may have been bugged. By whom? Who knows. Let's just say, the kind of people who feel they have a great deal at stake. And, yes, the planning process for Project Park had needed to progress for some time within a particularly stringent regime of confidentiality. Indeed, it had been made clear to Dominic that Robin was to be involved as little as possible. Why? Because of Marianne.

Dominic had been told in one phone-call that the business issues were too sensitive for there to be any risks taken in terms of the Church side of things. To put it bluntly, Marianne's co-ordination appointment by the Archbishop of Canterbury had been engineered by other interested parties – like Dr Conan – on the basis that her profile would be suitably low and uncontentious. Her relationship with Robin had also been considered a potential advantage, in that it limited the circle of people who needed to 'know'. Unfortunately (continued Dominic's revelation), the media had transformed both Marianne and Robin into minor celebrities – thereby making it difficult for them to retain the status of 'back-room fixers'. On the plus side, however, Marianne's pregnancy and the winding-down of Project Cath had provided an opportunity for 'diminishing her public role' – thereby reducing the risk that anything that she might say could be 'misinterpreted by the popular press'.

'So you've purposely been keeping me in the dark about Project Park because you thought Marianne might say something out of turn?' said Robin. Again, Dominic managed to look as contrite as it was possible for an advertising man to look.

'You must believe me,' he said, 'when I say how sorry I am. But Noel and I were put under a lot of pressure. I really can't tell you what a relief it is to be able to bring you back into the loop, as it were.'

'Now that Marianne's been conveniently pensioned off!' said Robin, his look betraying distaste rather than fury. Dominic tried to smile, but could not help looking back over his shoulder at the same time. Robin involuntarily did likewise, and thought he caught sight of a familiar figure staring fixedly at a shop-window.

'Well, I must say I'm rather flattered that anyone should think my views might carry so much weight with the Great

British public! But does this mean you now know all about Project Park?'

Marianne was sitting in bed, propped up with a couple of pillows.

'Not exactly,' said Robin. 'I've seen the plans for some of the rides. They're already being built in modular form at a number of locations. The plan is to assemble them on a site just a week or two before the grand opening. That's likely to be shortly before F-Day.'

'But you don't know where?'

'No,' said Robin. 'That's still a big secret. Even Dominic and Noel claim not to know anything about the location. They have a ground-plan for the layout of the site, so they can see where the rides and exhibits will fit – but that's all. Wherever it is, it's not very big – tiny, in fact, if you compare it to the size of *other* theme parks – which in itself suggests somewhere more metropolitan. Probably an inner-city spot. But where exactly is anyone's guess at the moment. Once again, the reason being used for the secrecy is "commercial confidentiality" – although I've been told that "all will be made clear" within the next few days.'

'Oh, Robin,' Marianne sighed, snuggling herself against Robin's body. 'I know I said we shouldn't hide away from what all this has become – but we really do have to give ourselves some space to think. Even if it *is* only for a few days. The more I think of it, the more your idea of rural Norfolk sounds just the job. The time and the space to get our heads straight. So can it be sometime soon? At least before Christmas?'

Robin did not answer immediately, and the pause was full of reasons why not. 'Don't misunderstand me, darling,' he said at last. 'I want a break as much as you do. And I'm especially keen for you to see the first parish church I ever entered. But I can't help thinking that a few things might keep me on the job until just before the baby is born.'

'But that's not until April!' Marianne almost shouted, sitting up quickly. 'You started talking about us taking some time out a month or more ago. And now suddenly it's moved off into the distant future. No, I'm sorry, Robin, but that's just not acceptable. We need to stand back from this – just for a few days. We need to get some perspective on life – on *our* lives. So, come on. Let's put something in the diary. How about New Year? How about we spend New Year in a nice cottage somewhere in Norfolk? New Year's a good time to take stock and think – and it's still more than two months away, for goodness' sake.'

'Well,' said Robin slowly. 'OK, then. Let's go for New Year. But I do think I need to stay close to what's going on at work. At least over the coming couple of months. I need to get closer to Project Park in particular. I need to know what's going on. I think *we* need to know. And we need to know more about what Conan is up to.'

He looked at Marianne intently. 'Do you think we might be able to get some answers by going over his head?' he added quietly.

'Over his head?' repeated Marianne. 'Over Dr Conan's head? You mean to the Archbishop of Canterbury?'

'Yes,' said Robin. 'Assuming, that is, we can get past Conan in the first place.'

'Conan,' Marianne repeated the name flatly. 'Even if I was wrong to be alarmed by his comments about the Archbishop "being taken care of", I think it highly unlikely that we'll be allowed anywhere near him. I get the distinct impression that he's being kept well out of the way. I mean, when was the last time anyone saw him in public, or heard him make any pronouncements at all about the changes? It must have been weeks ago.'

'In which case,' said Robin, 'you have to admit that my conspiracy theory is looking more likely as every day goes by. Why keep the Archbishop of Canterbury so obviously out of this, unless the whole enterprise is somehow threatened by him – by his honesty, by his leadership, by his wanting something else entirely? And before you answer that, let me tell you this. I think I saw my men in black again today. Or at least *one* of them. Whilst I was out walking with Dominic and Noel, I think I saw one of them following me. Conspiracy theory or not, you have to admit that a lot of this stinks to high heaven.'

'High heaven,' Marianne repeated, as she shifted back close to Robin, clinging even harder to his body so that she could feel his heart beating. She screwed up her eyes tight and prayed as hard as she could, 'Our Father, who art in heaven, hallowed be thy name, thy kingdom come . . .'

A week later Robin and Marianne set off once more by car for Lambeth Palace. Marianne remained sceptical about how useful such a visit would be, but Robin managed to convince her that they had 'nothing to lose'. He knew that Dominic had a meeting with Sir Victor Catchpole and 'various other interested parties' that very morning, and that one of those present would be Dr Conan.

'The timing will be ideal, with Conan out of the way,' said Robin, 'and it's certainly our best chance of finding out where the Archbishop of Canterbury is, and how we can get in touch with him.'

'But, even assuming we can get in to talk to a secretary or someone, what's our line going to be?' asked Marianne. 'Conan will surely have given instructions as to what the palace staff can and cannot say.'

'Well,' said Robin, 'The staff there do at least know who we are. It's not as if we were perfect strangers. So I think our best ploy is to suggest that we need to talk to the Archbishop personally as part of the agency's customer service programme around Operation Kingdom – on behalf of the Government, of course.'

'And does such a programme exist?'

'Not exactly,' continued Robin. 'So it does mean that we'll need to indulge in a very small deception of our own.

Just enough to enable us to meet up with him in the first place, of course. Once we're over *that* hurdle, then the deception can end. After all, at one level at least, we really *are* trying to provide the Archbishop with some genuine customer service.'

Marianne looked worried. 'I don't know,' she said. 'I understand that we have to work around Conan and whoever else is "taking care" of the Archbishop – but it all still feels so underhand. Given that it was the Archbishop who first appointed me to a formal role in this whole thing, I really ought to be able to go to him openly and speak to him honestly. I mean *really* honestly. About everything. About the vision, and the opportunity – and why it all seems to have gone ... well, ... wrong. And to understand where *he* is in all this. I want to be able to talk to him as my pastor and spiritual leader – not as some clandestine ally. I just don't want to be sneaking off to snatch a secret word with him. It's not right for all sorts of reasons. And, *another* thing, he's *not* a "customer" to be serviced.'

Robin remained silent.

'You know, one of the saddest things about all of this,' continued Marianne at last, with a slight sob in her voice, 'is that the Archbishop has been so obviously put to one side. If ever there was a time when we needed leadership, this is it. But the more I think about it, the more I can see how his vision is at odds with almost everything that's going on. *Outside* the Church, Government and business interests seem to have their own selfish agendas, and *inside* the Church, large numbers of evangelicals of a particular persuasion, such as Jonathan are seizing on the situation to undermine any authority the Archbishop might have had in the first place.'

She stopped suddenly. Robin paused before asking gently, 'But your own vision, Marianne. What about your *own* vision? You've always known there were huge risks in the changes that are sweeping through the Church – but all along you've been able to persuade yourself that it would lead to more good than bad. More people in church – and a bigger role for church in society.'

She smiled. 'Yes, I know,' she said. 'And on *good* days I can still see the positives. At least I *think* I can. But at times like *this* . . . Well, at times like this I begin to wonder whether or not I've been deluding myself all along.'

Robin reached out and touched her hand. 'I know it's not getting any easier,' he said. 'But that makes it all the more important that we – that *you* in particular – get to speak directly to the Archbishop. So this really *is* the right thing to be doing right now.'

'Yes,' she said. 'I know. I just hope we're not too late.'

Robin wasn't sure what Marianne meant by those words, but they prompted him to look up at the huge clock that towered above them symbolizing the might and endurance of the British constitution. They had stopped at the traffic lights in Parliament Square, heading south. Lambeth Palace should be only a few minutes away.

Back at St Thomas's, Stuart was scratching his head over the new church register that had taken the place of the old parish electoral roll. The parish reorganization was now almost complete, and the newly arrived vicar had asked him to 'cast an eye over it'. The interregnum after Marianne's departure had been mercifully short – certainly shorter than expected – and the Reverend Jack Spires had arrived to end the short period of uncertainty.

Jack – the son of the local estate agent who had been the original sponsor of St Thomas's commercialization – was one of a new breed of Church of England ordained ministers. Once it had become clear that the Church's new-found wealth and popularity required new models of ministry, a fresh approach to filling jobs was quickly adopted by the bishops. The old model (of full-time ministers living in free houses and spending much of their time attending tea-parties or surfing the Internet) had been in decline for some time. An alternative model of Non-Stipendiary Ministers (NSMs) or Ministers in Secular Employment (MSEs) had for some years institutionalized the idea of cheap labour in the Church of England's ordained ministry, and had suffered the usual problems associated with such a phenomenon: a combination of exploitation and lack of credibility. Far from establishing a real alternative, the NSMs and MSEs fell into the trap of modelling themselves on the outmoded parish clergy, and were therefore condemned to be regarded with even less respect than their full-time colleagues.

It was against this background that the bishops hurriedly introduced a real new model army of church ministers: Shareholder Clerks in Holy Orders – or 'Sharks', as they soon became known. It was the intention that Sharks should be people with a constructively critical view of the old Church order – and, at the same time, people with the energy and experience to drive the commercialization of the Church of England at a local level.

Sharks were therefore recruited from the ranks of the enterprising class, and were promised a share of the cash proceeds generated by their 'ministry'. They had all exhibited a kind of healthy disrespect for anything other than money, suggesting they would not be unnecessarily encumbered by any particular theological or pastoral sensitivities. Recruitment to this new breed of Sharks was by personal recommendation. Local business interests and even masonic lodges had offered to help in the introduction process, thereby cutting down on any unnecessary church administration. Selection was via a single interview with the local Shareholder Clerks Board. Ministerial training prior to ordination was considered to be desirable, but (given the urgent need for qualified resources) not obligatory: it was considered that 'on-the-job training' would meet most requirements, with newly ordained Sharks being encouraged to create their own pattern of ministry in response to local consumer needs.

Jack Spires had been one of the first to rise to the new challenge. His appointment as vicar of St Thomas's was seen as 'inspirational' – or at least, that was how the local Chamber of Commerce newsletter put it. Within weeks of his appointment, his impact on the structure of the building was very much in evidence. The giant SPIRES sheath over the church steeple had been replaced by permanent metre-high neon letters, and the churchyard was being cleared in readiness for a new extension which would house what the vicar described as 'workshops' – 'places of creativity and expression'. When the plans had been announced Mrs Murch had voiced some concern to the churchwarden that the building was 'simply being given over to use as office space' for the growing Spires business. Stuart had reassured her, however, that the new vicar would not be acting in such a 'parochial manner' – an expression that Mrs Murch found somewhat odd, given the circumstances. Mrs Murch felt sure that Stuart, for all his qualities, found it impossible to see anything untoward in the motives or behaviour of one of the Church's ordained ministers.

Stuart looked back at the new church register – a computer-generated list of everyone living in the parish, showing exactly who had attended which services over the last six months. Anything to do with computers would normally have sent him into a blind panic – yet here he was, 'casting an eye' over this new list. He scratched his head again, unsure as to quite why he was supposed to be casting an eye over it.

Robin and Marianne parked as close to Lambeth Palace as they could and then walked to the main entrance. It was locked. They exchanged looks and then Robin proceeded to knock. It was some time before they heard a bolt being slid across on the other side of the door, which then opened a few inches to reveal a man's face. The face was wide, red and unshaven. The head was bulbous and crowned with a yellow workman's helmet.

'Right then?' enquired the face, which Marianne now noticed was ingrained with dust.

'We're here to see the Archbishop,' said Marianne firmly, trying to see past the man's shoulder. 'Or at least to *arrange* to see him.'

The man looked from Marianne to Robin and back to Marianne, before speaking again. 'Which Archbishop would that be then?' he said.

'Which Archbishop?' said Marianne. 'Why, Canterbury, of course!'

'Canterbury,' repeated the man thoughtfully. 'That's in Kent.'

'Yes, I know Canterbury's in Kent,' said Marianne.

'Well, I'd be thinking that's where he is then,' said the man with imperturbable logic. 'At Canterbury. In Kent.'

'Look,' said Robin, just stopping himself from saying 'Look here, my man'. 'Look – this lady is the Archbishop's special adviser on large buildings. The Archbishop said that he might not be here, but that we were to be told where he was and how he could be contacted. So, if you wouldn't mind letting us in, I'm sure there will be *someone* who'll be able to help us.'

Robin glanced nervously at Marianne, whose face was a picture of concentration.

'Well, I don't know about that,' said the man, looking at Robin. 'I'm not supposed to let no one in. I'd better be having a word with the gaffer. What was it you said the lady was?'

'The Archbishop's special adviser on large buildings,' said Marianne solemnly. 'Cathedrals, palaces . . . and, er, other large buildings.'

'Even so,' said the man. 'I'd better ring the gaffer. You wait here.'

'I think you can trust us to stand *in*side whilst you ring the . . . the . . . gaffer,' said Marianne assertively. 'After all, we're hardly likely to make off with anything, are we?'

The man in the helmet looked confused by this and, after a few seconds, stood aside to let them pass. He shut the door behind them and, with another curt instruction to wait there, went off to ring the gaffer.

Robin and Marianne hardly heard his words. They were standing next to each other, staring ahead into what had been the courtyard of Lambeth Palace. The place was quiet and an eerie silence hung in the air with a great deal of brick dust. In one corner stood a large mechanical digger, immobile like a dinosaur frozen in time. In front of it was a pile of bricks. On the other side of the digger only a shell remained of the building that had stood there. To Marianne's right, in the part of the palace she had first entered for her meeting with the Archbishop, half the accommodation had been reduced to a pile of rubble. Other than the man who had let them in, the place seemed deserted. The only movement was made by two birds that were picking over a mound of rubbish in the middle of the courtyard.

'Where did he go?' said Marianne.

'Who?' said Robin vaguely.

'The man in the helmet,' said Marianne, pinching Robin's arm.

Robin started and said, 'Into that Portakabin, I think.'

He indicated a low, flat structure, along the side of which was the word 'Cassells'.

'Come on then,' said Marianne. 'I think we've seen enough, don't you? Let's go before he comes back.'

Robin was happy to follow Marianne's lead. He felt strangely remote, as if he had strayed somehow into a fantasy world where none of the rules of 'normal life' applied. By the time the man in the helmet returned there was no sign of the Archbishop's special adviser and her friend.

# VI

After stopping for a coffee with Marianne – 'and a chance to calm down' – Robin arrived at the agency an hour later. He brushed past the group of smokers huddled outside the entrance and walked purposefully towards the lift. As he bustled by, Charlotte the receptionist called after him, 'Mr Tredwell would like to see you as soon as you arrive.'

'Well, I've arrived,' he said. 'And I'd like to see Mr Tredwell! *And* Mr Fear!"

'Robin,' said Dominic earnestly as the three met in the boardroom. 'We've had a phone-call within the last ten minutes. About the site for Project Park.'

'Within the last ten minutes. What a surprise!' said Robin, looking sour and sitting down heavily. Dominic glanced across at Noel with a quizzical look on his face before making the full revelation.

'It's to be Lambeth Palace – or rather the place where Lambeth Palace is now. They're going to knock it down. Can you believe that? They're actually going to knock it down.'

'Oh, yes,' said Robin quietly. 'I can believe it. At least I can *now*. They've already started, you see. That's why I'm late. That's where I've been.'

It was now the turn of Dominic and Noel to sit down heavily. 'You've been to Lambeth Palace?' they said, almost in unison.

'I went with Marianne. We didn't know, of course, before we got there. But the work is already pretty advanced as far as I can see. There was some kind of foreman there in a Portakabin. He was on his own – and I can only assume that the rest of the demolition team hadn't yet arrived for the day. Oh, by the way,' added Robin. 'Can we run a check on Cassells?'

'Cassells?'

'The construction company – or perhaps I should say *de*construction company. I'd put money on it being part of Catchpole's empire.'

'Well, that's the other thing,' said Dominic, taking off his glasses and rubbing two very tired-looking eyes. 'The phone-call just now came from Catchpole's office. Someone claiming to be secretary of the Park Implementation Team.'

'Oh, yes,' added Noel, somewhat bashfully. 'The PIT. It was what I called the group that discussed the creative ideas for the theme park. Yes, there was a bloke from Catchpole's there – but he never said very much.'

For a few seconds Robin, Dominic and Noel all looked at each other as if they were trying to work out a crossword clue. None of them could quite decide whether this latest revelation was of major importance or just another step along the road of increasingly bizarre goings-on.

'The bloke on the phone,' said Noel, who was the first to feel uncomfortable with the silence. 'The bloke on the phone said it was because they wanted a central London site in a prime location. Of course, it's not very big. But then we'd been told some time ago – at the PIT – to assume a small site.'

'But the idea of knocking down Lambeth Palace and replacing it with a theme park . . .' sighed Dominic, throwing his hands into the air. 'Well, it's just ridiculous.'

'Except,' said Robin, trying desperately to think why it would have happened. 'Except that, unlike the cathedrals, Lambeth Palace as it *was* did not have any real potential to make a profit. Whereas *now* the site could become a real Mecca – if you'll excuse the expression – for the Church of England.'

'Even so,' said Dominic. 'Lambeth Palace is the traditional seat of Church of England power. The official residence of the Archbishop of Canterbury. Symbolically, at least, its demolition seems to signal the end of the Archbishop's influence.'

'And yet surely he must have agreed to it. Or agreed to *something*,' said Robin.

'Oh, I think he did,' said Noel innocently, as if he were announcing something that everyone was aware of. 'At the last meeting of the PIT, that Conan bloke came along to tell us that the Archbishop was prepared to make a great personal sacrifice to ensure the success of Project Park. Of course, we didn't know what that meant at the time – but I'm pretty sure those were the words he used. Personal sacrifice.'

'You're sure about this?' asked Robin.

'Yes, I'm sure I want to go back,' said Marianne as they neared St Thomas's for the first time in more than six months. 'I know the last visit was something of a shock. But at least they have a new vicar now – even if he *is* a Shark. I'm sure things must be more . . . well, more organized, I suppose. Less ad hoc – if you see what I mean.'

'I think so,' said Robin unconvincingly.

As soon as Stuart saw them approaching the main door, his ruddy face broke into a wide smile. Robin and Marianne stood chatting with him at the door for a couple of minutes. During that time a steady stream of people entered the church. Most of them were carrying what looked like credit cards which they swiped through a device that was linked to a computer just inside the porch. Stuart explained how this was all part of the new system to help keep the records in order.

'Them who've not been here before fills in a form – and then they get put on the computer. We then give out these here identity cards so that folks can record the number of times they come to church. He's quite nifty, eh?'

Marianne and Robin took only a split second to realize that Stuart was referring to the card, and not to the vicar or any other person.

''Course,' he said, reaching for some pieces of paper. 'As you're not yet on the church register – on the computer, that is – you'll have to fill in a form. You can let me have it back at the end of the service. I'm in charge of keeping an eye on the register, you see.'

His face betrayed a mixture of pride and bewilderment, and Robin and Marianne left him whilst they went to find some seats amongst the neat rows of soft-cushioned chairs that had replaced the old pews. The pieces of paper that Stuart had handed them included an open letter from the Reverend Jack Spires, vicar of St Thomas's. Robin and Marianne read it together.

*Dear Newcomer,*
*You are very welcome to St Thomas's – and we hope that we can look forward to your presence with us for a long time to come. To make it easier for us to stay in touch with you, we would ask that you help us (and ultimately yourself) by completing the yellow form. This will enable us to enter your name on St Thomas's church register. It will come as no surprise that, since the Government's announcement about the commercial freeing of the Church of England, there has been much speculation about how the new privatized enterprise will be established. The creation of Shareholder Clerks has encouraged the notion that shares in the new Church of England will be issued to Church members – in much the same way as they were issued to members of the building societies that converted to banks a few years ago. In the event of such a development happening, St Thomas's (in alliance with several other churches) has decided to keep a register of its members and their level of attendance.*

*Should the speculation about shares have any basis in fact, it is hoped that the new church register will enable us to ensure that any windfalls find their way into the right hands – and that we do not become prey to any carpetbaggers. Thank you for your co-operation.*

*Love and blessings,*
*Revd Jack Spires*

*P.S. Thinking of moving house? Spires has the widest selection of local homes to suit every budget. Just call in at the Spires office in the High Street – or alternatively talk to the vicar after the service.*

*Spires – Estate Agents you can have faith in.*

Within a few weeks of the visit to St Thomas's, Christmas had come and gone. And so had the New Year – without a trip to Norfolk, or anywhere else for that matter. Marianne was disappointed, but not surprised. She knew that sooner or later Robin's attention would turn back towards the prospect of family life. For the time being, however, he seemed more than usually concerned with trying to stay in touch with 'developments', as he insisted on calling anything and everything to do with Project Park. It was in this state of obsession one early January afternoon at the beginning of 'year three', that Robin picked up the phone in his office to be told by the agency receptionist that 'a strange man' had been asking about him.

'Is he still downstairs?' said Robin.

'No. He seemed a bit odd and disappeared as soon as I said I'd call you.'

'Did he leave a name or message of any kind?'

'No. He just said was Mr Angel in today, and I said yes I

thought so, and could I ask who wanted him. And then he said no, no, it was nothing important, and off he went.'

Robin thought for a second or two before saying, 'Was he wearing a black suit, this man?'

'A black suit? I don't know. He had a big, brown over-coat on. You know – the sort of coat that flashers wear. Well, that's to say, the sort of coat I would *expect* them to wear.'

'And how old would you say he was?' Robin continued, anxious not to be drawn into a conversation about flashers.

'Oh, he was well old.'

Robin knew that this meant over 50. He replaced the phone slowly and stared at the wall.

Leaving the office just before eight in the evening on that same bitterly cold January day, Robin began walking towards Charlotte Street where he had arranged to meet Marianne for a meal. Rather than take the most direct route from Covent Garden, he cut through to Charing Cross Road so that he could look in the bookshops that stayed open late. Not that Robin wanted a book. Once again he had the feeling that he was being followed. With several crossings of the road, a few pauses to peruse shop-windows, and a sudden dive into the labyrinthine depths of Foyles, the walk took about half an hour. By the end of that time he had identified no fewer than 14 people who might be following him. Allowing himself to smile at this impres-sive tally, he managed to shrug off his neurosis, turned left off Tottenham Court Road, and soon found himself at the designated restaurant. Twenty minutes later, as he relaxed with Marianne and a Montepulciano, she suddenly grabbed his hand.

'Well, would you believe it!' she said. 'You'll never guess who's just sat down at the table in the corner.'

'Surprise me,' said Robin wryly.

'The Bishop of Saxonford,' said Marianne. 'What a small world.'

'Isn't it,' said Robin, agreeing and frowning at the same time.

'And what does that face mean?' said Marianne.

'Oh, nothing,' replied Robin, who felt himself once again prey to his imagination. He had not said anything to Marianne about the stratagem for outwitting his 'followers' on the way from the office. 'If you want to ask him to join us, I don't mind,' he added.

'Oh, no,' said Marianne quickly. 'I'm sure he wouldn't want to. And, anyway, he's probably meeting someone himself. But I think I ought to go and say hello. I don't think he's even noticed us.'

Ignoring Robin's cynical grunting noise, Marianne went over to where the bishop was sitting. Robin heard the muted exclamation of surprise and, after a few seconds, turned to wave a greeting. Two or three minutes later Marianne returned to say that the bishop had arrived in London for an early-morning meeting tomorrow. No, thank you very much, it was a very kind offer, but, no, he wouldn't join them for dinner. He preferred to dine alone. He would, however, enjoy going somewhere for coffee or a drink afterwards. As a matter of fact, now that he thought about it, there *were* a couple of things he'd value their views on.

Ninety minutes later, with a few discreet signals between tables, the three of them gathered in readiness to leave the restaurant. As Robin stepped out into the crisp night air, one of the waiters came rushing towards the bishop, saying 'Your overcoat, sir. Don't forget your overcoat.'

And with that he handed the bishop a capacious brown overcoat.

Once outside, the bishop immediately suggested that it would be rather nice to have coffee at Robin's and Marianne's flat, and so the three of them took a taxi to Highgate. During the journey the conversation revolved around pleasantries and the swapping of basic facts – where the bishop was staying, how long Robin had lived in Highgate, and so on. As they neared the apartment, however, Robin steered the conversation on to the chance meeting in the restaurant. The bishop assumed a rather coy look, and then admitted that, yes, he had called at the agency earlier that afternoon and had then followed Robin to Charlotte Street.

'I knew your place of employment would be unlikely to give me your home address,' he said once they were inside, 'and I very soon found that your phone number was ex-directory.'

'But why the cloak and dagger stuff?' asked Robin. 'Why not just announce yourself at the office?'

'Yes, I'm sorry about that. It must all sound a bit silly. Perhaps I've been watching too many spy films. But the fact is, I wanted to see both of you – and I wanted it to be off the record. I think that's the term.'

'You mean you didn't want anyone to know,' said Marianne.

'Well, yes,' replied the bishop, looking slightly uneasy. 'Walls have ears, as they say.'

'And so might these,' said Robin, looking around the room.

'I know,' continued the bishop. 'But I hope they're not – bugged, I mean. And I feel I can trust you. Both of you. I think we might be on the same side. Despite appearances. I'm sorry. I'm not making much sense, am I?'

'Well, you are making it all sound a bit like something from *1984*,' said Marianne. The bishop looked confused by this comment, and Marianne had to explain that she had been referring to the book.

'Oh,' said the bishop – at which point Robin decided his

guest needed something stronger than coffee. A large glass of malt whisky had the desired effect, and the bishop began to be rather more articulate – indeed, loquacious – about why he had approached Robin and Marianne in such a way. He explained that he was looking for some independent advice about how he might handle the marketing and advertising of his diocese ahead of the Church of England flotation. He felt he had made a 'tolerably good beginning' with his newspaper and the related activities – but now that the Government had stolen his Freedom idea ('without a shred of acknowledgement'), he wanted advice on how he might differentiate ('I think that's the word') his position relative to what was happening in the rest of the country. It was now Robin's and Marianne's turn to be confused.

'I'm sorry, Bishop,' said Marianne. 'But I don't understand why. Why do you need anything to differentiate your position? Surely the whole point of the flotation is that it's designed to bring together all the commercial activities that were set loose by Project Cath.'

'That's right,' added Robin. 'The idea of handling the flotation as a single exercise – concentrating on the Church of England as a whole – is intended to preserve unity and consistency. With respect, Bishop, the last thing anyone wants at the moment is differentiation between dioceses.'

The bishop did not respond immediately. Instead he stared into the glass which Robin had just refilled. 'Well, let's just say,' he continued at last, 'that I have a few ideas for doing some extra things. A few things around the edge of the main campaign, as it were. A few things specifically targeted – yes, that's the word, isn't it? – a few things targeted at people in the Diocese of Saxonford. That's what I'd like your help on.'

It seemed clear to Robin and Marianne that, for whatever reason, the bishop had decided not to develop his original point. For their part, Marianne felt disinclined to interrogate the bishop further, and Robin was keen that nothing should be said that might compromise any of them.

The conversation therefore lost any potency it might have had. Instead, Robin responded to the bishop's revised agenda, and spent some time outlining the ways in which marketing and advertising might be used to achieve different ends. It was all rather conceptual, but the bishop seemed happy to listen and drink more of the whisky. By the time he picked up the hint that it was time to go, it was well past one o'clock. Robin called a taxi and despatched the somewhat pickled prelate back to his hotel near Russell Square.

It was only five minutes later, as Robin and Marianne were preparing for bed, that they discovered their guest had once more forgotten his large brown overcoat.

The situation became clearer within the next 48 hours. Two days after the bishop's visit, Robin and Marianne were watching the evening news on the television at home.

'. . . *with observers close to the Cabinet suggesting that the Education vote will simply prolong the split. This is Richard Dacre for* News at Nine, *Westminster.*'

The image of a callow youth in a raincoat outside the Houses of Parliament was replaced by that of a newsreader in the studio. Behind her, and to one side (or so it appeared) was a picture of the Bishop of Saxonford. There was barely time for Marianne and Robin to exchange glances before the newsreader began to speak.

'*Within the last hour there has been a dramatic development in the Church of England flotation saga, with the Bishop of Saxonford issuing a statement declaring his intention to go it alone. The statement was rushed out this evening by the bishop's press secretary to pre-empt the publication tomorrow morning of a story suggesting a misappropriation of funds within the diocese. The statement reads: "In view of the scurrilous comments which it is understood are to be published tomorrow in the national* press with respect to alleged financial irregularities within the Saxonford Diocese, the Bishop of Saxonford wishes to assert that the stories have no basis whatsoever in fact, and that they appear to have been initiated with the intention of discrediting and defaming the diocese's wholly legitimate exercise of its statutory freedoms within the Church of England. Furthermore, the bishop wishes to declare his intention to preserve the independence and integrity of the Saxonford Diocese in the face of those unconstitutional forces which appear set on removing the Church of England's traditional powers of self-governance."

Our Church correspondent, Gwyn Clarke, is with me now. Gwyn, the wording of the statement appears somewhat cryptic. What's it really saying?'

'Well, Jane, it appears to be pretty much a UDI – a unilateral declaration of independence. The story that I understand will appear in tomorrow's Daily Mail suggests that, since the initiation of Project Cath – the commercial freeing of the Church of England's cathedrals – the Saxonford Diocese has failed to declare all its income. Now, whether or not that is true – and clearly this statement seems to dispute the charge – the bishop has seized on it to declare his opposition to the whole flotation plan which is, of course, being run centrally – and is, in essence, a Government privatization initiative.'

'But presumably, Gwyn, the bishop's stand is more symbolic than real. I mean, the Government can't allow one diocese to do its own thing.'

'Well, that's right. The last thing the Government wants is a no-go area. The Government's been very clear throughout all this in saying that the Church of England would maintain its integrity as a national institution. Now what we have here is the Bishop of Saxonford using those very words to defend his own position. The financial accusations complicate the picture because it's unclear whether the bishop has overstepped the mark in asserting his diocese's independence.'

'*Gwyn Clarke, thank you very much. And now the Middle East, where the latest round of talks has . . .*'

Robin pressed the button on the remote control and turned the television off. 'Bloody Nora!' he said, standing up and running his hands through his hair.

'You can say that again!' chimed in Marianne, who was still staring wide-eyed at the blank screen.

They travelled to Saxonford the next day, after checking that the bishop would be there. The message they left with a member of his staff was that they would 'be passing by, and could therefore return the bishop's brown overcoat'. A message very soon came back, via the same member of staff, saying that the bishop was looking forward to getting his coat back, and had expressly asked that Robin and Marianne call in for a drink at his office in the cathedral close.

It took them some time to find a parking space when they arrived. The centre of Saxonford seemed more than usually busy, and several of the roads appeared to have been closed off. As they walked the last half-mile to the cathedral, they passed several police vans. It looked as if preparations were being made to marshal or control some kind of public demonstration. Compared to the bustle of the town centre, the cathedral close itself was eerily quiet. A huddle of tourists was being marched away from the west door of the cathedral by a stout guide who was holding aloft a bright yellow umbrella. A solitary cyclist was riding in a wide arc across the grass to the north. Although it was nearly mid-day, the winter sky was dark with heavy clouds.

Inside his office, the bishop glowed in the orange light of a standard lamp. He received the brown overcoat with a wide but weak smile, and invited his visitors to sit on two winged chairs.

'You know what's going on, I presume,' he said, with no attempt at small talk.

'We heard the news last night, if that's what you mean,' said Marianne.

'And we've caught up with the story in this morning's *Daily Mail*,' added Robin. 'Is any of it true?'

The bishop looked temporarily taken aback by Robin's bluntness, but then recovered with a smile that appeared more relaxed than the one with which he had greeted them.

'It's true that the diocese has attempted to keep its financial position under wraps,' he said. 'Since the C of E flotation plans were announced, every diocese in the country has had accountants and merchant bankers crawling all over it. My colleagues and I decided we did not want that to happen here. We've made great progress in our efforts to make this cathedral and large parts of the diocese self-sufficient. That is not something I want to give up easily. The accusation of financial impropriety is a stratagem aimed at undermining the commercial confidentiality that we've been maintaining – even if it did involve the exclusion of the Government's own advisers. In the eyes of many it declares us guilty until proved innocent – and, of course, it forces us to open our books simply in order to have any chance of re-establishing our reputation. It's a thoroughly underhand device, whichever way you look at it.'

The bishop paused whilst coffee was brought into the room. He offered his guests some lunch, but they refused, although Marianne could not resist saying 'Well, perhaps just a biscuit.'

When they were alone once more, Robin returned to the main point of discussion. 'Again, I have to say, Bishop, that we are not unsympathetic to your cause – as you yourself suggested when we talked at our flat. But, at the same time, it is all too easy to see why the stand you are making might be interpreted as a threat to the Government's plans.'

'A threat,' repeated the bishop, smiling again. 'I hardly

think this turbulent priest could ever be regarded as a threat.'

'So why don't you simply accept the inevitable?' said Marianne. 'Why can't you go along with a plan that will at least preserve the Church of England intact as a single entity – even if its future financial health will be dependent on the marketplace? Is that really going to make that much of a difference? I'm sorry, Bishop. Perhaps I'm sounding naïve and possibly even rude, but you do seem to be risking an awful lot for what looks rather like a symbolic gesture.'

'A symbolic gesture?' Again, the bishop repeated the words slowly to himself. 'A symbolic gesture. It's strange, you know. At one point I thought I was in the vanguard of the quest for freedom. And yet now I am cast as the reactionary. A rather cranky cleric manning his own little barricade against the advancing hordes of a new world order. A symbolic gesture. Well, perhaps it is. Who knows how history will view this whole thing? Except . . .'

The bishop paused, and Robin and Marianne looked at him expectantly.

'Except,' the bishop continued, 'once they have won, I suppose *they* will be the ones to write the history books. And so this probably *will* be seen as a symbolic gesture. The last spasm of a moribund body for whom resurrection will be a rude awakening.'

Robin and Marianne were becoming increasingly confused by the bishop's words.

'Once they have won?' pressed Robin. 'Who do you mean by "they"? Is it the Government? Or the financiers? Or Catchpole? Who is it?'

The bishop's head had sunk on to his chest, but at Catchpole's name he looked up suddenly. 'Ah, Sir Victor,' he said, letting the two syllables of 'Vic-tor' form slowly in his mouth. 'The tip of the iceberg. But, of course, a very good tip. And a very big iceberg.'

The bishop smiled once again, and this time there was a

slightly manic gleam in his eye. Robin was leaning forward, quite literally on the edge of his chair. 'I don't understand you, bishop. What are you getting at? What *is* this iceberg?'

Robin was to receive no answers to his questions. At that moment there was a light knock on the door of the study, immediately followed by the appearance of a white-faced man in a cassock.

'I'm terribly sorry to disturb you, Bishop,' said the white face. 'But there is an Inspector here to see you, and he said it was important enough to interrupt any business you might be conducting.'

Behind the speaker's shoulder, Robin and Marianne could see the looming bulk of a plain-clothes policeman.

'I'm so sorry,' said the bishop mournfully. The words were addressed to Robin and Marianne. 'But you are going to have to excuse me. I very much regret that our conversation will have to be concluded another time. I suspect that this, er, gentleman's business cannot be postponed.'

Robin and Marianne rose from their seats and, shaking hands with the bishop, left with hardly another word. The Inspector's silent presence seemed to have inhibited any further comment. It was only when they emerged back out into the fresh air that Robin and Marianne spoke to each other.

'What's going on?' said Marianne. 'What on earth's going on?'

Her questions related to what was happening in the areas immediately surrounding the cathedral itself. Various police vehicles had taken up positions on the grass, and a number of officers were erecting barriers around the west end of the building.

'Come on,' said Robin. 'Let's get out of here.'

So saying, he took Marianne by the hand and pulled her in the direction of the town centre. As they passed a policeman who was supervising the unloading of metal barriers from the back of a truck, Robin stopped and addressed him.

'Excuse me for asking,' said Robin. 'But what's happening here? Is it a bomb scare or something?'

'No, not a bomb scare, sir,' said the policeman, who seemed very keen to reassure Robin of his safety. 'Nothing at all for you to worry about. We're just looking after the place. Just securing the assets, that's all. Making sure everything's safe, sir.'

Robin thanked him and tugged once more at Marianne's hand.

'Securing the assets?' said Marianne, once they were out of earshot. 'Securing them for whom? The police – are they doing this for the bishop? Are they on the bishop's side?'

'Somehow I don't think so,' said Robin. 'I rather get the feeling that nobody's on the bishop's side any more.'

February – and Noel was obviously 'up for this'.

He was wearing a very striking black and white check suit, an orange shirt and green tie. A year before, the thought of meeting with Government officials would have sent him searching through his large wardrobe for a sadly neglected dark and sober suit. But now he felt confident of his, and the agency's, creativity. The very idea that representatives of the British Government should be sitting down with members of a major business consortium, a host of City financial advisers, and two of the directors of Angel, Fear & Tredwell to discuss the future of the Church of England . . . well, it seemed the most natural thing in the world.

That there were no representatives of the Church there *might* perhaps have been seen as something of an oversight. But, as one leading consultant put it, '*They* should be free to focus on their ministry. They shouldn't need – or want – to concern themselves with matters of *ownership*.'

A hush descended on the gathered assembly as Noel and Dominic rose from their chairs and stood at the head of the table. As they looked around the room they saw about 20 faces, half of which they recognized. Dominic, unlike Noel, was dressed as if he were a member of the Cabinet – an ambition that he still cherished alongside his desire for a knighthood, which now appeared a distinct possibility. He opened the proceedings by welcoming everyone and summarizing briefly the overall objectives that underpinned the communications strategy. The idea, as everyone knew, was to build on the 'Freedom' theme. The Church of England would be 'liberated' through the flotation. This transition would, of course, necessitate certain changes in the C of E's structure. It was at this point that Dominic handed over briefly to the Minister without Portfolio who was able to outline the main alterations to what he described as 'the management'.

First of all, it was felt inappropriate that the monarch should remain as nominal head of the Church of England and retain the title of 'Defender of the Faith'. After all, with the Church effectively disestablished – 'I'm sorry, I mean privatized. Or, rather, simply *freed*' – there would be no need for a titular head in quite the same way. Instead, the monarch would take on the role and title of 'patron' – with the same relationship towards the Church of England as he or she would have towards any other charity.

Second, the Archbishop of Canterbury would be replaced as the full-time head of the Church of England by a Chief Executive Officer (to be known as the C of E CEO). The Government was already looking at several eminently qualified candidates from the private sector – one of whom (the retired head of a public utility) had already been approached about the job. ('The only snag,' Dominic had confided to Noel before the meeting, 'is that he's Jewish – although the Government doesn't think that will be an insurmountable problem, given his other qualifications. After all, Jesus was a Jew, wasn't he?')

'The key,' insisted the Minister, 'will be in providing a management team that will attract continuing outside investment, and maintain confidence abroad. That task will be important as we build on the initiatives begun through Project Cath in strengthening the Church's role in our very valuable tourist industry. Which is also why communication, marketing and advertising will continue to be so vital.' So saying, the Minister handed back to 'our friends at Angel, Fear & Tredwell'.

'Thank you,' said Dominic, clearly relishing the pivotal role he had been given within this particular communications forum. 'And so to the details of the final stage of Operation Kingdom and the supporting advertising campaign, which will go public just before the flotation itself – in other words, immediately prior to the great day. F-Day!'

Robin was not at the meeting. He was well aware that, as the day drew near, he was not being invited to take a central role in the presentation. Suspecting that this was part of a continuing attempt by certain individuals to 'freeze him out', he decided to pre-empt any apparent exclusion. He therefore announced his decision to accompany Marianne to hospital for some routine prenatal tests that she was due to have that morning, and, as he expected, Dominic's reaction, if not palpably one of relief, was certainly not one of disappointment.

Robin was still unclear as to what exactly was going on at the heart of Operation Kingdom – especially as he was now devoting most of his time to help ensure the success of Project Park. The lack of information and involvement was specific to the Kingdom business: it was certainly not the case that his influence in the agency had waned in other important areas. On accounts as diverse as toothpaste and airlines, his word was still law. No one disputed his skills and insights as Planning Director. It was just that, on the specific subject of the Church of England flotation, there was a definite sense in which his presence seemed 'surplus to requirements' when it came to high-profile meetings. Surely, he reasoned, this was not still due to his relationship with Marianne. After all, she was now safely ensconced at home, with no formal role in the Church's affairs, well away from the glare of any publicity. Might it, then, be due to *another* perceived relationship? Had someone perhaps been tracking his movements in relation to the Bishop of Saxonford? *That*, reflected Robin, was surely the reason.

Soon after he and Marianne had returned from their day-trip to Saxonford, it had been announced that the bishop was retiring early on health grounds, and that the cathedral would be closed temporarily whilst a structural survey of the building was conducted. The suggestion was that money earmarked for improvements to the fabric of the building had been used for other purposes, and that the cathedral now constituted a possible hazard and risk to visitors. In order to maintain public confidence and safety, a Government-appointed administrator had been installed in the cathedral close to oversee any necessary developments in the period up to and including F-Day.

There was a part of Robin that was relieved not to be required at the communications meeting with the Government officials and the businessmen who were carrying through the details of Operation Kingdom. As Marianne's appointment at the hospital took less time than expected, the occasion gave the two of them the chance to spend some daylight hours together. They decided to travel together into central London for a short walk and some lunch, after which Robin would go to the office for the afternoon. The sun was shining in a cloudless blue sky, which helped to make Robin feel that he had been right to absent himself from the agency for a few hours. He even managed to admit to himself that the idea had been Marianne's in the first place.

As each day passed, and the birth of their child drew nearer, Robin felt increasingly that Marianne was right in encouraging him to spend more of his time away from the relentless machinations of the combined agency and Church worlds. Thus it was that the two of them travelled by tube from the hospital, and arrived at Charing Cross by mid morning, with the intention of taking a gentle stroll around St James's Park. They wandered through Admiralty Arch, turned left off the Mall, and stopped for a coffee in a small pavilion overlooking the water. Robin seemed more at ease than Marianne had seen him for some time, and so she was particularly surprised when he suddenly squeezed her hand and said, 'Good God! They're back!'

She knew too well what he meant to ask 'Who?' She simply waited a few seconds, and then turned casually to survey the people who were visible through the window behind her. She didn't want to believe what she saw – but there, sure enough, about 30 yards off, standing together on the path, were two men. Both were wearing long black overcoats and scarves, and one had on a wide-brimmed black hat. She knew she couldn't be certain, but she felt she could believe that they were the men that Robin had pointed out on that sunny day in Kensington Gardens nine months before.

'Yes, I see them,' she said. 'Come on. Let's get moving.' Marianne decided that it was now a time for solidarity on the subject of the men in black.

'You *do*? You do see them?' said Robin, who was noticeably taken aback by her swift and decisive reaction. He rose and followed her towards the exit.

'Yes,' continued Marianne, matter-of-factly. 'And there's only one way to test this theory of yours. Let's see if they follow us now.'

So saying, she took his hand and led him on to the path and directly towards where the two men were standing. The smaller of the two men cupped his hands to light a cigarette, and the taller man looked away across the water. Robin and Marianne walked past them at as brisk a pace as Marianne could manage, and kept going for 100 yards or so before sitting down on an empty park bench. It was only after they were seated that they looked back along the path. The men in black were now walking slowly towards them, coming nearer and nearer. Robin and Marianne, familiar with the way these things seemed to work in films, sat back, fully expecting the two men to pass by, as they had done in Kensington Gardens, with scarcely a glance in their direction. They were therefore dumbfounded – and somewhat worried – when the two men stopped and sat down on the bench on either side of them.

'Mr Angel, Mrs Angel,' said the smaller of the two men immediately, throwing his cigarette on to the path and treading on it with an immaculately polished black shoe. 'We are truly sorry to disturb you – in more ways than one. But it is now increasingly urgent that we speak.'

The man had a slight accent but Robin and Marianne were not sure of its origin.

'I realize this must seem very strange and discourteous behaviour,' continued the smaller of the men, looking ahead at the ducks that were waddling to and fro at the water's edge, and hardly turning to look at either Robin or Marianne. 'And my colleague and I apologize profoundly for any discomfort we may have caused you. But there is so much at stake that secrecy has been, I regret, an integral part of this operation.'

'Operation?' thought Robin. 'Operation Kingdom? Or some *other* operation?'

'It is not fitting that we should talk here. In the open,' continued the man in black. 'But we would ask for your indulgence and understanding, Mr Angel, Mrs Angel. We would, indeed, ask that you meet us for a proper discussion of the issues. You must believe us when we say that there really is no pressure on you to comply. You must do what you feel is best. But we would be most appreciative if you would agree to meet with us in a rather more private environment.'

For the first time the man turned to look directly at Robin and Marianne. He had a small, neat face with high cheek-

193

bones and a dark complexion. Robin and Marianne simply nodded in unison. Whilst the thought of meeting the men again hardly filled them with excitement, neither of them could bear not to know more.

'Good,' said the man with obvious relief. 'Hanging Sword Alley meets Fleet Street close to Ludgate Circus. We will meet you there at eight o'clock this evening, and then conduct you to one of our houses. Please do not tell anyone else. And please believe me, you will be perfectly safe. On that, you have my word. Be guided by the one true faith. Until tonight then.'

With that, the two men rose from the bench, and with no more than a slight parting nod, walked away in the direction of Buckingham Palace.

'One of our houses?' repeated Marianne.

'Be guided by the one true faith?' muttered Robin. 'Why does that sound familiar?'

'The letter,' said Marianne, who now suddenly felt cold in the winter sunshine. 'The letter that was delivered to the flat.'

Lunch was over.

'I think it went well enough,' said Noel, passing the bottle of brandy back to Dominic. 'I think they liked the ideas.'

'They *loved* them,' said Dominic, slurring his words just a little. 'They *loved* them. They just didn't want to say, that's all. Not in front of everyone else. They particularly loved your "Born Again" idea, Noel. *"The Church of England has been Born Again."* That is just such a good line. Such a bloody good line, if I may say so.'

'And . . . what . . . about . . . the . . . posters?' said Noel, who was now hiccupping with some regularity.

'The posters,' said Dominic. 'The bloody posters! They

*loved* them. *Loved* them. Especially that one with the parents and the baby. What did it say?'

'They must think it's Christmas,' said Noel.

' "They must think it's Christmas",' repeated Dominic. 'Bloody good line. An absolute cracker.'

'Well, it's rebirth, of course,' said Noel confidentially, as if he were communicating something previously unknown to his colleague.

''Course it is,' echoed Dominic, his eyes nearly closed. 'Birth. Rebirth. Didn't we always say that would do the trick? Didn't we always say that?'

He looked across at Noel who appeared to have become unconscious.

Robin and Marianne were at the north end of Hanging Sword Alley a good ten minutes before eight o'clock. Fleet Street was still busy with people hurrying from offices to stations or bars. Robin and Marianne stood scanning the faces that came towards them from both directions, and yet neither observed the approach of the men in black, who appeared as if from nowhere at eight o'clock precisely.

Their greeting this time, whilst being quite formal, carried a hint of warmth even though it made no attempt to convey names or purpose. The men were clearly genuinely glad that Robin and Marianne had accepted their 'invitation', and even the taller of the two spoke briefly. His accent was most definitely English, and what Marianne later described to Robin as 'top-drawer'. It was the smaller man, however, who was clearly the nominated spokesman, and he it was who talked most as they walked towards their destination.

The route threaded through the streets and alleys directly to the north of Fleet Street. They passed by Lincoln's Inn, and soon found themselves in front of a tall house with a discreet exterior midway along an elegant terrace. The smaller man opened the front door and led them through to a study which was a traditional blend of dark wood, leather, books and mustiness. A drink ('some water, or perhaps a glass of wine?') was offered and politely refused, and the four of them sat down awkwardly on chairs that looked as if they had once been part of a West End gentleman's club.

'We should introduce ourselves,' said the smaller man with something approaching a smile. 'I am Father Rosso, and this gentleman is Father Catesby.'

He paused and waited for his guests' reaction. He knew that, whatever Robin's and Marianne's assumptions had been, this introduction would confirm or convey some significant information.

'You're Catholics,' said Robin, not sure whether he was surprised or not. '*Roman* Catholics, I assume. You're nothing to do with the Government, then. Nothing to do with big business.'

Father Rosso smiled again and glanced across at his tall colleague, who was sitting silently with his fingers interlaced. 'My friend, our motives are religious,' said Father Rosso. 'Strictly religious. And we would like your help.'

'Our help?' said Marianne. 'How can we help *you*?'

Her comment brought forth another smile from Father Rosso. He offered them a drink once more, and this time both Robin and Marianne said yes. A few moments passed, during which time Father Rosso poured four glasses of very fine red wine whilst commenting briefly and most properly on the weather. Once he had resettled himself on his leather chair, he began to speak in a more expansive way about what he and Father Catesby had envisaged in terms of 'help'.

He explained how the Roman Catholic Church had watched with great interest the developments that had been happening in England. He commented on how the Catholic bishops had taken steps to make sure that, at a local level, Catholic churches were not drawn into the tide of change that had swept through so many other parts of the Christian community. He was at pains to point out, however, that this was not due to basic objections to the concept of change in the Catholic Church. (Robin and Marianne must have looked slightly questioning at this statement, because Father Rosso clearly felt obliged to make the point again.) No, he continued, it was because the Catholic Church wanted to be able to take a considered view of the merits or otherwise of the various initiatives before committing itself one way or the other.

'That is why we have been so intent on watching. On watching, from a distance you might say, the ways in which your original "virtuous circle" has developed into what has now become your Government's plan for commercial independence, or "privatization".'

It was the first time in a long while that Robin and Marianne had heard the words 'virtuous circle'. They were words which, at once, reminded them of the small beginnings that launched what had now become a major religious, commercial and political enterprise.

'But you've not just been watching all these developments from a distance, as you put it,' said Robin. 'You've also been watching *us*. Often from quite close quarters.' There was a clear note of annoyance in his voice. 'Why has that been necessary? Why have you needed to follow us so secretively? Why couldn't you have just asked for a meeting? Like this.'

Father Rosso made a gesture which was half apologetic and half bemused. 'I cannot pretend that everything we have done has been – how do you say? – quite proper,' he said. 'But I hope that we have not strayed too far from the bounds of acceptable conduct.'

Robin winced slightly. There was something about the man's turn of phrase that made him feel uneasy.

'If I am honest,' continued Father Rosso, 'I have to say that, in the early months, we were hoping to observe the *collapse* of a series of schemes which some commentators saw as replacing the Church of tradition. Of course, it has not quite happened in that way. The "virtuous circle" appears to have been just that – virtuous, and a circle. Far from collapsing, the initiative that you began would seem to be on course for a crescendo which even you could not have imagined a year ago.'

Was this flattery or cynicism? Robin and Marianne were unsure, and were put on their guard by their host's eloquence.

'Nevertheless,' continued Father Rosso, after pausing to sip his wine, 'we have observed certain differences between yourselves and those people who are, let us say, the ultimate authorities in the matter.'

He paused again as if to allow for some response, but Robin and Marianne remained resolutely silent.

'And that has encouraged us,' continued the priest, 'in our hopes that we could persuade you to share with us some of your thoughts concerning the way the initiative is being managed. So that we may learn from you some form of, let us say, "best practice". You see, whilst it may come as a surprise to you, it is the case that the Catholic Church wishes to embrace the spirit of your initiative in many ways. However, as you might expect, there are some areas where we have particular misgivings. We are therefore looking for some informed evidence on which elements of the overall programme are working most effectively and which are working least well.'

Robin felt a sudden rush of outrage, which he vented through tightly controlled lips. 'You mean you want some inside information,' he said. 'You want to get an inside track on what's going on. And you reckon on us as your most likely route for getting it. That's it, isn't it?'

Robin felt Marianne squeezing his arm, but he continued nevertheless. 'That's why you've been following us, isn't it? You knew that we were not comfortable with everything that was happening – and you were looking for something that might compromise us. Something that might give you some leverage over us. I imagine you followed us to Saxonford. You did, didn't you?'

Robin's barely restrained outburst clearly took Father Rosso by surprise, and his cheeks reddened. Father Catesby twitched, crossed and uncrossed his legs, and then looked across at his colleague. It said something for Father Rosso's skills that he took only a few seconds to recover his colour and his composure.

'I'm very sorry that you should feel that way,' he said mildly. 'For I really have to say that your speculations are not well founded. I hope you will believe me when I say that there is absolutely no question of us wanting to solicit any . . . inside information from you. Indeed, I find it difficult to imagine what advantage such information might provide – given that your various pursuits have received so much publicity. I can only repeat that we were hoping that this meeting would provide the basis for a continuing dialogue between us. But clearly, if trust is absent on one side . . .'

He paused again, but neither Robin nor Marianne felt inclined to contradict him. Marianne was gripping Robin's arm even tighter than before.

'. . . then,' continued Father Rosso, 'it is probably best that we terminate the interview now. Except . . .'

This last word temporarily stopped Robin and Marianne from rising to their feet.

'. . . except that my esteemed colleague and I were truly hopeful that the current circumstances might have provided the basis for greater unity across the traditional pillars of the Christian Church.'

Robin and Marianne looked briefly at each other. It was a look that signalled a silent agreement that they would not be cajoled by promises of greater Church unity. They rose to their feet together.

'Look,' said Robin, through taut lips. 'Perhaps I over-reacted. But you have to admit that your conduct is hardly likely to engender the kind of trust you claim to be seeking. And so I really do think you must excuse us.'

Father Rosso and Father Catesby stood up immediately and bowed their heads slowly to show their icily polite acceptance of the situation.

'I am sorry,' said Father Rosso, 'if I have been precipitate or misjudged the situation. Perhaps you would allow me to contact you again in the future. After all, things may change.'

Robin eyed him suspiciously before saying, 'They may indeed.'

Once outside again in the cold night air, Robin and Marianne walked in silence towards the West End for some minutes, before they stopped to look behind them. There was no one there. Finally Marianne spoke. 'Do you think they're *really* Catholic priests?'

'I think they are almost certainly part of a large and secretive organization with Italian origins,' said Robin, feeling himself shaking in the icy darkness. 'But whether that is the Roman Church or not, I really couldn't say.'

Marianne looked at him to see if he was being purposely mischievous. He was not smiling.

'You don't mean . . .' she said.

But Robin shook his head quickly before she could say any more.

By the beginning of March the Lambeth Palace Experience (as the Bible theme park was to be known) was almost finished – and in record time. Robin and Marianne were among a select few hundred people invited to preview some of the major attractions. As they sat having breakfast at home, however, their minds were focused on a different aspect of the new Church of England.

The morning's newspapers were unanimous in their choice of lead story: the announcement by the Prime Minister the previous day that churchgoers would be entitled to free shares in the new C of E PLC. Speculation about such an issue of shares had been rife ever since the first announcement of the Church's impending disestablishment. Various 'mutual' building societies had converted to PLC status in previous years, and in each case long-standing customers had benefited through a distribution of free shares. Against this background it had been assumed that the Church's privatization might also provide an opportunity for the supporters of 'share-democracy'. It had been expected that the Government would want to do *something* to reinforce public opinion in support of the proposed change, and a free-share scheme appeared to be everyone's favourite option. Whilst various ecclesiastical authorities had tried to deflect public attention away from the likely financial gains of such an initiative – insisting that the Church had always believed in common ownership – it was generally agreed that some kind of 'windfall' would be in everyone's interest.

In one of his last television interviews, the Archbishop of Canterbury had clearly not wanted to be drawn on the subject. In answer to a direct question about free shares, he had talked about the need for everyone – including himself – to be open to all kinds of possibilities. It was a statement that had widely been interpreted as confirming that the Anglican primate no longer commanded any real authority, and that he had been sidelined in the rush to let market forces dictate the future of the Church.

At the local level, parishes and deaneries had already taken steps to prepare for a distribution of shares. St Thomas's had been by no means untypical in setting up a mechanism aimed at controlling the likely reaction to the Prime Minister's announcement. That reaction was hardly surprising: church attendances increased even faster as the predictions of personal gain became ever more exaggerated. When the announcement finally came, the details were generally in line with expectations, and many of the newspaper headlines heralded the story as hardly more than a confirmation of what they had been saying all along.

'Congregations to Share in Church Windfall' was how one sober broadsheet put it. 'Pennies from Heaven' was the headline used by a more populist paper. Of the tabloids, the most striking front page was probably the one across which ran, in very large letters, the two words: 'Thank Christ!'

Robin and Marianne sat surrounded by all those newspapers, and many more besides. On the whole, they both felt as if they were reading about things that were happening to other people, well outside their own realms of experience. The past weeks had created something of a split between their own domestic world and the developments surrounding the Church flotation. To a large extent that was because Marianne no longer felt any real enthusiasm for what was happening. Her comments to friends suggested that this was mainly due to the central place that the pregnancy was taking in her life. Both she and Robin, however, knew that it was more fundamental than that – and that the forthcoming birth of their child was simply making it easier for them to distance themselves from those things they found least acceptable about the latest developments. Whilst Marianne had not completely lost her sense of mission and opportunity, she now had the distinct feeling that she was hanging on to it *in spite* of the various enterprises, and not *because* of them. Operation Kingdom, which originally had suggested itself as the fulfilment of the 'virtuous circle', now seemed rather to have hijacked it – and she found it difficult to imagine that things might somehow be put back on their original course.

The prospect of visiting the completed Lambeth Palace Experience therefore filled her with anxiety, rather than excitement. She definitely wanted to see what had been made of the site since her last visit during the partial demolition of the buildings. She was also interested in seeing how some of Noel's more bizarre thoughts had been brought to life by the various teams of designers and engineers who had been labouring day and night to develop and deliver the various 'experiences'. But she could not hide a real nervousness and sense of unease about what she might find there.

'Have you got the tickets?' she said, as they were about to leave the flat. Robin stared down at two pieces of gold-edged card.

'Please present yourself at the Pearly Gates at 11.00 a.m.,' he read aloud.

'Pearly Gates?' exclaimed Marianne.

'The new main entrance,' said Robin with a slight shake of the head. For all that he had managed to involve himself in some aspects of Project Park, he was quick to admit that he had had very little to do with the creative executions.

'Noel's idea presumably,' said Marianne, closing the door behind them.

'I'm afraid so,' replied Robin.

'I had a dream last night,' said Marianne.

'About the Pearly Gates?'

'No,' she said, almost laughing. 'No. it wasn't that. I dreamt that I was Pandora. And that you came along and opened my box . . . and let all this out.'

'All *this*?'

'All this . . . stuff.'

'Oh, dear,' said Robin dolefully. 'I should have known it was all *my* fault.'

This time Marianne did actually laugh. 'Come on,' she said. 'Let's get moving. We don't want to find the Pearly Gates closed when we get there!'

The inside of the transformed palace was unrecognizable. Having entered through a real set of pearly gates, Robin's and Marianne's senses were bombarded with sights, sounds and smells – none of which was remotely linked to what the place had been like in its former life. The path from the Pearly Gates led to a small piazza, at the centre of which a fountain cascaded water over a coloured sculpture showing the biblical story of Creation. The air was filled with the sound of hymns, relayed through loudspeakers disguised as boulders. Around the fountain were ranged tables, chairs and benches. At the edge of the piazza were various kiosks dispensing champagne and canapés, as well as colour-coded paths that led to the facades of the different experiences that were on offer.

Robin scanned the various options that were available and noted the four things he had already heard discussed at the agency: *The Elijah Trip*, *The Jonah Experience*, *The Virtual Last Supper* and *The Ride of Revelation*. As he and Marianne moved slowly forward in the direction of the fountain, he focused his gaze on the select band of people who, drinks in hand, were standing or sitting in twos and threes around the piazza. He recognized quite a few of the faces: members of the Government, businessmen, the odd bishop, colleagues from the agency, a smattering of celebrities, and what looked like some representatives of other faiths.

'Robin! Marianne!' Dominic managed to make it sound as if he were greeting two long-lost friends. 'Good to see you both! Do come and meet the Egyptian ambassador and Air Vice-Marshall Pickering.'

The two faces that until then had been listening to Dominic turned to look at the two newcomers.

'Well, my dear lady,' said the Air Vice-Marshall, addressing Marianne in his most gallant tone. 'I imagine that for you, like me, this is a first time on the hallowed ground of Lambeth Palace!'

'Yes,' said Marianne. 'I'm sure you do imagine that.'

The Air Vice-Marshall looked slightly puzzled by this reply, but Robin was already pulling Marianne away on the basis that they were urgently required to accompany a group of diplomats on the first trial run of *The Elijah Trip*.

'*Are* we?' she asked, as Robin steered her across the piazza. 'Are we urgently required?'

'Not exactly,' replied Robin. 'But I somehow felt that

you and the Air Vice-Marshall would not be good for each other.'

At the entrance to *The Elijah Trip* they met Noel who was smiling broadly, having already topped up his good humour with several glasses of champagne. Robin's comment about the imminence of the first trial run of the *The Elijah Trip* was not far from the truth, although the group of people being marshalled in a jocular fashion by Noel was made up of newspaper editors rather than foreign diplomats.

'Ah!' said Noel with a gleam in his eye. 'Two angels prepared to join a gang of demons! Step this way please!'

'You go ahead,' said Marianne to Robin. 'I'm not sure this is the sort of thing for a heavily pregnant woman.'

Noel looked at Marianne as if noticing for the first time her ample proportions, before leading Robin away with a conspiratorial wink.

Robin was strapped securely into a kind of small car next to Noel. There were four cars in all, each of which seated four passengers, and they were lined up one behind the other about four metres apart at the side of a 'quay'. When everyone had been strapped in, the cars started to move forward into what appeared to be the opening of a black tunnel. Robin knew that *The Elijah Trip* actually took up a relatively small amount of space within the total complex, and that therefore any further movement was likely to be simulated rather than real.

The first part of the trip was real enough, as the cars moved forward sedately, winding from side to side along a narrow track which could have been no more than 20 or 30 yards long. As the cars triggered sensors on the track, lights lit up various scenes displayed in hollows and caves that had apparently been cut into the synthetic rock walls on either side of the track. The tableaux showed scenes of

Elijah's life, from his feeding by the ravens, through to the contest with the prophets of Baal on Mount Carmel. Finally, as each car approached the dark doorway at the end of the track, a deep voice filled the place with the following words: 'Prepare to be taken up to heaven with Elijah!'

At this point the cars were each propelled into separate small chambers. Robin could hear Noel breathing loudly in anticipation as their car came to a halt in the gloom of a room which appeared only slightly bigger than the dimensions of the vehicle. For a few seconds, nothing happened. And then he felt a gentle breeze on his face. Two newspaper editors who were in the same car, and sitting immediately behind Robin and Noel, were making dismissive comments about the whole thing being 'OK, I suppose, if you're a kid'.

It was then, however, that the gentle breeze began to get stronger. The chamber was suddenly filled with dazzling light and the car appeared to pitch forward violently, catch fire, and then rise into the air at great speed and at an acute angle. All the time the wind in their faces grew stronger and fiercer, whilst strange and colourful images flashed in front of them and past them on the walls which had been transformed into a kaleidoscope of fast-changing sights and scenes. Robin was completely taken aback by what was happening. At one level he knew that they could hardly have moved anywhere at all. He knew they must be in some kind of wind tunnel. That the carriage was being manipulated by computer-activated hydraulics. That the flames – surely? – could not be real. That the intense sensation of airborne travel was being simulated by the images projected all around them. But at another level, he believed that he was indeed being carried up to heaven on a chariot of fire in the midst of a whirlwind – and it was as terrifying as it was absorbing.

The whole experience lasted for less than one minute, but it was enough. Perhaps more than enough. Just at the point when the sensations were about to become overwhelming –

just at the point when the editors' cries of amazement were about to turn to screams of terror, just at that point – it ended.

The flames fluttered away, the wind died down, the car tipped back to a level position, and the space around them was once more cloaked in darkness. Almost immediately, however, the doors in front of the car opened wide, and Robin found himself moving back towards the brightly lit quay from which the journey had started. It was noticeable that the two men in the seat behind had fallen silent, and were making no comments, critical or otherwise. As they all stepped shakily from the car, the second vehicle was emerging back into the light with the faces of its four occupants showing the same combination of shock and relief that Robin and his fellow travellers were feeling.

'Are you all right?' asked Marianne, as Robin walked giddily into the open air.

'I think so,' he said, smiling and breathing heavily. 'But I think you were right to give it a miss. And I must say, on the evidence of that little trip, I think we should *both* sit out *The Ride of Revelation*!'

'Amen to that,' added Marianne. 'I'm happy to leave Revelation to another time. But there must surely be *some* experiences here that aren't likely to increase my chances of giving birth on the spot! Don't you think?'

When Noel finally disentagled himself from the group of newspaper editors, he was slightly ruffled but still smiling broadly.

'Well, what did you think of *that*?' he said proudly.

Robin looked thoughtful before saying, 'Very effective.'

'*Effective*!' exclaimed Noel. 'You bet it's effective! By the end of it even *I* was praying!'

Robin and Marianne looked at each other, unsure as to quite how serious Noel was being.

'Jolly good,' said Robin. 'Well, I think we'll try something a bit gentler now. If you'll excuse us . . .'

Leaving Noel to prop himself up against a life-size representation of Elijah, Robin and Marianne followed the path around to *The Jonah Experience*. As expected, this made far fewer demands on the human nervous system. Entering a dark cavernous interior through the large and open mouth of a giant fish, they found themselves confronted by a sequence of exhibitions and installations, all targeted at an audience seeking an altogether more sedate and sober experience. Various videos and interactive displays dramatized facts and fictions of sea life. Interestingly, Jonah himself hardly got a mention, and the real heroes of the piece appeared to be the whales, dolphins and other sea species that moved across the ceiling and walls in a never-ending, 360-degree, three-dimensional display.

'Well, that was very nice,' said Robin, grateful simply for the fact that the experience had had a calming effect on the two of them.

'Hmm.' Marianne's response carried more than a hint of cynicism. 'I'm not sure I see much of a biblical connection.'

'No,' said Robin. 'You're right, of course. But people aren't really going to come here for a religious experience, are they? They're going to come for some fun, with perhaps a little bit of information thrown in too.'

'I suppose you're right,' she replied. 'Except that Noel's comment as we left *The Elijah Trip* – his comment about praying – made me think that perhaps there *is* scope in something like this for making people more aware of the variety of religious experiences. I mean, it's not always going to be a chariot of fire – but *some*times, perhaps, it *will* be. And other times, of course, it will be quite, quite different.'

Robin put his arm around Marianne, conscious of how much she still desperately wanted to see the spiritual positives in all of this.

'That sounds like a cue for our next experience,' he said. 'Do you think you can face *The Virtual Last Supper*?'

Marianne looked distinctly concerned by the prospect. The skin around her eyes was taut, and she was biting her lip.

'I can't say I'm looking forward to it,' she said. 'But I can't not do it. It's just that . . .' She paused. 'It's either going to be the future's answer to the Eucharist, or . . .'

'Or what?'

'Or it's going to be a travesty.' She breathed heavily. 'Or even a blasphemy. Whichever way,' she continued, 'it's hardly something I'm able to feel comfortable about.'

'Do you want to sit it out?' asked Robin, as gently as he could.

'I couldn't,' she replied. 'We have a duty. *I* have a duty. This place, this whole approach, has somehow come about because we tried to stop a small parish church from closing. To some extent this place represents the future – or at least *a* future – that we and everyone else, it seems, have chosen. Whatever else may have changed, I'm still an ordained church minister. I have to go on hoping that the new way is a more positive way. So, no – I don't want to sit it out. Until I've had the experience, I will not know.'

'Will not know what exactly?'

'Where God is in any of this.'

Half an hour later they removed from their heads the virtual reality helmets which were key to the whole experience. Robin looked drawn. Marianne's cheeks were marked with tears. They linked hands, rose from their seats and filed out with several other people, back into the midday sunshine.

'Well?' said Robin weakly. It was a half-hearted attempt to break the silence that had engulfed them since they had left *The Virtual Last Supper*.

'Share in Christ's last meal!' the banner outside the entrance had proclaimed, and the whole experience had been based around that. Quite how it had been managed,

Robin and Marianne were not sure – except they knew that the bread and wine they had received had most certainly been real. They could still feel the crumbs in their mouths. They could still taste the bitterness of the wine on their tongues.

Marianne simply shook her head mournfully – her body still convulsed with small sobs. Robin was not sure what this meant. Had Marianne experienced the future – or a travesty? He did not want to ask the question so directly. He squeezed her arm and prompted once again, 'Are you OK?'

By way of reply, Marianne looked up at him and stared deeply into his face with eyes that were tired and tearful. 'We really must get away,' she said. 'Robin, we really must. I don't care where we go. Your Norfolk or the back of beyond. I don't care. But we must go. *Some*where. The baby is due in just over a month, and we need some space before then. And some time. Away from all this. You must promise me, Robin. Promise me that we will go away.'

'I promise,' said Robin. 'We *will* go. F-Day is only three weeks away. Let's go somewhere then. OK? Just *before* then. That will mean we can make sure we're away when all the hullabaloo is in full swing – and we can still be back in time for junior's arrival. How does that sound?'

Marianne was about to answer, but her response was swallowed up by a series of cries and shouts as several people began to run past them towards *The Elijah Trip*. Something was obviously wrong, and so Robin and Marianne joined the general movement towards the crowd that was forming outside the entrance to the ride.

'What is it?' Robin asked of the people who were standing closest to them.

'A malfunction,' volunteered a very earnest-looking young man. 'One of the carriages has got stuck in the last phase of the ride. Looks like the poor buggers on board have been getting the chariot of fire and whirlwind treatment for more than five minutes.'

Suddenly Noel's large face was looming in their direction. 'Christ!' he shrieked. 'Do you know who's in there? It's the Minister. The Minister without Portfolio. He's in there with three of his staff – and that chariot's been up and down more times than is good for anyone!'

By now almost all the guests had gathered around the entrance to *The Elijah Trip*. Some of them noticed wisps of smoke escaping from the roof.

'Dear God,' said Dominic, pushing his way to the front of the crowd and looking as worried as Robin had ever seen him. 'Let's hope it's not another St Paul's. The public electrocution of the Bishop of London was regrettable enough, but the premature bodily assumption of a prominent member of the Government might be altogether too much!'

At just that moment, sirens could be heard approaching the palace. Heads turned to see the Pearly Gates swing open wide to admit two fire engines which then careered across the piazza towards *The Elijah Trip*, scattering dignitaries and celebrities in their wake. Noel, who still liked to pretend that somehow he was in control of the whole thing, flapped his hands in the direction of the entrance as if giving permission for the axe-carrying firefighters to enter his domain. As they rushed past him, the air was filled with the noise of a helicopter that appeared in the sky immediately overhead. Ropes were thrown from the sides of the fast-descending aircraft and, almost immediately, men wearing combat fatigues and carrying rifles began to descend on to the now flaming roof of *The Elijah Trip*.

As various small explosions started to go off in the vicinity of the building – and as the police moved in to shepherd the guests away – the loudspeakers in the piazza added to the general cacophony by blaring out a brass band version of 'Give me oil in my lamp, keep me burning'. It was, Marianne remembered thinking, an unfortunate choice of hymn.

# VII

For all the drama surrounding the malfunction of *The Elijah Trip*, there had been no real injuries, much less any fatality. The Minister without Portfolio and his aides had all been recovered – albeit in a somewhat traumatized state – and advised to rest for a few weeks 'to regain a sense of equilibrium'. The damage to the ride had been significant, but repairs began almost immediately with a view to it being restored in time for the park's public opening before F-Day. The problem had been traced to an electrical fault, and satisfaction was being expressed that the fire had been so well contained.

'What are you thinking?' asked Marianne as Robin lay in bed, staring at the ceiling.

'Well, it is all a bit odd, isn't it? You remember those silly stories about sabotage and murder when the Bishop of London was killed? I wonder . . . Don't you think two electrical faults might be a bit coincidental?'

'You mean they weren't accidents?'

'I don't know,' said Robin. 'It just seems a bit odd, that's all. But I can't think of any reason for it. I can't think why it might have been planned. Except that the emergency services arrived at Lambeth Palace so quickly, it was almost as if they were waiting for it to happen.'

'They did arrive quickly,' agreed Marianne. 'But I assumed that was just because there were so many important people there. That sort of reaction is probably quite normal when it's somewhere so close to the seat of Government.'

Robin looked unconvinced. 'All the more reason for us to

go somewhere else, then,' he said. 'If all these goings on are "normal", I'm even more convinced that we should be well out of the way when F-Day comes along. The way things are going just now, I'd be scared to switch on the toaster in case it burst into flames! Yes, I'm sure we'd be safer somewhere away from all this coincidental activity. And, anyway, we should be focusing on each other at this stage – not on the future of a giant commercial enterprise.'

'Darling,' said Marianne patiently, 'I've been saying that for as long as I can remember. But, even when you've agreed with me, you've still managed to find reasons why you've been needed at the agency. Personally, I can think of nothing better than being away for F-Day – but won't you be needed then more than any other time?'

'Well, with any luck, everything will be done and dusted by then. When the day arrives I suspect Dominic and Noel will spend the whole time pacing up and down, biting their fingernails. No. We need to be away from all that.'

'So, that's settled then,' said Marianne, smiling broadly.

'Yes,' said Robin, turning over to switch off the lamp on his side of the bed. 'Norfolk, here we come!'

*'With less than 24 hours to go until the official flotation, excitement is rising across the country. The very last of the letters were sent out at the end of the week – which means that everyone who is entitled to participate should by now have received notice of their individual share allocation. Anyone who has maintained a regular pattern of worship at an Anglican church over the last 12 months is guaranteed a minimum of 50 shares, with some long-term churchgoers getting up to 2000. Estimates of the opening share value on F-Day differ, but most observers put the likely price at something between £2 and £5. All of which means that some people who sell on the first day will stand to make capital gains in the region of £10,000. And remember, you*

*can find out the very latest on everything to do with the flotation by visiting the Church of England online at www.kingdom.com.'*

Marianne leaned forward and retuned the car radio so that the newsreader's voice was replaced by the strains of some baroque music.

'Ah, that's better,' she said, resettling herself on the passenger seat and trying to get tolerably comfortable.

'Is it still hurting?' asked Robin.

'It's not so much a hurt. More an ache. In my back. As long as I shift around every so often, I can deal with it. But I'm afraid I don't think I'm going to be up to doing any of the driving. Sorry.'

'No problem,' said Robin. 'I was a bit worried about this being too long a ride for you in your current condition.'

'No, it's all right,' said Marianne. 'I'm fine. Anyway, we're nearly there now.'

Over the next half-hour Marianne began to think that perhaps she had spoken too soon. They left the main A-road, and started to make their way cross-country on a series of smaller roads. The route seemed to be particularly winding and bumpy, and it was all she could do to maintain any semblance of enjoyment. In fact, she began to feel decidedly unwell as they breasted a small humped bridge, and so she was very relieved to hear Robin declare that they had arrived. He slowed the car to a crawl as they entered the village where he had spent the first years of his life.

'Will anyone remember you?' asked Marianne, trying hard not to grimace.

'I very much doubt it,' said Robin. 'The family moved out almost 30 years ago. And, anyway, I think I'd rather travel incognito.'

'Isn't that rather difficult?' continued Marianne. 'There can't be many Angels around.'

'More than you think!' replied Robin.

He may have been right. There certainly appeared to be very few *people* about. The stone buildings looked bare and rather bleak in the thin, early spring light. She tried to imagine the village in midsummer, bathed in sunshine and with each cottage and garden clothed in colourful flowers and wrapped in a warm glow and the perfume of roses.

'I'm sure it's not always this grey,' said Robin, as if reading her thoughts. 'At least, not in my memory.'

'Where are we staying?' asked Marianne, who was beginning to understand that the village Robin really wanted to visit perhaps no longer existed anywhere other than inside his head.

'At the village inn,' said Robin. 'Well, it's primarily a pub – with a few rooms. Except that the word "inn" always seems more appropriate in a place like this. "The Green Man".'

'Excellent,' said Marianne. 'And is it old, and do we have a room with a four-poster bed and a sloping ceiling?'

Robin looked rather sheepish. 'I don't know, I'm afraid,' he said. 'I haven't booked.'

Marianne immediately flashed a look at him as if to say, 'You've brought your heavily pregnant wife all the way from North London to Norfolk – and you haven't booked?'

Robin felt the accusation burning into the side of his face as he continued to drive at a very sedate pace along the main village street, and so he kept talking.

'That is, I didn't ring ahead. I thought it would be more . . . romantic just to turn up. I'm sure it will be all right. After all, who's likely to want to stay here of all places on the night before F-Day?'

'Well, *we* do!' said Marianne.

Her physical discomfort had returned, and she was having to try very hard to see the excursion as anything at all like a romantic adventure. With no traffic before or behind them, Robin slowed the car even more – to walking pace – as they turned a corner where a small Norman church stood.

'What did that big, pink notice say?' said Robin, accelerating slightly. 'Was it about the services, or a fête or something?'

'I rather doubt it,' said Marianne, who was now fearing the worst. 'It said "Beauty and Cosmetics". Something about a course.'

'Ah,' said Robin, who was feeling that perhaps there was, after all, no such thing as an escape from manifestations of 'the virtuous circle'.

'But,' he added optimistically, and pointing ahead, 'in a changing world, at least "The Green Man"'s still here!'

The woman behind the bar was cooly polite. She was most terribly sorry, but there were absolutely no rooms available. It was the Beauty and Cosmetics Course, you see. At the church. All the rooms had been reserved months ago. The church was very 'into' beauty and cosmetics. There was a course held every month, and the delegates always stayed at 'The Green Man'. Sorry, but there it was.

Robin felt wretched. He had completely misjudged the situation, and now there would be nothing for it but to drive on further to a larger village or town where they could find some acceptable accommodation. Marianne, however, felt *more* wretched – and her feelings were far more physical than emotional.

'Robin,' she gasped, clutching his arm and almost falling on to the chair that stood next to the reception desk. 'I think it's starting.'

The woman behind the bar looked slightly disconcerted by this announcement, and then said, through her fixed smile, 'I'm sorry? What is starting exactly?'

Her look changed palpably to one of horror as Robin explained quickly and somewhat incoherently what was likely to happen. He calmed down slightly when Marianne admonished him for faffing about and told him in no uncertain terms to 'do something'. Robin's response was to start muttering about 'the nearest hospital' as he helped Marianne – at her request – on to the floor, and started trying to settle her with a few cushions from the sofa on the other side of the room. The woman behind the bar dampened his enthusiasm with a high-pitched and strained comment to the effect that the nearest hospital was almost 20 miles away 'along a very bumpy road'. Marianne groaned at this revelation, and gave Robin another withering look as she shifted her weight once again. The woman behind the bar decided at this point that she needed reinforcements, and disappeared along a corridor, calling 'Simon' as she went.

Only a few seconds elapsed before she returned with a sandy-haired and stocky man in his forties who took in the situation at a glance, rubbed his hand across his broad face, and declared at once, 'Let's try to get the young lady across to the stable.'

'The stable!' Robin almost cried, feeling that his wife was in danger of being dealt with in a less than appropriate way.

'It's a converted stable,' added Simon quickly with a smile. 'I've just turned it into a small flat for letting out this summer. It's not been aired and the bed's not been made. But I'm sure we can fix that. That is, if you don't mind staying in our stable, sir.'

Robin apologized for everything – several times – and then thanked the man for his help. Yes, of course, he assured him: they would be delighted to stay in the stable . . . Except . . . Except . . . What about . . .?

'Don't you worry about a thing,' said Simon, addressing himself to Marianne. 'There's a midwife, Belinda, lives about a mile away. She's my cousin, as it happens. I'll give her a ring, and see if she can come over.'

It was just after five o'clock in the afternoon when Robin and Marianne arrived at 'The Green Man'. By a quarter past six Marianne was ensconced in the stable with Robin and Belinda in attendance. At midnight, as the baby's head first appeared to Robin's astonished gaze, a muffled cheer could be heard coming from the bar. At eight minutes past twelve, a baby boy was born. Just after one o'clock Robin went back across to the bar to tell the news to anyone who might still be around.

Dorothy – the original woman behind the bar – had gone home some time before, but Simon was still clearing up and looked delighted by what he heard. By half past one, Robin had wet the baby's head three times and was feeling as if he were king of the world. It was about then that Simon suggested that Robin should perhaps rejoin his wife and son.

Arriving back at the stable, he found that Marianne had just drifted off to sleep. He gave Belinda a hug that threatened to break the poor woman's ribs, before gazing dumbfoundedly at the small bundle of life that was now a full 90 minutes old.

'I heard a cheer,' he slurred. 'In the distance. Just as he appeared. Were they cheering for my son, do you think?'

In the soft light of the single lamp, he could see that Belinda was putting her coat on. 'It might have been,' she said kindly. 'Although I suspect it was for something else.'

'Something else?'

'Simon had a few friends stay on to see in the special day,' Belinda continued. 'F-Day. It's a day that will put quite a few pounds in their pockets, if I'm not mistaken.'

'F-Day,' repeated Robin, almost to himself.

'Yes,' said Belinda, who of course had no idea who Robin was, and therefore assumed that the birth of his son had wiped away all awareness of any other newsworthy event. 'F-Day,' she said once more. 'It's the day when the Church of England becomes a PLC, or whatever you call it. When the shares are floated on the stock market. There's a lot of folk around here who've been looking forward to this day for quite a while, I can tell you.'

Robin appeared not to be able to take in what the midwife was telling him. Belinda was hardly surprised by this and so she made no attempt to further the conversation.

'Well, I'm going to get back home now for some sleep myself,' she said. 'I'll be back in a few hours. But, in the meantime, give me a call if you're worried about anything. I've left my number over by the phone.'

She walked to the door of the converted stable.

'By the way,' she said. 'Have you and your wife decided on a name?'

'What? Oh, yes,' said Robin, smiling awkwardly. 'Yes, we have. We're going to call him Theo.'

Marianne was asleep in bed and Robin did not want to disturb her. He curled up on the sofa under a spare blanket and dozed fitfully until about four o'clock when Theo woke them all with his demand for milk. The proud parents spoke a little to each other, but communicated mostly by looks and touches. Robin brought his blanket and lay down on the duvet next to Marianne, where they both snatched another hour's slumber before Theo disturbed them once more. As his son was rocked back to sleep again, Robin heard a key in the lock, and Belinda whispered 'Good morning' from out of the shadows. It was just after six o'clock in the morning, and still dark. Whilst the mid-wife directed all her attention towards mother and baby, Robin took the opportunity to freshen up with a shower and shave, before unpacking the single suitcase they had brought with them.

'I'm assuming we'll be here for at least the rest of today,' he added by way of explanation.

'Oh, I'm sure you will,' said Belinda. 'Mother here needs plenty of rest and a proper check-over from the doctor before you think about driving off anywhere. I've brought you some nappies, and I know that Simon's happy for you to stay here for as long as need be.'

'Simon. Of course,' said Robin, remembering how much they all owed to the landlord's calm and thoughtful attentions the night before. 'I ought to go and see him. Do you mind . . .?'

'No, of course not,' said Belinda firmly. 'You leave me and mother here to sort out the young one. Go on. You get over to the main building and get yourself some breakfast. After all, you've had quite a night!'

Robin picked up the very slight hint of sarcasm in her voice, and noticed the knowing looks passing between the two women. He wasn't sure whether he felt rebuffed, ridiculed or quite rightly put in his place – but he *did* know that he had an enormous appetite, and decided that his hunger was not helping his feeling of confusion.

'Right then,' he said tamely. 'I'll go and sort things out with Simon. See you all later.'

Once outside in the cobbled yard that separated the stable from the main part of 'The Green Man', Robin could see that the sky was showing signs of the new dawn. He paused in the crisp morning air to fill his lungs, before walking purposefully across to the side entrance of the public house. Simon was not there, but a young woman who was sorting some newspapers in Dorothy's place behind the bar had obviously been briefed on the events of the night before. She greeted Robin with warmth and assured him that breakfast would be available from seven o'clock. As this was still 15 minutes away, would Robin like to take a look at the morning newspapers? Robin almost said 'yes', but then remembered that they would all be full of news about F-Day. Even before Theo's birth, this trip had been planned to give them an alternative to F-Day.

'Er, no, no, thank you all the same,' he said. 'I think I'll take a short stroll. It will give me an even better appetite.'

As he walked through to the front of the building, he reflected that it was rather too cold for a stroll, and he thought about going back to the stable for his top-coat. He did not want to disturb Belinda and Marianne, however, and so – buttoning his jacket against the chill air – he set off at a brisk pace back up the road that led to the church.

The church was square-towered and squat. It crouched on the bend of the road, quiet and black against the now luminous sky. The soft pink of the dawn contrasted with the garish magenta of the large sign that proclaimed the advent of 'Beauty and Cosmetics'. Robin looked past the sign at the church building, which seemed now to be hunched like a black cat, indignant but tolerant of the liberties a child might take with its fur. Quite unexpectedly he heard a voice breaking the silence. He was doubly surprised because the voice was his own, and the words were something of a prayer. 'Dear God, If you're there or thereabouts I'd just like to say thank you. Thank you.'

He suddenly found that he could say not a single word more. There was an enormous something in his throat, his eyes were burning, and his cheeks were wet. He was obviously ill. He paused to see if the sensations would pass, and, when they did, he added a few more words. 'Please look after them.'

But the sensations came back again, and he felt as if the large black cat had turned to look at him with curiosity before resuming its impassive position against the brightening sky.

Back at 'The Green Man', Simon had arrived at the stable to welcome his newest guest.

'I had a few mates stay on for a private drink after closing time last night,' he told a tired-looking Marianne who sat propped up in bed with Theo in her arms. 'We were seeing in F-Day, as it were. Toasting the coming of a new age. You see, we've all put a lot into making the local church what it is today. And Mel – that's one of the lads – he said he reckoned it was a good omen that a little 'un had been born in our place only minutes into the big day.'

Marianne managed a smile at the thought that this was being seen as 'a big day' by everyone.

'In fact,' continued Simon, 'we toasted your young man several times, and we wanted to give him something as well. But, of course, being so late, there wasn't anything we could buy him. So, what I've done instead is put together a basket of cosmetics and bits and pieces from the church beauty thing. They're for you, of course – not the baby. That is, not that you need beautifying, if you see what I mean.'

At this point, Simon's words trailed off into something of a mumble as his embarrassment got the better of him. 'Well, if you'll excuse me,' he said at last, putting the basket in a corner, and backing towards the door, 'I'd better go and make sure that breakfast is coming along all right. Your husband took himself off for a little walk, and so he'll be back pretty soon with a fair old appetite, I shouldn't wonder.'

'Like father like son,' said Belinda, as Theo began to make his own hunger apparent. At the suggestion that Marianne might start feeding her son there and then, Simon make his exit with alacrity. As he crossed the stable-yard he could see Robin, shoulders hunched against the morning breeze, making his way determinedly back towards the 'The Green Man'.

Robin and Marianne tried to insulate themselves from the events of F-Day. They did not listen to the radio or watch the television, and Robin left the mobile phone switched off. Instead they concentrated their attentions on Theo and thoughts of their future together as a family. Early in the afternoon Robin drove to the nearest town to buy more nappies, baby clothes, a Moses basket, and other related accessories that had all been written down for him on a list compiled by Marianne and Belinda. He also bought a few things unprompted, including two large bouquets of flowers – one for his wife and one for the midwife. By the time he returned to the stable, the doctor had been to see Marianne and given her the 'all clear' to travel home. Robin therefore started planning the return journey, which they had agreed should start around the middle of the next day.

That evening Robin and Marianne enjoyed a light meal together in 'The Green Man', whilst Theo slept in the Moses basket beside them. They then retired early to bed for what they hoped would be a less eventful night. Their baby son woke about every three hours, but Robin (at least) enjoyed a reasonable amount of sleep – finally waking at nine o'clock to organize breakfast and start the preparations for the drive back to London. By one o'clock they were all packed up and ready to go. Belinda had been called to another delivery at a nearby farm and had made her farewells more than an hour earlier. It was therefore left to Simon to say the parting words.

'So you didn't really see much of the village and the country hereabouts, did you?' he said, his face beaming with good humour.

'We saw enough for it to have a very special place in our hearts,' said Marianne warmly.

'Yes,' added Robin. 'And you can be sure we'll be back.'

So saying, he reached for his wallet and asked Simon to let him know what they owed him.

'Nothing,' said the publican. 'You owe me nothing. Your being here has been a real blessing, and – although I know you don't want to hear anything about you-know-what – I have to say that my little windfall has worked out at rather more than I might have expected. So this one's on me.'

There followed the kind of gentle altercation, laced with profuse thanks, that often follows an offer of this kind. 'No, really . . .'; 'No, no . . . really . . .'; 'No, you mustn't . . .'; 'No, I insist . . .'; and so on. Needless to say, it ended with smiles, handshakes and hugs all round, as Robin and

Marianne finally – and graciously – accepted their host's generosity. As they made their last preparations to leave, two or three members of 'The Green Man''s staff came out to wave to them. Marianne felt as if she were in a scene from a latter-day *Pickwick Papers*, as she climbed into the back seat of the car where Theo was already strapped into place. With all passengers (as it were) wrapped up warm against the elements, and with the onlookers shouting their good wishes for a safe progress, the carriage made its exit from the cobbled yard of the coaching inn, bound for London and, no doubt, a whole new series of adventures.

Once they were on their way, Robin and Marianne began to make the mental adjustments needed for re-entry into the real world. As a first step, Robin switched on his mobile phone, which responded almost immediately by announcing through the hands-free speaker that he had six recorded voicemails waiting to be heard. He pressed the button to retrieve the messages, and was not at all surprised to find that all six were from his two partners at Angel, Fear & Tredwell. The recordings spanned a period of some 24 hours, and grew increasingly desperate in their tone.

'I know you're on holiday,' said Dominic, in the last of the messages, 'but why the bloody hell do you keep your phone switched off? What would happen if there were an emergency? What would happen if I'd died, for God's sake? No, don't answer that. Just get in touch when you can. Please!'

'It's nice to know they miss you,' said Marianne. 'But I suppose you ought to give them a ring. Just to tell them that your son and heir has been born. You can let them know that you *might* be in the office next week, all being well!'

Marianne's last comment was made with a wry smile. She knew that she had effectively already lost her husband back to the world of the advertising agency. For all his talk about wanting to get away from it, she knew that the constant buzz of his job was something he could not be without for very long. Even without an F-Day, that would have been the case. Listening to the phone messages represented the first real step back towards that world of total communication, and there was now no point in trying to prolong their escape from 'the news'. They stopped at the first service station they came to and bought two broadsheets and two tabloids. Back in the car they tuned the radio to an all-news station. They had hardly managed to take in the main points of the last day and a half's developments, however, before the car-phone rang again. It was Noel. Despite his obvious urgency, Noel was less single-minded than Dominic, and sounded genuinely touched by the news of Theo's birth.

'That's . . . amazing, Robin,' he said through the crackles of a bad line that managed to mask a somewhat colourful use of language. 'Our first real . . . step towards the creation of the next . . . generation,' he said, clearly assuming some joint ownership of the new life. 'It puts everything else in . . . perspective, eh?'

'Well, yes, I think it does, actually,' said Robin, who was delighted but surprised by his partner's evident emotion. Noel waxed lyrical for another minute or two – which reinforced the impression that perhaps his emotion had already been enhanced by the effects of alcohol. Noel's evident concern, however (especially for Marianne) was warming, and Robin began to feel that the excursion into Norfolk had perhaps been an important creative act for the business, as well as for himself and his wife.

'You're up to date with what the . . . going on, I suppose,' Noel said, bringing the conversation around to F-Day at last.

'We know about the frantic buying and selling, if that's

what you mean,' said Robin. 'We've just caught up with that on the news.'

The actual flotation of the Church of England had gone pretty much as planned the day before. At midday the share price had been announced, and immediate trading had been reasonably brisk as individual small investors moved to capitalize on the windfalls of their free shares. The real excitement, however, had only started towards the end of the first day, when a new buyer entered the market, securing large numbers of these shares at a marked premium over what had been assumed to be the price's upper limit.

This new force was something of a mystery. It was not one of the recognized institutional fundholders, but rather a broad-based and somewhat faceless industrial holding company. No one seemed to know very much about it at all, except that past performance would not have suggested it as an active buyer of traditional 'blue-chip' stocks – which was how the new C of E PLC was being viewed. It was certainly not a business with any obvious interest in the ecclesiastical field.

Consolidated Holdings (or 'Cons-Hold' for short) was one of those large nebulous corporations that was a collection of operating companies spanning a wide range of unglamorous mineral and engineering activities. It had no real identity outside a fairly specialized area of the financial markets and, as far as could be seen, was managed largely on a regional basis, the co-ordination of which was controlled by an international consortium based in Singapore. What seemed *not* to be a mystery, however, was Cons-Hold's apparent intention of building up a sizeable stake in 'Church of England PLC'.

With Cons-Hold seemingly happy to see the share price rise fast on the first day of trading, the majority of the small shareholders who had not immediately sold up, decided that this really was too good an opportunity to ignore. By the time trading closed in London, it was clear that Cons-Hold had established a strong position as the single biggest shareholder in the Church of England. Widespread enquiries overnight had unearthed little more information about the extent of Cons-Hold's ambitions, but when several international banks declared in New York and Tokyo that they were backing the buying spree, the scene was set for a tempestuous second day of trading in London. When the stockmarket opened it also became clear that some of the big institutional pension funds were likely to sell their holdings ahead of what many now assumed would be an equally rapid fall in prices. The situation that followed on that morning, as Robin and Marianne were leaving 'The Green Man', could only be described as chaotic, as millions of shares changed hands, whilst so-called experts argued about the legality of what was now fast becoming an extraordinary chapter in the history of both the Church and the City.

'So what does it mean?' asked Robin.

'I'm not sure that anyone knows exactly,' said Noel. 'The latest estimates suggest that Cons-Hold may have amassed almost 50 . . . per cent of the shares. But they've only done that by shelling out some gargantuan amount of money. And now everyone's rushing around trying to find out whether the . . . stories are true, and – if they *are* true – whether the events of the last 24 hours meet all the technical and legal criteria for a successful takeover bid.'

'Is this what's known as a corporate raid?' asked Robin, who found himself, against his will, being drawn in to the excitement of the whole episode. 'Because if it *is*, it seems quite extraordinary to me that anyone might actually want to *manage* the Church of England.'

Noel's voice continued to crackle away over the airwaves. 'The talk at this end is that it's all about . . . asset-stripping,' he said. 'They're saying that the . . . real residual value of the Church's property is far, far higher than was made public . . . that Cons-Hold is just the buying front for a worldwide alliance of . . . banks who want to get their hands on a huge slice of relatively recession-proof goodies.

You know . . . land, prime sites, lots of gold and other precious metals . . . All that sort of thing.'

'But I thought the whole C of E flotation was tied up with all sorts of legal restrictions,' responded Robin. 'Restrictions that mean that not even a single parish church hall can be sold off without Government approval. Surely the only thing that Cons-Hold have bought themselves is the dubious honour of claiming some kind of technical ownership of the Church. Won't they simply have to keep it for forever and a day as a going concern – effectively maintaining it pretty much as now, but having to make up any shortfalls in income? I can see that the current spread of commercial schemes guarantees a reasonable dividend for the foreseeable future. But that bubble could burst pretty quickly. I'm not sure it necessarily makes much sense as an investment for income, *does* it?'

'I don't . . . know about any of that,' said a weary-sounding Noel. 'I really don't . . . know. Despite the briefings those . . . Government chaps gave us, you could write everything *I* know about stocks and shares on the back of a . . . postage stamp. Perhaps they *can't* break it up. The . . . Church, I mean. But that's what Dominic seemed most concerned about yesterday. And, after all, he's closer to the . . . powers-that-be than we are. Perhaps the Government is going to wash its hands of the whole . . . thing – and let market forces decide.'

The road began to dip, and Noel's voice became a series of broken squawks and squeaks.

'Look,' said Robin, 'I'll be back home some time this afternoon. Tell Dominic he can ring me then if he wants to. Otherwise I'll be in the office first thing tomorrow.'

Noel's reply was barely audible, but Robin felt that he had got the message.

'Do I take it that you won't be spending tomorrow at home with your new family then?' said Marianne, who had to admit to herself that she was now as eager as anyone to know what was going on.

228

'I'm sorry,' replied Robin, 'but I can't jump ship now. Whatever it is that's happening is at least partly down to me. I'm afraid I'm going to have to see this through.'

Robin arrived at the office before eight o'clock the next morning to find that Dominic was already there. Dominic congratulated Robin quickly on the birth of his son, assured him that the agency would be sending some flowers to Marianne, and proceeded to brief him on the latest news.

'I would have called you last night,' he said confidentially, 'but there were moves afoot – and I spent most of the time on the phone to various people who claim to be close to the action in the Government, or the Church or the City.'

'With what result?' asked Robin.

Dominic leaned forward to whisper, although it was clear that there was nobody else around. 'Just one thing. I've been told to expect a special visitor at nine o'clock.'

'A special visitor,' repeated Robin, who had also started to whisper. 'How special? Who is it?'

'Well, I'm not absolutely sure, of course,' said Dominic. 'After all, many of the messages I received yesterday seemed rather coded. But I think it's the Archbishop of Canterbury.'

'The Archbishop of Canterbury?' blurted Robin. 'Here?'

'Sshhh! Keep your voice down. He doesn't want anyone to know about it.'

'But the Archbishop of Canterbury,' Robin said again, this time in more of a half whisper. 'Why on earth does he want to talk to *us*? And why *now*?'

'I don't know,' said Dominic. 'But we don't have long to wait before we find out!'

At nine o'clock on the dot, a figure shrouded in a long, grey overcoat, and wearing a wide-brimmed grey hat, was shown into the agency boardroom. And, yes – when he had thrown off the coat and hat, it was clear that he was indeed the Archbishop of Canterbury. He sat one side of the table, his brow furrowed, his eyes flickering nervously. Every now and again he glanced towards the door as if he expected to be interrupted and apprehended by somebody. Opposite him sat Dominic, Robin and Noel, who had joined them only minutes before the Archbishop's arrival.

'I suppose I just feel I've let people down,' said the Archbishop, after the usual pleasantries had been exchanged rather stiffly. 'By not being more . . . active. Perhaps I was too trusting in the way I let others deal with the matters in hand. But, at the time, they all seemed to know so much more about it.'

'If you don't mind my asking,' said Dominic, 'was there ever a time when you felt you could have changed things – compared to how they have worked out now, I mean?'

'You know, I think about that all the time. And I honestly don't know,' replied the Archbishop. 'There were certain points where I could have made a stand, as it were. But it was never clear what the stand would have been *for*. On every side there were groups with apparently different agendas and objectives. As long as they were heading in generally the same direction, it seemed as if it were at least the will of the Church, if not always so obviously the will of God. But now it's so difficult to determine any clear will at all . . . other than . . .' He paused.

'Other than?' Dominic prompted. The Archbishop sighed, stroked his beard thoughtfully, removed his glasses and screwed up his eyes.

'I don't know,' he said, clearly not wanting to articulate his train of thought through to its logical conclusion. He replaced his glasses and stared at the sky beyond the large window that ran along the side of the boardroom before continuing, 'But I think things will soon become clearer than they have been.'

Dominic, Robin and Noel glanced at each other.

'In fact,' the Archbishop went on, 'I was rather hoping you might be able to tell *me* something that might help clarify matters. You see, I have to admit that it is proving very difficult to find out . . . things. I seem to be what's called "outside the loop".'

'Well, I have to say,' said Robin, 'that we've all been wondering for some time now as to . . . well, to put it frankly . . . as to where you *were*.'

The Archbishop smiled ruefully and looked at each of the partners across the table. 'You will understand my reticence even now, I hope, on some of the details relating to the recent past,' he said. 'And I could never bring myself to use words like "prisoner". But I think it would not be a great exaggeration to say that I have been detained for periods of time, and encouraged, let us say, to remain silent on certain key points.'

'But the fact that you're here now . . .?' Noel probed.

'Yes,' said the Archbishop – the rueful smile once more just visible beneath the grey beard. 'I *am* here now. No longer a threat, you see – if ever I *was* one. No longer able to throw any kind of spanner in the works. Free, in a sense. Perhaps for the first time in a long while. Certainly free to move about . . . to some extent – and to make some enquiries. Although it would appear that my driver, who waits below, is answerable to another authority.'

'And who is that exactly?' asked Dominic.

'Once again,' said the Archbishop, 'I was hoping you might be able to tell me. I have my suspicions. I'm trying to piece the puzzle together. But – so far at least – no one is making any attempt to help me discover the . . . the truth.'

'But what about Dr Conan?' pressed Robin. 'What about Sir Victor Catchpole? We thought they were both close associates of yours in taking this whole thing forward.'

Another sigh from the Archbishop. 'Associates?' he said.

'Yes, I suppose it must have seemed that way. But the fact is that I was never really a player in any true sense. And yes, I may reproach myself for that – there were certainly opportunities I missed, or failed to grasp as well as I should. But, in summary – and for one reason or another – my apparent authority counted for nothing. To put it bluntly, I was "used" – or at least the position I occupy was used. Conan? Well, on the basis that this conversation is either "off the record", or meaningless – both of which, in this case, amount to the same thing . . . Conan was my chief "keeper". It was he who suggested I should appoint Marianne to the notional post of co-ordinator. A way of keeping things "tight". I think that's how he put it. But the venerable doctor seems recently to have disappeared – presumably because I no longer require "keeping" in quite the same way. His secretary claims he went abroad the day before the flotation, and she doesn't know where he is. And Sir Victor Catchpole? Well, he refuses to take any calls from me. I've been trying to make contact with him for the last three days and have just been given one excuse after another. And of course the Government's no better.'

'I'm sorry,' said Dominic, who was not sure where the Archbishop's train of thought was leading. 'What exactly is the Government doing – or not doing?'

'Well, I have no proof, of course,' said the Archbishop calmly, 'but they do all seem to be part of the same . . . the same game. Having the Minister without Portfolio on sick leave at such a crucial time has been, of course, wonderfully convenient. They're now referring all my calls to civil servants on the Minister's staff. In fact, I haven't been able to find a single member of the Government willing to talk directly to me. You know, I'm beginning to think that the Bishop of Saxonford was right all along. This does rather look like something of a conspiracy – and I think its roots must go deep. I just wish I'd trusted my instincts the very first time that Sir Victor came to see me, with his earnest request that his identity should be kept a secret from everyone, and that he should be seen as no more than "an anonymous donor" to the cause of Church unity and growth.'

'I'm sure you're right in your assessment of Catchpole,' said Dominic. 'I suspect his interests in this go much wider and deeper than any of us could currently guess. But if you're right, and if there *is* some kind of conspiracy, don't you think that *we* might be part of it as well?'

The Archbishop laughed quietly, and poured himself a glass of water from a bottle that was on the table. 'Of course, you're *all* part of it,' he said. '*We're* all part of it. But I suspect that you're less tainted than the others. At least, that's the interpretation I put on the fact that you were at least prepared to talk to me. I surmise that you too feel you are in possession of less than all the facts, and that you would like to know more.'

'Well,' said Dominic, 'you may be right in your assumption that we would like to know more – but, at the present time, I have to say that there is little further light that we can throw on any matters concerning the individuals you've just named. Dr Conan is not someone we have had any contact with for some time. Perhaps he *has* simply taken a holiday, now that the flotation is over. Nor for that matter have we seen or heard from Sir Victor Catchpole – although he is, of course, a client of ours in a number of ways. As far as the Government is concerned . . . well, like you, the enforced absence of the Minister without Portfolio has meant a decrease of information from that quarter, but I have to say that that hasn't affected us dramatically. After all, in many respects, most of our work was completed well before F-Day. If I'm honest, I have to say that the events of the last few days have surprised us as much as they have surprised you and most other observers.'

The Archbishop looked tired. He lifted his head and ran his fingers slowly through his grey hair. Dominic stared across at him and, for the first time, saw clearly a figure of dignity and wisdom. But it was the image of a King Lear who has belatedly realized what he may have given away. It was also a picture of reverence that looked out of place against a garish poster for the C of E website which, stretched out across the wall behind the Archbishop's head, proclaimed baldly 'Thy kingdom.com – the Church for you. Virtually.'

The Archbishop looked at his watch. 'The car will be waiting for me,' he said slowly. 'It seems I can do no more. It appears that I am powerless in the face of forces about which I can guess, but which are still undeclared.'

He stood up and wrapped himself once more in the all-covering grey coat. Suddenly, and incongruously, he chuckled. 'Do you know?' he said. 'I think I would resign this morning – except that I don't know from *what* I would be resigning, or indeed to *whom* I should hand the letter. Now isn't that absurd?'

Dominic, Noel and Robin felt unable to join in the Archbishop's strained laughter. They rose silently from their seats and shook his hand in a warm but formal way. Dominic then led their guest out of the boardroom and downstairs to where the driver was waiting, ready to carry the country's most senior churchman to an uncertain future.

At midday a hastily convened press conference in the City of London confirmed that Consolidated Holdings had now acquired a 51% stake in 'Church of England PLC'. The spokesman for Cons-Hold deflected most questions about the company's intentions, insisting that statements would be made as soon as possible after the UK Government had given its blessing to the situation. In the meantime, he said, Cons-Hold was 'looking forward to securing a united future for the Church of England'. It was with that in mind that the company was pleased to announce the appointment to the board of Cons-Hold of one of the figures who had been most influential as a 'consultant' during the previous 12 months. Indeed, Sir Victor Catchpole would not simply join the board, but would 'manage directly the transfer of interests relating to the next stage of corporate development'. When pressed on what exactly this comment referred to, the spokesman once again insisted that all would be made clearer once approval had been given by the Government.

Twelve hours later Robin changed channels to a late-night film. It was, after all, the third time he had watched the same news clips on the television, and the third time he had heard the same phrases used. Marianne sat on the sofa next to him, feeding Theo.

'Looking forward to securing a united future for the Church of England,' Robin said almost to himself. 'Are you thinking what I'm thinking?'

'Possibly,' said Marianne, looking down at the small head that was nuzzling against her breast. 'But I don't think I care very much any more.'

It was 48 hours before the Government finally gave its formal approval to the Cons-Hold takeover. Robin wondered if the delay indicated some last-minute doubts in the corridors of power. When the statement came, however, it was short, to the point, and gave few clues about the machinations that may (or may not) have gone on behind the scenes.

'Her Majesty's Government is satisfied that the share transactions during the last week by and on behalf of Consolidated Holdings PLC fulfil all the conditions set by the terms of the Church of England Freedom Act.'

It was, Marianne reflected later, no more than a pre-amble for what was to follow. The more important announcement only came a week later. At Angel, Fear &

Tredwell it was a week of guessing and speculation. Since the flotation, no one had made any attempt to involve them in the communication of the latest developments surrounding Cons-Hold. The visit by the Archbishop of Canterbury had merely confirmed the advertising agency's apparent position outside the inner circle of those who were 'in the know'. For most people, however, any mystery surrounding Cons-Hold was of no great matter. The vast majority of former Church of England shareholders continued to exult in their windfalls and retained only a passing interest in the nature of the new owners. It was only those individuals and institutions who had hung on to their shares that now waited impatiently for any available information as to the purpose and intentions of the somewhat anonymous Cons-Hold. For many of them, the news, when it broke, was startling.

Fate, or good planning, meant that the announcement was made on the same day that a member of the Royal Family was captured on film exposing himself to a group of foreign students. Needless to say, the Royal exposure was given top billing on all the news programmes, and the communication by Cons-Hold was therefore relegated to second place. Sir Victor Catchpole made the announcement himself, surrounded by several men in black suits. His words were matter-of-fact, businesslike and totally without any hint of either drama or emotion. Indeed, viewers and listeners alike might have been forgiven for thinking that this really was nothing other than factual confirmation of the latest predictable and practical development – a wholly sensible resolution of what had clearly been a somewhat disruptive chapter in the Church's recent history. Sir Victor's heavy-jowled face was a model of seriousness, as he looked across the top of his spectacles at the assembled pack of press men and women gathered in one of the grander halls of a prestigious London hotel.

'And therefore,' he continued, after a series of introductory remarks detailing a variety of reasons why the 'freeing' of the Church of England was genuinely the most democratic and far-sighted move that could have been envisaged, 'it will probably come as no great surprise to the citizens of this country to learn that Consolidated Holdings has been acting throughout this short and tempestuous period with the full backing of the one true and universal Church, by which, of course, I mean the body commonly referred to as the Roman Catholic Church.'

He continued for some minutes more, but already the world's press were relaying the essence of the story back to their editors across the globe. There were a few reporters who could hardly believe their ears even then, and who felt the need to ask the sort of questions that would leave no hint of ambiguity.

'Does this mean, then,' asked a portly and very young-looking man in the front row, 'does this mean that, in effect, the Vatican now owns the Church of England?'

Sir Victor invited one of his colleagues to answer this question. The colleague was obviously a lawyer and spent some considerable time setting out an answer which – by the expression on the portly young man's face – was anything but clear. Sir Victor, seeing the look of incomprehension spreading itself across the faces of several more of the assembled journalists, decided that now was not a time for circumlocution.

'To answer your question directly,' he said, when the lawyer had finished, and looking straight into the eyes of the portly young man, 'yes. The Roman Catholic Church now owns the Church of England. The full legal transfer may take some time – but, yes, in effect, the wounds of the so-called English Reformation can now be healed. The Catholic Church in England is once again a single entity. The Church *in* England – as I think we should now call it – has been reunited with its sister churches around the world. It is clearly a time of great celebration.'

'Stone me!' said Dominic, as the news was relayed to the agency boardroom. Noel and Robin simply looked at each other, speechless.

'Stone me!' said Dominic once again, as he flopped on to a chair. It was clear that his usual eloquence had deserted him. 'Does that mean,' he continued, 'does that really mean that the English Reformation has been cancelled? Does it mean that all that Henry VIII stuff and the split with Rome all counts for nothing? Does it really mean that all those people who thought they were Protestants are now Catholics?'

Noel and Robin looked at each other again blankly. Robin felt he ought to say something, but didn't feel equipped to offer any kind of informed comment.

'I guess so,' he said at last. 'As far as I can see, the Vatican has control of Consolidated Holdings' 51 per cent of the Church of England shares – and the Pope is therefore now the boss.'

There was a long silence before Dominic said once again 'Stone me!'

It was at this point that Noel finally found his voice. 'You know,' he said, suddenly looking quite animated. 'This could be really good for us?'

'Good? For us?'

Neither Dominic nor Robin had begun to consider what the news might mean for the agency, and they were frankly surprised that Noel was already thinking along such lines.

'Well, that is to say,' continued the agency's Creative Director, 'Sir Victor is one of our clients – and so is the Church of England. Oops! Sorry! I mean the Church *in* England. Surely the combination of those two facts means that we've got a damned good chance of picking up some business from the guys in Rome.'

The slight hesitation that showed in Dominic's face indicated that he wanted to agree with Noel, but that he felt the neatness of his colleague's analysis to be overly simple.

'In which case,' said Dominic, 'why have we been kept in

the dark about the whole Catholic Church thing? We've not been told anything since the flotation. Don't you think Catchpole would have talked to us by now if he wanted us on the case?'

In one of those coincidences that sometimes persuade cynics that perhaps there is a God after all, the door of the boardroom opened at this point and Dominic's secretary entered with what she described as 'a mega-urgent message'.

'Sir Victor Catchpole's office has been on the phone,' she declared. 'He's apparently going to be giving interviews all afternoon about this morning's announcement, but would like you all to meet him for dinner this evening at eight o'clock. There's a private room booked at a West End hotel. I've been asked to ring back to confirm that you'll be able to go.'

She looked expectantly at the three partners. Noel's jaw had dropped open. Dominic was staring at the ceiling and seemed to be mouthing the words 'Stone me!' Robin was the first to be able to articulate a reply on behalf of them all.

'Yes. Yes. Definitely, yes,' he said excitedly. 'Tell him – tell them – tell whoever it is – that we'll be there.'

Dominic, Noel and Robin arrived at the hotel at eight o'clock precisely and were immediately shown into a small private room where a round table was laid for five people. As a member of the hotel staff served them glasses of champagne, Sir Victor marched into the room accompanied by a smaller man in a black suit.

'I believe that at least one of you has already met Father Rosso,' said Sir Victor, as he shook hands with the directors of his chosen advertising agency.

'I have,' admitted Robin, who was slightly unnerved by seeing one of his 'men in black' once again. 'Although I have to say that our conversation on that occasion was not especially productive.'

Father Rosso smiled broadly as he greeted Dominic and Noel for the first time. 'Unfortunately,' said the priest, 'we were having to conduct ourselves in a covert manner at the time. I'm so glad that the situation has now resolved itself, and that we are able to speak freely about the great opportunities that lie before us.'

From his apparently relaxed manner it appeared that Father Rosso would like to have spent the next few minutes engaging Robin and his colleagues in a more informal and less obviously pressured conversation. Sir Victor's approach, however, was decidedly brusque and businesslike. He waved his guests into their places at the table, and immediately started to tell them why they had been summoned there.

'What I'm about to say is all strictly confidential, of course,' he said, turning his large face from Dominic to Noel and then to Robin. 'If any one of you breathes a word of it, the understanding between us will be at an end. Is that clear? So you're going to have to keep the agency team as tight as possible. We'll want everyone to sign confidentiality agreements. And I don't want anyone involved in this who you think might leave your team within the next six months. Do I make myself understood?'

'Yes,' said Dominic, who had assumed his natural role as agency spokesman. 'Very clear indeed.'

Noel and Robin nodded their agreement.

'Good,' continued Sir Victor. 'Because this is big. Really big. We need a campaign – a really big campaign. We need to sell the idea of the Church of England's reintegration into the Catholic Church.'

'The Church *in* England,' added Father Rosso helpfully.

'The Church *in* England,' repeated Sir Victor. 'Yes. In fact I think the new name will be an important interim step in winning public support. It's both a sign of change, and a declaration of continuity and English faith.'

'I'm sorry,' interrupted Dominic, who felt the need for some clarification. 'You talk about winning public support, but I thought the whole thing – the reintegration, or whatever it is you want to call it – I thought it was all a *fait accompli.*'

'It is,' asserted Sir Victor. 'That is, in terms of ownership – and, in some places, operationally as well. But there's still a big job to be done in winning over the hearts and minds of the British people.'

'You see,' said Father Rosso, choosing his moment to re-enter the conversation, 'large groups of Anglicans have already declared their independence. The evangelical wing of the old C of E has, as we expected, already published its intention to carry on as a so-called "free" church – like the Methodists and the Baptists. Indeed, many of the evangelicals had started to move in this direction even before the flotation. They saw, in the English Church's commercial development, the opportunity to break loose from what they felt had been, let us say, unenlightened episcopal oversight. Now, that in itself is not a problem. Our calculations – if I might put it so baldly – allowed for that. After all, the evangelicals are prevented by law – by the Church of England Freedom Act – from taking any Church property with them. Our most tangible assets – the land and the buildings – are protected. But this is not just about property.'

'It isn't?' said Robin, almost involuntarily.

Father Rosso looked towards Sir Victor, who waved his hand as if to indicate that the priest should continue his own explanation.

'No, Robin,' said Father Rosso, trying his best to sound like a sympathetic ally and friend, 'it is not about property. It is about people. Yes, whatever you may think – this is about people. The Church – that is, the Catholic Church – has not embarked on this great crusade, this great investment, simply to regain the land it lost during the so-called English Reformation. This entire enterprise has been pursued with the missionary intention of securing for the one true faith the maximum number of *souls*. If we were to be left with every church building in the land, but with no people to worship in them, then we would have failed.'

'Which is why we need a campaign,' said Sir Victor, looking at his watch. 'A campaign which makes everyone think this really is the best thing since . . .'

He paused, and Noel said, 'Sliced bread?'

Sir Victor glowered at him and continued, '. . . since St Augustine first brought the Christian faith to this place in . . . in whenever it was.'

'Right,' said Dominic, who glanced quickly at Noel as if to suggest that the Creative Director should leave the talking to him. 'Yes,' continued Dominic, 'I can see that it's a great challenge – a chance to say something really important, in a way that is appropriately creative and motivating. We might, for example, choose to position the development as one more step on the road towards international – particularly European – integration. After all, with the exception of our foreign policy, which is of course run from the Pentagon, most of our political institutions are now controlled from one place – Brussels. It surely makes sense, therefore, for our spiritual will to be controlled from one place as well. Rome. It's another stage in helping us all to be free of the historical notion of national independence that we've laboured under for the last 500 years. It really should be seen as the beginning of a new age.'

'Possibly,' said Sir Victor, who did not look particularly impressed with Dominic's first thoughts on the matter. 'I don't know what exactly the positioning, as you would put it, should be. That's *your* job. But I would say this. The Church of England's own worst enemy has always been itself. By being everything to everybody, it ended up being nothing to nobody. No other church would have gone in for all this commercialism stuff in quite the same way. If it says anything at all about the Anglican Church, it is that it has been floundering without any kind of strategy for as long as I can remember. That's why it's ended up in this mess. And that's what we're going to put right. Not overnight, of course – but certainly within the next three to five years. We've got to turn off the overt commercialism without turning off the people who've done so well from it. We've got to centralize resources, make more of our combined strengths, and not allow every Tom, Dick and Harry with a dog collar to rush off and do whatever he likes. And, in the course of doing all that, we've got to build up the Church in England as a true, faithful, effective and efficient expression of the Roman Catholic Church. That's the brief – direct from the Vatican. As far as the management of the campaign is concerned, the Holy Father has devolved the responsibility to me – and I want an outline creative strategy on my desk within two weeks. Is that clear?'

Sir Victor's tone suggested that questions would not be welcome at this point. Dominic, Noel and Robin therefore nodded in unison. This seemed to be the sign for Sir Victor to leave, even though only the first course of the meal had been served.

'Good,' he said abruptly, standing up and throwing his napkin on to his chair. As his guests began to rise themselves, he waved them back into their seats. 'No,' he said firmly. 'You stay here. The food is good. And Father Rosso will be able to answer some of the many questions which I'm sure you have. I'm catching a plane first thing in the morning and need to straighten out a few issues before I leave. I'll see you all in two weeks' time.'

And with no more ado, the large frame of Sir Victor Catchpole marched out of the room, leaving the agency team wide-eyed and in a state of some shock.

'I think he really likes you,' said Father Rosso, after Sir Victor had left the room. Dominic, Noel and Robin, having regained something of their composure, all looked at the priest in a way that clearly showed they were unsure about this. 'No, I mean it,' continued Father Rosso, noting their expressions. 'He was always very clear when he spoke to me that he would have no other agency in charge of the first big advertising campaign. "They're a bunch of cranks," he told me, "but they're *original* cranks – and they will have learned a lot from the way they've already helped transform the Church in England."'

'A bunch of cranks,' mused Dominic. 'High praise indeed!'

'In its own way, it is,' said Father Rosso. 'I'm sure you know that Sir Victor is not an easy man to please, and most of the people who have been involved in this great mission have, at some stage or another, been castigated by him.'

Father Rosso was obviously keen to expand on this and any other point that Sir Victor's guests were likely to raise, and so the meal continued at a leisurely pace, with much wine being drunk and a good deal of information being exchanged on all matters related to the situation in hand. For example, Father Rosso was quite forthcoming in explaining how Sir Victor had always been a committed Catholic, but how he had kept his faith as very much a private concern – indeed, often giving the impression that nothing could be further from his mind than ecclesiastical affairs and spiritual well-being. It was this apparent dis-interestedness that had helped him to win the confidence of the Archbishop of Canterbury just as the commercial exploitation of the Church in England was beginning to establish itself. The Archbishop had regarded him as a man of professional integrity and clear business acumen, and had been persuaded by others to accept Sir Victor's advice as objective and unbiased.

One of those others was Dr Conan – perhaps the key mover in limiting the influence, and ultimately the move-ments, of the Archbishop. Father Rosso explained how Dr Conan had been working closely with the Vatican for more than ten years. The decision by the Church of England to ordain women to the priesthood had persuaded him that he must join the Roman Catholic Church, but friends in the Vatican had convinced him that he could be more instrumental in securing 'true Catholic unity' if he remained within the Anglican fold, especially as he had (at that time) just been appointed to the staff of the Archbishop of Canterbury.

'And where is Dr Conan now?' asked Robin, who, since Sir Victor's departure, had become the main focus for the agency team's questions.

'Cardinal Conan is currently in Rome,' said Father Rosso, smiling broadly. 'He is being briefed for a senior position in this country. But I really can't say any more about that for the time being.'

Despite his apparent discretion concerning future developments, however, Father Rosso seemed only too willing to fill in some of the gaps in Robin's knowledge of what had already taken place. It was because of this that Robin was finally encouraged to touch on the subject of the electrical accidents at St Paul's and Lambeth Palace.

'Let me tell you just what I have heard,' said Father Rosso confidentially. 'This information has no more authority than a rumour, you understand – and if you ever claimed you had heard it from me, then I would, of course, feel obliged to deny it.'

Robin pursed his lips and nodded as if to signal his acceptance of the implied conditions. Dominic frowned but said nothing. Noel refilled his glass.

'The lamentable occurrence at St Paul's Cathedral was an accident – so I hear,' said the priest. 'As far as I can ascertain, there was absolutely no malice aforethought, as I think your English language so beautifully puts it. Whether or not greater powers took a hand, I really could not say. You are asking me to comment, I assume, on the acts of men, and not on the acts of God.' He paused to sip his red wine. 'As to the matter of the troublesome fault at Lambeth Palace, however, the rumour suggests that there was a

245

certain amount of planning involved. The story is that the earlier unhappy demise of the Bishop of London gave some people an idea – and that this idea was then used to engineer a situation which would ensure that the Minister without Portfolio could be temporarily removed from the scene. The Minister had, so the story goes, dealt with the errant Bishop of Saxonford in a rather unnecessarily heavy-handed way – an approach that was likely to endanger public support for the centralization of the various Church initiatives. He had also begun to enquire rather too closely into some areas that really were matters for the Church rather than for the State. Of course, no long-term physical or psychological harm was intended for anyone – and, so I am told, the British intelligence and security forces were very co-operative in making sure that everything was made safe within a particular time-scale. There are those who would say that Sir Victor is very well connected in those quarters – and, of course, it is no secret that the Minister without Portfolio is a man who does not elicit obvious support within your so-called establishment. Anyway, Robin, as I say – that is the rumour. Whether any of it is true or not, I really could not say.'

It was two years, almost to the day, since Robin had noted the thermometer standing outside St Thomas's Parish Church. In those two years his life, and the lives of those closest to him, had changed dramatically. It was a clear and sunny Saturday in early May. Robin and Marianne took turns pushing Theo in his pram as they walked across Hampstead Heath.

'So you've decided, then,' said Robin. 'You're going to give up the church.'

'I'm not looking at it in terms of giving anything up,' said Marianne. 'My feelings are much more positive than that. I'm going to devote as much time as I can to Theo – and to you, of course.' She threaded her arm through Robin's as he took charge of the pram. 'Anyway,' she continued, 'I think it might be a good thing to take a proper break for a while. Some time to reflect. After all, we've yet to see what the Church in England is going to do about women priests. So I think it would make sense for me to see where the Catholic Church is heading before I decide exactly where and how I'm going to practise my ministry. In fact whatever else I do, I've got to remember that it's not *my* ministry. It's not even the *Church's* ministry. It's really *God's* ministry – and I'm still not clear in all this turmoil just what it is that he would have me do. And I'm certainly not sure yet how easy it's going to be for me to start thinking of myself as a Roman Catholic.'

'Well,' said Robin, 'if Noel has his way, people are going to be queuing up to join the club pretty soon. In the taxi on the way home last night he started regaling me with his top-of-the-head thoughts.' Robin stopped walking and started to chuckle.

'Come on, then,' said Marianne. 'You've got to tell me. You can't just stand there chortling. Come on!'

'It's supposed to be very secret,' said Robin at last, adopting a serious expression. 'But then Noel *was* very drunk – and I don't suppose the idea will stay in his head for very long. Well, I hope not at least!' He started walking again. 'It's based on something we tried a couple of years ago on another piece of business, and would involve the Church giving people free jackets,' he said. 'Good-quality ones, of course. On the back of each jacket would be a big reference to the website, www.kingdom.com, and below that it would say "Be part of a new Mass Movement".'

'A new mass movement?' said Marianne, pulling a face. 'I suppose that's meant to be a joke.'

'I suppose it is,' said Robin, laughing.